Loving Life:
Five decades in radio and TV

by Gene Loving with Joe Coccaro

ISBN 978-1-63393-272-2

Published by

 köehlerbooks™

210 60th Street
Virginia Beach, VA 23451
800-435-4811
www.koehlerbooks.com

LOVING

Five decades in radio and TV

LIFE

GENE LOVING

WITH JOE COCCARO

VIRGINIA BEACH
CAPE CHARLES

TABLE OF CONTENTS

INTRODUCTION

don't know exactly why I liked the song, *She Loves You,* when I first heard it. Maybe it was the simplicity of the lyrics; maybe it was the harmony of the four young Brits singing and playing electric guitars to a steady backbeat. All I knew at the time was that I liked the sound, and that it was different. When you're a DJ in his early 20s and you're paid to pick winners, you had better have good musical instincts. At the time, it's about all you had to go on. So, I went with my gut and chose that catchy tune as my featured record of the day.

It was September 1963, and I was the first DJ in the country to report *She Loves You* as a potential hit following its release in the US by Swan Records. I liked the band so much that I booked them to perform at a 2,000-seat venue in Virginia Beach. To my chagrin, and Swan's, the song went absolutely nowhere—a total flop. Five months later we would be vindicated, in a big way. The lads from Liverpool, with their Edwardian suits and strange haircuts, appeared on *The Ed Sullivan Show.* They performed *She Loves You* " "yeah, yeah, yeah" at the end of their first set in front of screaming teens in the live audience and 73 million people watching from home. That performance triggered a musical tsunami that helped launch the most storied rock 'n' roll band of all time. Being the first to pick *She Loves You* in a national trade paper as a future hit, and later book that group before they were big, gave me entrée to the Beatles when their fame erupted. They wound up canceling the Virginia Beach gig, as their manager decided to abandon the whole spring 1964 tour. But being among the first, if not *the* first, in the US to discover this band put me on the map with the group's US agent, and that relationship ultimately kicked open other doors of opportunity. That success taught me, very early in my career, that timing in show business was, in fact, a springboard to bigger possibilities. And who you know certainly does matter. As I look back on that good fortune now, it's clear I was the right age, in the right market, and on the ground floor at a pivotal time in rock 'n' roll history.

I have spent five decades evolving with the music business, first as a DJ and promoter during the golden days of Top 40 radio, then as a founder and executive of broadcast corporations. I've been a principal owner and operator of radio stations all over the US and founded a company that became the nation's largest group of independent TV stations. My life has been, and continues to be, a whirlwind of meetings, phone calls, logistics and connections.

I got hooked on music as a young boy growing up in central Virginia. With encouragement and support from my parents, I simply followed my passion, forgoing more sensible careers. Along the way, I have accumulated hundreds of stories involving big-name celebrities or those kingmakers handling marquee performers. I've been backstage with John, Paul, George and Ringo, and countless others as they made their fame: Mick Jagger, Jimi Hendrix, Cher, Muhammad Ali, Jack Benny, Dick Clark, Norman Lear, James Brown, The Beach Boys, The Temptations, Three Dog Night . . . It's a very long list. I even managed a band— Bill Deal and the Rhondels.

Oftentimes my wife, Angie, or close friends prod me to share some of my wistful moments chauffeuring around big stars, or hanging out with them backstage or taking them to dinner. I have just as many stories about co-workers and investors who helped build significant businesses in radio and TV. On occasion, I oblige Angie (and others who nag me) with a story or two, and every once in a while I even show pictures.

Telling stories and name-dropping to entertain family members, business associates and friends is one thing; having the gumption and the resources to chronicle them in a book is quite another. I would have been happy to keep all of this within the family. But my lovely wife—my unrelenting lovely wife—pushed me hard to share. Angie shamed me by first asking that I do a book just for her, and said it was the only gift she wanted from me for many Christmases to come. Next, she enlisted friends to join the chorus and then found a publisher to be her accomplice. I finally ran out of excuses.

Except for saying "My radio show ratings were always higher than yours," in never-ending arguments with my longtime friend and partner, Dick Lamb, I have tried to avoid glorifying my accomplishments, believing that only *today* and the future are important. I still believe that. But I'm at least willing to admit that some may find use for, or interest in, my professional travails. In many ways, what I experienced is bigger than me. One of the reasons I capitulated and did this book was to chronicle Virginia's broadcast history in the second half of the twentieth century, especially in eastern Virginia. Peter Easter, Executive Director of the Virginia Association of Broadcasters, says I have archived more success in over-the-air radio and TV than any other Virginian, or any other pure broadcast company headquartered in the state. Other Virginia families have founded and built major diversified communications companies and headquartered here, but those riches grew out of the newspaper business—Landmark Communications in Norfolk, Media General in Richmond, and the *Daily Press* in Newport News are among four or five big ones. My roots have always been in broadcast.

My earliest years were as a radio DJ and after that, TV show host. Then I became an owner of radio stations, getting in on the ground floor of the exploding popularity of FM radio. Television station ownership came next. My colleagues and I were among the first big investors in UHF-TV and we grew a company that became the largest chain of independent TV stations in the country. I'm still amazed by this success. Statistically, it shouldn't have happened. I started out with empty pockets on the lowest rung of the broadcasting ladder. I ascended a pretty fair distance, risking all my own money while relying on connections to raise the rest. My only inheritance was my parents' support, good nature and strong moral compass.

I have pictures hanging in my office that reflect certain periods in my life—handshakes and hugs with stars, media honchos, and politicians. These photos memorialize, in a small way, some of my good fortune. But I have taken equal pride in aspects of my life outside the office. I have believed that everyone needs a personal life and other interests to provide balance and perspective to your time on earth: the way one earns a living is just one part of who he is. Another important part of my life is my Christian faith and passion for helping children. Few endeavors have brought me more satisfaction than serving as temporary CEO of Operation Smile, an international children's health organization.

Writing on the computer, which I do almost every day at work, does not lend itself to my stream-of-consciousness style of communicating. I've been told—and fully admit—that my e-mails and memos are twice as long as necessary. I find editing myself difficult, which means I believe every thought I have is worthy of being shared. When you're a DJ, you learn to love the sound of your own voice, so doing an oral history would have been easier, but my wife wouldn't have it. I am sure my colleagues would also say I am too long-winded to tell my own story, especially in writing. Most of them have learned to pick out the important sentences in my e-mails and ignore the rest, especially the grammar and spelling.

I tried explaining my verbosity to Angie, but she took care of that excuse, too, by introducing me to Joe Coccaro, the executive editor of the publishing company she found for this project. Joe promised he would not let me embarrass myself—or his publishing firm. So, what we have here is a collaboration of words between Joe and me, anchored in rambling content spanning five decades. Joe tried his best to keep my stories chronological, but as you'll see, I meander in places. My ace assistant, Debbi Babashanian, suffered along with Joe on this project. She helped manage the flurry of multiple drafts of my manuscript passed back and forth via email, constantly reminding me to pare down my expressive style. God bless you, Debbi, for enduring my wordiness for twenty years.

I cannot tell you with absolute certainty that every date, fact or sequence is exact. Most of what this book holds is personal recollections, media accounts, files, photographs, and a tad of original research. The book is built almost entirely on my perspective, and nearly every story or anecdote is my firsthand account. I can assure any reader that my intention is not to embarrass anyone but myself, with maybe one exception—my longtime friend and business partner, Dick Lamb. Dick, by the way, is still on one of our stations, WAVE, 92.9 FM.

The truth is, I am extremely proud of Dick and the work we've done together. The same holds for staff and associates I have been privileged to work with. I'm especially beholden to my other longtime partner, John Trinder, president of MAX Media. None of what I take credit for would have been possible without John, Dick, Larry Saunders and countless others.

The roots of all our companies are deep in Virginia soil. I was born, raised and educated in Richmond, the state capital. My DJ career started there and migrated just slightly southeast to the coastal area known as Hampton Roads.

My life is an amalgamation of many small events that, over fifty years, have added up to something big. Doing this book has forced me to retrace many of those steps, and give them broader context. Typically, you don't realize you're part of a bigger picture when you're doing it. That's partly true in my case.

I think back now to my love of music as a kid, of the friendship I formed with *American Bandstand*'s Dick Clark, of being the first in the US to interview the Beatles face-to-face, of syndicating radio shows, promoting acts, dealing with big shots, buying a string of broadcast stations, and taking a large communications company public. I sincerely hope that those of you who indulge these memories recall your own favorite station, DJ, or concert, and my path contributes to the narrative of the music and TV business as it evolved in the 1960s and bolted forward in the following decades. Music, radio, and TV have shaped much of our culture and who we are. I feel privileged to have played some small part as listeners and viewers embraced the electronic media evolution. I was able to watch it happen from the front row.

CHAPTER 1

HIGHLAND PARK, RICHMOND

From as almost far back as I can remember I loved to listen to records and the radio.

As a kid, especially during the cold Richmond, Virginia winters, I would sit in front of our living room radio and phonograph console listening to Glenn Miller, Tommy Dorsey, Bing Crosby, The Andrews Sisters, Patti Page and other soothing or upbeat songs intended to put the nation in a good mood. In the kitchen, my mom would be doing the same thing, listening to the radio while she prepared our meals. Her radio was always within reach, sitting on the counter next to the sink. In my youngest years it was the radio that brought the outside world to us.

I was born in November 1942, and in those very early days in my life, milk in glass bottles was delivered to the house and kids played in the street. Many of us didn't have refrigerators, but we did have record players. There was no TV anywhere. Back in the late 1930s and 1940s, most songs were on ten-inch shellac 78 RPM recordings, those fragile discs with the small hole through the center and a single recording on each side. My mom had a small collection—maybe a couple of dozen—that I listened to over and over. When I was about six, my father bought me a radio to go in my room. Most nights I fell asleep listening to shows like *Jack Benny* or *Your Hit Parade*. Radio seemed glamorous, and I tried to picture the people behind the microphones.

Unbeknownst to me at the time, my mom's 78s and those early radio shows kindled in me what would become a lifelong ambition. By the time I reached my pre-teen years I had a hefty record collection of my own that included 45 RPM recordings by of some the pioneers who reshaped the musical landscape—Fats Domino, Little Richard and Elvis. Soon the record companies took aim at the kids and teens as their primary customers. I still remember singing along with early 1950s novelty songs like *That Doggie in the Window* or *The Ballad of Davy Crockett,* songs which captured perfectly the innocence of my young life.

We lived in an emerging suburb, the Highland Park section on the north side of Richmond. Our brand-new house cost $5,000 in the late 1930s, one of three duplicates next to each other on Arnold Avenue. Each was two stories with a stucco façade. Ours had a basement. We were only a few miles from downtown, but our neighborhood had a small-town feel. Kids rode their bikes everywhere and across the street was even some remaining farm property—with chickens.

Aubrey Eugene Loving, Jr. at 18 months shortly after being
vaccinated with a phonograph needle.

At age two, an early indication that I will develop a bunny fetish. My favorite movie is *Who Framed Roger Rabbit*

My cousin Patsy and me (age four) in the back yard at my Highland Park home in Richmond, Virginia. A true white picket fence, too. 1944

• • •

I was three when World War II ended. I remember using ration coupons when we shopped for groceries. I also remember the black-out lights and air-raid drills at night, not understanding that what seemed like a game to me was serious. From those early days I recall ice was delivered from an orange-colored horse-drawn wagon to put in our ice box. My parents could have afforded a refrigerator, but refrigerators weren't available because nearly all heavy manufacturing had gone into the war effort.

Our family car was a large black Cadillac, most likely about a 1940 model. Dad drove that car for years because GM and other automakers were then building only war products. But when GM started manufacturing for consumers again, my father bought one of the first Cadillacs to roll off the assembly line. I recall going with him to Jones Motor Car Company to pick it up. And my dad's love of cars definitely rubbed off on me.

My mother didn't have a driver's license in the 1940s. She rode the bus to work, walking to a stop three blocks from our house. Lots of people rode the bus in the 1940s and 1950s. Second cars were a luxury, and my dad needed the family car for his daily commute to a more rural location just outside the city.

Because both my parents worked, they could afford to spoil their little boy. My father bought me a Lionel train set one Christmas, which led to model railroading as a major hobby. I developed an impressive layout of tracks in our attic. It became a big attraction for my friends who spent hours every week helping me build and rebuild our miniature towns and working industrial sites. I still have boxes and boxes of my Lionel collection, which I expect to set up again someday. I have been waiting for the right moment to resurrect those great childhood memories.

My parents invested wisely when they decided to buy on Arnold Avenue. They purchased three adjacent lots, using one as a large yard. They eventually sold the others, which remained wooded during my childhood. Like the train set, that big yard and woods became a magnet for my neighborhood pals. My parents enclosed the yard with a white picket fence. It was like having a private park. My friends congregated there to play, and neighbors came to barbeque on a brick fireplace my dad had built. Few homes had outside fire pits back then.

Aubrey Eugene Loving, Sr.

Lillian Mae Loving

• • •

As the only living child of Mae and Aubrey Loving, I was happy to have so many other neighborhood kids around. There were about ten of us—boys and girls—constantly running up and down the street to each other's houses, playing hide-and-seek, and going to school together. Life was different then; safer, friendlier and more community-oriented. Parents watched out for each other's kids and for each other.

I was about a year younger than most of my classmates in elementary school because I was skipped a grade. But don't get the wrong idea; I was no whiz kid. When I started school there just weren't enough school buildings, so students were put on what they called half-year semesters. Some kids finished the school year in January and some in June. When that system changed to one academic calendar year for everyone, I was bounced forward a grade, being among the few Highland Park Elementary School seven-year-olds placed with eight-year-old second-graders. Like so many times in the years ahead, I was in the right place at the right time. The net effect of this change was that I graduated from high school at age seventeen. Being moved forward a grade had forced me to learn more quickly, and at times I struggled to keep up—but I managed.

Outside the classroom my life was pretty normal and carefree. With friends from my neighborhood, I walked eight blocks to school for the first several years, and later we rode bicycles. I fondly remember walking home down Meadowbridge Road with maybe four other boys, following a few girls—one I really liked—stopping at High's Ice Cream for a five-cent lime-sherbet cone. We also got around by riding the city bus which stopped about every four blocks. The bus was often crowded, so kids would stand to make room for adults. In those pre-Rosa Parks days of the early and middle 1950s, African-Americans were still riding in the back.

When I was nine, along with friends of a similar age, I often took the bus to downtown Richmond to just walk around the stores, and we visited the capitol buildings and historic monuments or we'd go to the movies. We'd be gone for hours, and our travels as young kids were considered completely safe. During my elementary school years, one of my best friends and travel buddies was Kenneth Fleet. He was a year older than me, which would one day figure into my first radio job. He lived about three blocks away and had a snub-nosed Pekingese dog. Seems most afternoons I was at his house or he was at mine. His father once won a new Buick and I went with them to pick it up.

As youngsters, Ken, other friends and I rode our bikes all over. Highland Park was a post-World War II Norman Rockwell world. Those were calm, happy years.

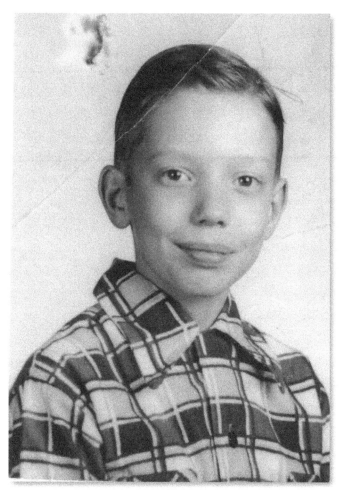

Age six, my official elementary school picture.

Billy Minsen, Danny McFadden, me, Mickey Gentry, Raymond Miller.
Highland Park Elementary School, Richmond, Virginia.
My first experience in "show business." 1949

• • •

One difference in my house from many of my friends' was that I was the lone child at the dinner table. A brother had died at birth five years before I came along. I did get to know and spend time with my grandparents on my father's side. My grandmother lived into her early nineties; granddad died at seventy-two from smoking-related issues. My mother, Lillian Mae, was thirty-two when she had me, which was late in those days to have a baby. Mom was also a working woman, a buyer for Miller & Rhoads, the downtown Richmond department store. Her job involved periodic trips to New York and other exotic cities, and she looked every bit the fashion plate. I remember how stylishly she dressed each day for work, and for church on Sunday. When mom and dad were working, a black woman cared for me after school and would bring her kids along. We all played together.

I had a protective pet—for a while. He was a black-and-white collie named Pal, who began the habit of jumping the fence, killing chickens at the farm across the street. One day my father said it was time to take Pal to a friend who had a lot of land outside of Richmond. Parting with Pal was tough, especially for a four-year-old only child. My parents quickly tried to heal the wound when a neighbor, who was moving, gave us her Persian cat, Lady Gray. For a couple of years my father also kept a pony at the small regional airport where he worked. One of the airplane mechanics, a guy who lived in a trailer at the edge of the airport, took care of the pony, but it was always available to me and my friends when we visited.

My father was a co-owner, with Floyd Clark, of Central Airport which was in the county just outside the Richmond city line. Dad taught people to fly, restored wrecked airplanes, and owned a variety of aircraft that he rented to others or used on weekends to take Richmonders on joy rides. He took me on more than few joy rides. I remember being in an open cockpit bi-wing plane with my dad flying it wide open, upside down. It was a blast and very scary.

My father didn't start off as a pilot. He was a plumber and served in World War I on a Navy oiler. He got into the airplane business after the war. When WWII came he was commissioned as a colonel in the Air Reserve.

The airport was a dream hangout for me as a kid, and I always thought my career would be in aviation or, based on some ads on TV in the early 50s, raising chinchillas in the basement. I did learn to fly but never got a license, which is one of my big regrets. Now I have a flight simulator in my office and subscribe to two flying magazines, and I tell my associates that if we ever get another company plane, I will be the pilot. That's probably why our company doesn't have a plane.

My father, on the right, and his partner Floyd Clark, early 1940s.

My father did not go to church with Mom and me on Sunday because the airport was open every day and my dad's days off were Thursdays and Saturdays—that was when he did things with us. And though absent from the church pew, he was an ethical man of faith. He supported my time at church activities, including Sunday night youth meetings and social outings, by driving me and others whenever he could.

Some of my best times with Dad and Mom were during summer vacations. My parents owned three cottages in Buckroe Beach, a suburb of Hampton. They rented the cottages to vacationing families during the summer, and reserved one for two weeks for us starting every Fourth of July. During those visits we would drive all over the Chesapeake Bay area, sometimes crossing the James River on the bridge or taking the ferry boat from Old Point Comfort to Willoughby Spit in Norfolk.

My dream spot was near Grandview Beach in Hampton's Foxhill neighborhood. New homes had been built on canals where people tied up their boats at docks behind their houses. Little did I know that I would one day live in Grandview.

In the summer I loved going with my father on his regular visits to a major Richmond junkyard that sold everything imaginable. We also went to the C&O Railroad dent-and-scratch warehouse where they actually had goods damaged during train transport. He would buy things to be used at the airport or the cottages in Hampton. He could fix anything.

My father loved the most cutting-edge technology. So, when TV became available we got the first set in the neighborhood. My parents knew the manager of Miller & Rhoads, so one night after hours we went to the big store on Broad Street to see the first television they would offer for sale. It was made by RCA and was basically a large box with a very small screen. We ordered one, and a week later our neighbors and my friends came over to see it. Soon every afternoon a few of us watched *The Howdy Doody Show,* and every Tuesday night several neighbors came over to see Milton Berle host his variety show.

• • •

Neither Dad nor I were into sports. I liked playing softball with the kids in the neighborhood, but following professional teams wasn't part of our routine. Back in those days, Richmond didn't have any major league teams to follow, or even local college teams. So my parents encouraged my interest in other things—especially music.

My love of songs may seem an odd choice for me because I am basically tone deaf. I can't sing *Happy Birthday* in tune. I was so tonally inept that I was the only kid asked to drop out of the chorus in elementary school. Yet, somehow, I developed a sixth sense for great songs. I understood melody, lyrics and whether a song had resonance. I was able to hear how tightly and harmoniously the pieces of a musical puzzle fit.

My early musical tastes were influenced by a radio program from Richmond radio station WRNL, a network affiliate. The music on WRNL most of the time was crooner tunes and schmaltzy love songs performed live on shows like Arthur Godfrey's. But for two hours each Saturday, a local DJ would play audience requests. Back then, there was no calling in; you had to submit your choice in writing the week before, which I did. Ears glued to my radio, I would jot down the names of songs and artists that I thought would make a good addition to our family record collection.

Radio stations were springing up around the country in the mid-1950s, which led to more musical choices for listeners. I would soon learn that the programming available for these new startup stations was relatively cheap. A disk jockey would take a stack of records in a studio and spend several hours talking about what he liked and telling something about the artist. Soon Richmond had several of these new upstarts. I delightedly skipped around the AM dial, regularly listening to WXGI, Richmond's first country music station, which at the time only broadcast during the day. I also gravitated towards rhythm and blues on W*ANT*, whose call letters stood for *All Negro Talent*.

The country may have been racially frayed at the time, but black artists were becoming increasingly prominent among white listeners. And, many popular white performers were mimicking or collaborating with the great black jazz and blues musicians from the South. Obviously, Elvis is the best known from that transition period. Others I liked in the 1950s include Bill Haley and the Comets, Ruth Brown, and LaVern Baker. Elvis, Buddy Holly, plus Don and Phil Everly were of the *rockabilly* ilk and inspired by Nashville and its famous Grand Ole Opry. Elvis first recorded on Sun Records out of Memphis, as did Johnny Cash, Jerry Lee Lewis and Carl Perkins. In fact, Carl had the original *Blue Suede Shoes,* which Elvis took pop once he moved to RCA records.

My two favorite artists when I started junior high school were Fats Domino and Little Richard. I loved their sound from the first time I heard it. I immediately bought a copy of Fats' 1955 hit *Ain't That a Shame,* and then drove my parents nuts playing it over and over. (Little did I know that six years later I would be sitting on the piano bench with Fats for his entire show at the Thunderbird Night Club, broadcasting his set live on WLEE, talking to Fats between songs, and asking, "What's next, Fats?")

• • •

My parents encouraged my musical exploration. They gave me a modest allowance for assigned jobs like cutting the grass or raking leaves. I also earned money mowing neighbors' lawns. On Saturdays I got to spend some of it. Very few homes had air conditioning when I was a boy, but a lot of stores and commercial buildings in downtown Richmond did—including the movie theater. My dad liked cooling off on those soupy Richmond summer days, so we would go see a movie. Afterwards, I'd go next door to a small record store owned by Pat Cohen. The store wasn't much bigger than a typical living room, and had records in trays divided into categories, including a Top-Hits section. I usually knew what I wanted before I entered. I would select two or three 45 RPM discs and then listen briefly to each in a small soundproof booth in Pat's store. I would typically buy one record a week for 49 cents. By the time I was nine or ten I had nearly three dozen records.

Collecting and listening to records wasn't something many boys did back then, at least not that I knew of. Girls idolized singers and collected their songs—but not boys. That didn't matter to me. In fact, it made me popular with the girls, and even with some of my male buddies. Friends started to come to my house to listen to my newest records. By the time I was twelve, I took my record collection public. I hauled a box with about thirty recordings to a neighborhood park that hosted outdoor dances on summer nights. There was a record player and speakers and kids danced on a large cement floor outside. Some of the girls I liked from school, or the neighborhood, danced with each other, and a few older ones with boys, while I changed the 45s. The kids would come up and request their favorites, and I enjoyed the attention. I'm guessing it kept me from being tagged as just some geeky kid who didn't play sports. The seeds of musical show biz sprouted as I was spinning records on those balmy nights.

My academic skills throughout junior high remained pretty average, so I was not in the language clubs or vying for the honor society, and, as I said, playing sports just didn't interest me.

Music and entertainment was my niche, one that provided me with a bit of status. I liked the attention I received from friends and strangers who knew I was the guy who showed up in a class to bring the movie projector or set up the audio equipment, and played records at the occasional gym sock hop after school. I was also a volunteer, during study periods, in the school library and the principal's office, often running notes to various classrooms—anything to stay out of study hall.

In 8th grade I joined the Chandler Junior High School safety patrol, wearing a white belt and badge, getting out of class three minutes early, and arriving three minutes late as I had to take up my post in the halls to keep students left or right. It was very organized and orderly in 1957. When school let out, I stood at street intersections stopping traffic and directing my classmates to cross safely. I became a lieutenant on the Chandler Safety Patrol, which made me responsible for the direction of several other lesser ranked thirteen-year-olds. The safety patrol reported to the toughest teacher in the school, English class teacher Miss Rawlins. Being on her good side helped, especially for a C-plus student like myself.

Toward the end of my junior high years I found out there was a stage crew for school shows. I tried to get on that crew, but there was never an opening. But I realized stage work was something I wanted to learn more about, so I made a mental note to pursue it in high school, a decision which would prove fortuitous.

One of my best friends in junior high was Ronald Peters. I started hanging out and riding bikes with Ronald—never Ron—in those playing-records-at-the-playground days. We had a mutual interest in some of the same girls and would ride our bikes to their neighborhood, sitting on their porch and trying to impress them.

I credit Ronald for pointing me to a morning radio show on WLEE that would greatly influence my life—*The Harvey Hudson Show*. Harvey's co-host at that time was George Prescott. Harvey and George would invite listeners to call in to win movie tickets or a 45 RPM record—not expensive prizes. Most of the questions had to do with music: they would play some little bit of a song and then ask for the title and singer. I was pretty good at knowing the answer, but the real challenge was getting through on the rotary-dial phone before someone else did. The first time I got through, the voice on the other end said "Harvey Hudson." I could not believe I was actually talking to the man who was on the radio. I won and was thrilled when he announced my name on the air. They offered to mail the prize, or I could pick it up. I chose to pick it up, not thinking about how I would get there.

A day or so later my mother agreed to drive Ronald and me way out on West Broad Street to the station office and studios so I could collect my prize. When we arrived, one of us asked if we could see Harvey and George broadcasting. Someone in the office took us back to the studio. We got to look in through a glass wall that separated the main studio from the newsroom, but what I saw didn't match my vision of what a radio show looked like. I guess my expectation was of big-time New York radio studios like I saw in the movies, with a full orchestra, engineers running controls, and others hanging around the stars doing the show, handing them scripts or creating sound effects. Instead, I saw two men in a studio with microphones in front of them, behind two sets of a lot of interesting looking equipment with turntables on each side of them. They were in constant movement—changing a record, or handling big discs that contained commercials or jingles. They were operating everything themselves, occasionally turning on the mic to say something out over the air. Harvey looked like the real star of the show, dressed in a suit and tie, while George was more casual, minus his suit coat. They did not seem to notice us. I guess they were used to people looking in all the time, or walking through where we were. After about ten minutes our escort led us back out to the parking lot, and my mother drove us home, all the way listening to the guys we had just seen in person in the WLEE radio studio. That experience changed my life. I no longer expected to be an aviator like my father; I wanted to be in that radio studio like Harvey Hudson.

· · ·

When I think back on those impressionable days, I can still hear my mom's 78 RPM vinyls spinning on the phonograph, or the voice of some crooner on the radio, the DJ playing the song I requested on WRNL. It seemed magical to me. I didn't know it at the time, but I was about to experience a seismic shift in the radio and music business.

Music hadn't changed much from 1935 to the 1950s. Most of it was studio produced, sanitized and aimed at previous generations. It was the Sinatra-Bing Crosby era of big bands and deep voices, of crooners and pretty love songs. By the mid-1950s, the roots of rock 'n' roll were spreading like weeds. Electric guitars joined pianos and saxophones. And, the same people singing the songs—and sometimes writing the lyrics—were also *playing* the instruments. This new breed of musician was a rising tide and, eventually, I would ride the crest with them.

Harvey Hudson (right) and George Prescott doing the morning *Harvey Hudson Show*, when Ronald Peters and I first visited WLEE in 1957.

CHAPTER 2

RADIO BUG

The thrill of seeing DJs in action during my visit to WLEE never left me. I started to fantasize that I could do a radio show, further flouting my musical interest of playing records for the masses, and not just for kids at the playground and at school sock hops. I started listening to *The Harvey Hudson Show* and the other WLEE programs—not to win contests but to hear what they were saying and playing. I became a full-fledged radio student and DJ wannabe.

My church inadvertently kindled that flame when it purchased a reel-to-reel tape recorder to capture the Sunday service. During the Sunday night youth meetings I arrived early to record my voice, playing it back, envisioning being on the radio. Being able to listen to yourself on tape was a new deal at that time. I did not know anyone who owned one of those new electronic gadgets. Soon I was hounding my parents to buy me a tape recorder. Having agreed it was to be my birthday and Christmas presents for the next few years, we went to Sears and paid around $100. It was the best investment my parents ever made.

A few months after getting the tape recorder, my friend Ronald and I recorded our thirty-minute version of *The Harvey Hudson Show,* imitating Harvey and George, reading commercials we had written, telling jokes and playing records by holding the mic in front of the record player speaker. We mailed the tape to WLEE. When George Prescott called me, I almost dropped the receiver. He said he and Harvey liked the tape, but it would not play on the station's professional equipment, asking if we could come in and do it again at the studio. Guess what I answered.

George did the overnight show on WLEE Friday and Saturday evenings, from midnight to 6 in the morning. The station normally signed off Sunday through Thursday nights from 2 a.m. until 6 in the morning. Ronald and I were asked to come in about 9 p.m. on a Friday so George could help us make the repeat recording before he went on the air at midnight. He said he didn't know when they would play our tape or how it would be used. The two of us would just have to listen and wait. It was summer and we were off from school. I'm sure we told friends we were going to be on WLEE.

One morning Harvey Hudson said on the air, "See what you think of this," and suddenly Ronald and I were doing a joke, then a commercial. Unbelievably, I was listening to myself on WLEE. Harvey and George then explained that Gene Loving and Ronald Peters had recorded a takeoff on their show, that we were junior high school kids, and they would play some more in a few minutes. That morning they played a couple more two—or three-minute clips, saying they were going to send us passes to the movies, thanking us for the tape—and probably never expecting to hear from us again.

My friends, and my parents' friends, started saying they heard me on Harvey's show. The same was happening for Ronald, but he didn't seem to be as excited by his new fame as I was. Ronald worked at a grocery store, the A&P, had two younger brothers and a sister for whom he had some responsibility, and he didn't have the time to pursue radio dreams. For him the WLEE appearance was a lark; for me it was a game-changer.

I recall speaking with George Prescott afterward. I may have called him to say thanks for helping us make the tape and playing it. During the conversation I asked if he ever allowed people to visit him on the all-night show. He said he'd be happy to have me as a guest.

During this time I had been enjoying going to local stock car races on Saturday nights with my next-door neighbor Mary Ann

Lindner and her boyfriend, Bill. She was about five years older than me. The three of us usually went to Bill's Bar B Q after the races, getting home late. One night, Mary Ann and Bill agreed to take me to WLEE when the race ended around 11. My mother and father trusted Mary Ann, Bill—and me. It didn't take a lot of persuading to convince my parents to let me spend the night at WLEE. I think they understood the depths of my interest in radio after they heard Harvey play the recording Ronald and I made. Maybe their own friends commenting on my brush with stardom helped push them to see if anything else might happen. My father agreed to pick me up 6 a.m. Sunday.

I took coffee in a very hot glass container to George Prescott. Most likely it was my mother or Mary Ann's idea. Coffee in glass was the way they sold it at White Tower, which was about 2 miles from WLEE, located at 6200 West Broad Street, on the outskirts of Richmond. About the only thing out there besides a Reynolds Metals office building were the four WLEE towers, the station offices and the studios, all on a big property that someday would be worth more than the radio station.

When I visited that first night, I entered through the transmitter and engineering section of the WLEE building. I was greeted by a short, gruff, round guy named Marlin Scribner, one of WLEE's engineers. These technicians always had to be on duty while the station was broadcasting. He checked with George before I was ushered to the studio. I sat quietly watching while George mostly talked to female fans on the phone as records played. George tasked me with filing records in the racks along the studio walls. My time volunteering at the Chandler Junior High library came in handy, as I quickly picked up on the filing system WLEE used. By the time that early morning visit was over, I understood what a DJ did and how he worked the equipment to make a blended stream of entertainment flow from the radio speaker in a car or at home. George let me sit in the central chair while he took bathroom breaks during newscasts. It wasn't necessary for me to watch anything while George was on break; he let me sit there because at some point earlier in his life he must have been where I was—anxious to get behind the microphone. My visits to George became a regular thing—about two trips to WLEE a month. But before long George was moved to a different shift and I had pretty much exhausted the all-night show visits.

• • •

My neighbor Mary Ann's twenty-one year old boyfriend, Bill Allen, understood my interest in radio. As an engineer with IBM, he knew a lot about electronics and offered to help me build a radio station in my attic. He had visited my model railroad and knew we had space to spare. Bill ordered everything we needed from a Radio Shack catalog, as there were no retail stores in those days. My father must have agreed to pay for it. The necessary switches, knobs, turntables, microphone and amplifier arrived. I already had the tape recorder. Bill bought a phono oscillator, a small low-power radio transmitter, which he amplified. My "signal" could be heard for about a half-mile from my house, which was more than enough to span my neighborhood. People could hear WBUG on their radios, and more than a few listened. I played records and talked mostly about school events or gave shout-outs to friends while on air. It was all very innocuous, fun and very part time.

I didn't know that it was illegal to amplify the oscillator and make it a radio transmitter, and Bill, who most likely did, never mentioned it. I would find out the hard way later. My original plan had been simply to be on a radio set in the next room— not to transmit to the entire neighborhood. But thanks to Bill, WBUG was actually "broadcasting," and I was happy to be the voice of Highland Park.

BUG Radio took to the air almost every afternoon after school, up until about seven in the evening, with one-hour shifts divided between me and several buddies. I was on most of the time Saturdays and Sundays. I had just finished junior high, and at age fourteen, spent a great deal of my time trying to improve my DJ skills on my home radio station. People were listening and responding.

During my visits with George Prescott at WLEE I learned how radio stations got the records they played: for free. I saw stacks of them in the studio. I found out about local record distributors who wholesaled the disks to record shops and department stores. They gave promotional copies to radio stations in hopes they would be played, creating sales. After WBUG went on the air I wrote to about five Richmond record distributors. Nancy Moran, who worked for the Allen Brothers, must have liked something about my letter because she started sending new releases to me at WBUG. She knew it was only a neighborhood station, but at some point I was invited to the distributorship. I started a Saturday morning ritual of going to collect all the new releases from her. Nancy also gave me copies of hits I didn't have. It felt like WBUG was a real station.

I wanted to get a bigger transmitter so I could be heard all over the city—further proof of my naiveté. I knew that real radio was run by paid professionals, but I figured that we were just kids having fun. And even though my friends and I were having a great time *playing at* radio, it felt real and we were gaining experience talking over the air. My parents were happy, too. I was totally occupied and they knew exactly where I was.

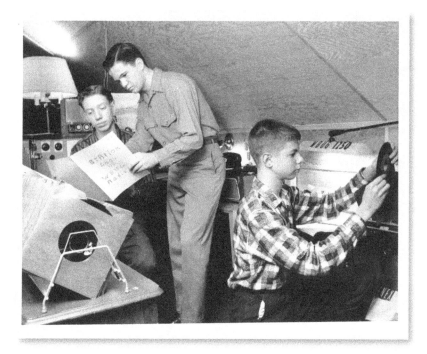

Me and my friends at WBUG. Not pictured is WBUG staffer Ronald Peters who originally suggested I listen to *The Harvey Hudson Show* on WLEE. He could not be there that day, most likely working at the A&P. Both Aubrey Ward (center) and Kenneth Fleet (right) were also part of my stage crew at John Marshall High School.

• • •

I was starting high school while all of this was going on, expecting to be in the Cadet Corps. It was prestigious in those days to wear a uniform—about one in four guys did—and the girls liked it. A lot of the social activity at John Marshall High School revolved around the Cadet Corps, which also helped ready young men for possible military service.

John Marshall High was in downtown Richmond, a thirty-minute bus ride for me. In 1957, you rode the commercial bus because there were no school buses in Richmond. I would buy a book of bus tickets at school. Students paid 15 cents a ride and everyone else a quarter. Many adults used the bus to commute to work. Most of the time there were no seats, so students would stand holding their books.

John Marshall High sat beside the eighteenth-century home of the school's namesake—the Virginia-born fourth Chief Justice of the United States Supreme Court. The Marshall house was, and remains, a major tourist attraction, but today the school is gone. My friend Ken Fleet and I protested the destruction of the beautiful school building. In 2016 the Richmond paper reran the original photograph of our protest, fifty-five years after it was demolished. We had a true campus with an athletic field, and an armory for the Cadet Corps about a block away. The armory was also used for proms. Two academic buildings, John Marshall and the George Wythe, were across the street from each other connected by an underground tunnel. Another separate building down the street was used to teach the trades, skills like auto mechanics and plumbing. Those students also worked part of the day as apprentices in a real workplace. Why they don't do that today is, in my opinion, one of the real shortcomings of our current educational system.

—Staff Photo by Deane Parrish

About 25 John Marshall Alumni Gathered to Protest Demolition of Building
They Moved on to City Hall Where Council Listened, Declined to Change Plans

JM Alumni Lose Plea To Council

Sentimental graduates of old John Marshall High School lost last night in a last-ditch attempt to prevent the building's demolition.

City Council rejected a move to block plans for tearing down

Landings Reported By Brazilian Troops

SAO PAULO, BRAZIL, Aug. 31—(P)—Brazilian naval infantry units Thursday night were reported landing on the coast of Santa Catarin state on orders from the nation's military chiefs to subdue the south-
————————————————tern cowboys and troops sun-

John Marshall High protest to save the building. You can see Kenneth Fleet (circle left) and me (circle right) along with others appearing in favor of preserving the structure. This is where Kenneth and I would set up the PA equipment for morning pep rallies, on the front steps of JM.

My stint as a cadet was short lived. After just two days of drilling, I was asked to leave. I had fainted in formation from low blood pressure. This episode would later save me from the Vietnam draft, but at that time being rejected was a major disappointment. My parents had already purchased all my gear, even the shoes. I think we sold everything to another cadet.

I rolled with the disappointment. I was already planning to volunteer for the stage crew as a follow-up to my missed opportunity in junior high. Thelma Keen, an assistant principal of John Marshall, was in charge of the auditorium. Miss Keen had never married and, like many educators of that time, her life was the school. After going by to offer my services, I got a note to see the stage manager, a senior who would be graduating in January. Most of the crew members were his friends in the same class. Soon I would become the senior member of the stage crew, enabling me to recruit my friends.

John Marshall High's football rival was Thomas Jefferson. Their annual clash was among Richmond's biggest sporting events of the year. Pep rallies were broadcast live on WLEE from the John Marshall and Thomas Jefferson auditoriums. The station switched back and forth to see which student body could out-yell the other. George Prescott was the announcer assigned to John Marshall, and it was great to reconnect with him. He treated me like a long-lost friend, much to the surprise of that semester's senior stage crew. I told George about our neighborhood station, WBUG, and he invited me to again visit him at WLEE.

My little enterprise was gaining notoriety. Lots of folks in the neighborhood listened to my friends and me playing DJ. My school newspaper, *The John Marshall Monocle,* eventually heard about WBUG and did an article on it. I was a mere ninth-grader but in the limelight. A reporter from *The Richmond Times-Dispatch*, the city's big daily newspaper, read the *Monocle* story and was intrigued. It took me a half second to say "yes" when the reporter called and asked if he could send a photographer and do a weekend feature on WBUG.

The story came out and I was over the moon. Unfortunately, my shooting star flamed out fast. Not long after the *Times-Dispatch* article, the FCC sent a certified letter to my house. WBUG was illegal, operating without a federal broadcast license—or any license for that matter. WBUG needed to "cease and desist" immediately or else face hefty daily fines. Within minutes of reading those ominous words my dad pulled the plug on WBUG—permanently.

• • •

Despite its abrupt ending, the WBUG experience only stoked my desire to be in radio show business. That fire was further fanned when I visited WLLY, the first station in the Richmond market to play Top 40 music in competition with WLEE. The station was located in the Broad Grace Arcade basement under a tall bank building in downtown about five blocks from John Marshall High. A week or so after the WBUG article ran in the *Times-Dispatch*, I visited WLLY after school to see if they would let me watch the DJ. The station program director, Gene Creasy, allowed me to go into the studio and sit with the afternoon man, Bob Joyce, who had read the WBUG newspaper story. Gene Creasy would later become program director of WGH in Newport News, Virginia. During time with my parents at the cottage in Buckroe Beach on those summer vacations, I often listened to WGH.

Bob Joyce was the station's music director and responsible for publishing the WLLY Top 40 sheet each week, which was distributed in record shops all over town. Bob told me I could come back as often as I liked. When I did, he had me run a couple of errands for him each visit, things like going upstairs to Peoples Drug to get him coffee, or filing records in a big rack in the hallway behind the main studio. One of my best memories was going with Bob to a record hop in his new T-Bird. I had the honor of setting up the equipment and he paid me $5 after the dance. That was my first paid radio-related gig. Soon I would be distributing WLLY's Top 40 lists to record stores, taking calls from listeners and even reading newscast over the air. I was just fifteen at the time and didn't even have a driver's permit.

• • •

The other part of my early showbiz education came when attending Richmond's biggest theater, which at the time was called The Mosque. The 3,500-seat venue located at Monroe Park was built in 1926 and had been used by the Shriners until the city bought it and renamed it The Landmark. It's now called the Altria Theater.

I'd go to The Mosque and to see the recording stars I had listened to on records and over the radio. Irving Feld of Washington D.C., whose family now owns The Ringling Brothers Circus, started promoting touring concerts at The Mosque featuring several big names in one show.

In those days, seating at The Mosque was divided down the middle from the top balcony to the orchestra pit by race: blacks on the left, whites on the right. Tickets were sold through local record shops and department stores. John Marshall High was about three blocks from the key ticket selling store, Thalhimer's. The day the tickets went on sale, I would go at lunchtime to get the best seats. Most of the time I got tickets for the front row. The Mosque often drew some of the biggest musical stars of the mid—to late-1950s. I was thrilled to be sitting just a few yards from American R&B artists like Clyde McPhatter, Fats Domino, Brook Benton, Sam Cooke, and the Drifters. Other entertainers on a typical bill would be The Everly Brothers, Brenda Lee, Frankie Avalon, the Shirelles, Fabian, Buddy Holly & the Crickets, or Bobby Rydell.

• • •

Being up close at The Mosque gave me a chance to study staging and sound, which dovetailed nicely with my school responsibilities. In January 1958, I was promoted to stage manager of John Marshall High. I was given keys to the school front door and all of the locked-up spaces that contained audio-visual equipment. Part of my job was to set up the big portable public address system on the school front lawn for morning pep rallies during basketball and football seasons—and we did a lot of rallies at John Marshall.

I had a crew of five people, whom I was allowed to pick. Three of the five selected just happened to be friends. It was a who-you-know world, even back then. I had a private office backstage where I could park my books and other personal belongings. Being in charge, I quickly learned the art of delegation. Someone from our crew had to be there whenever the auditorium was used, which was all the time.

With the exception of The Mosque, John Marshall's

two-thousand-seat venue was the largest theatre in the city. Outside groups often rented the auditorium for speeches, dance and music recitals, special movies, and group meetings. Most of these rentals were at night or weekends. To use the auditorium, outside groups had to hire me and other guys from our crew, which meant we were paid to be there.

I didn't really understand how much money I could make from this when I originally volunteered. It turned out to be very good monthly income. I mostly did it because I wanted to be around show business. I had no theatrical or musical talent, so I knew early on that my contribution to the performing arts was going to be behind the scenes. Managing that auditorium stage ended up being the best education I got in high school. I learned how to provide the logistics for concerts and dances, which would eventually earn me more money than being on the radio. Most importantly, I learned how to manage people.

A letter from the federal government saying "Shut down your son's illegal radio station." 1958

. • • •

I remained apathetic about playing sports, so much so that my gym teachers cut me some slack. They recognized my pathetic lack of hand-eye coordination and took pity. The coaches let me skip about 90 percent of gym classes. They must have figured that I was getting plenty of exercise setting up the equipment for pep rallies, which were held a couple days each week. It was a quid pro quo: the coaches gave me credit for what I did for them and the teams' morale, and I got to skip gym class. My crew and I also did the lighting for all the school proms, which involved lugging heavy equipment from the main building up to the third floor of the cavernous armory. No elevator.

The girl I took to the prom my senior year was the girl I would later marry. Susan Onyschuk and I were in a typing class together. She was a freshman and I was a junior. Susan lived on the south side of Richmond; I was on the north side and without a car, I didn't envision a date beyond trying to talk to her at school. I liked her, but she paid little attention to me. She was in the Russian Club and learning the language, she was smart and obviously more academically inclined than I was. I was bumping along making mostly Cs and some Bs. (I rallied in my senior year and made honor roll.) Luckily, I had supportive and sympathetic high school teachers and accepting parents.

Undaunted, I was determined to impress Susan. I knew that the Russian Club occasionally used the auditorium. So, when she was there I would speak to her, making sure she fully appreciated my importance as stage manager. At some point soon after we became friendly, I realized Susan was dating another guy in our class, and that they went to the same church. Very disappointing news, as I felt my chances fading. But, as I had learned so many times already, good things can happen when you pursue your dreams. I was nothing else if not persistent.

CHAPTER 3

GENE-O

My after-school visits to WLLY had started to blossom into something much bigger. Bob Joyce, the afternoon DJ who started me off running errands, had been promoted to program director within weeks after I started hanging out at the station. Bob was still responsible for delivering the station's weekly hit chart to local record outlets. So, he did what managers do—delegate. Bob asked if I was interested in doing the delivery job. It would take a few hours every Saturday. I gave an emphatic "yes," not considering at that moment that I needed a car to drop the list to stores around town.

I got home and told my mother I had accepted the job and asked if she would drive me around every Saturday morning. Let's just say she did not leap at the opportunity on her day off. Instead, she pointed out that I was within days of getting my learner's permit and could drive if someone else with a license was in the car with me. My sixteen-year-old friend Kenneth Fleet, who already had his license, came to mind. Maybe he would do it, I thought, provided we could use my mother's car. By then we were a two-car family. Kenneth agreed, so he and I became WLLY's Top 40 delivery team.

In those days, the music list was typed up on a stencil, which was then wrapped around a big drum full of ink. We would hand-crank the blank preprinted letterhead paper through the machine to get a final version that looked somewhat professional. This was all done at the station, and it was time-consuming and messy. WLLY was competing with WLEE on the air musically, so it also had to compete with other music charts at record outlets. I later found out that WLEE's chart was professionally printed. Both stations tried to predict the next Top 40 hit song, and the stores used the sheets to help decide what records to stock. Sometimes the stations had the same selections, but most of their musical prognostications related to "pick hits" were different.

Between buying gas and paying Kenneth, I don't think I made any money driving around town delivering WLLY's list. But, I was working in radio—sort of. It was way more impressive than a paper route. Kenneth and I would split up and walk the deliveries to all the downtown locations before getting back into my mother's red-and-white Buick station wagon and deliver elsewhere in the city. We would finish up around two in the afternoon, then go back to the station and hang around with Bob Joyce while he did his show, which was the big Saturday afternoon countdown of the top hits as listed on the music charts we had just delivered. Bob also played some requests and birthday dedications. I would help answer the phone and write down the listener names, passing them on to Bob in my bad handwriting. On occasion, Bob would ask me while he was on live, sort of over his shoulder, "What does this say?" My distant voice replies were heard on the air. I was on the radio.

One afternoon after school when I went over to WLLY, Bob told me he had decided to make his program all request-dedications; no one else in town was doing that. People called in, requested a specific song, and wanted it dedicated to someone like their mother, girl or boyfriend, or for a birthday or anniversary. What Bob and I had been doing casually on Saturdays was going to be the main feature of his daily show, which ran from three in the afternoon until the station went off the air. That worked for me because school let out at three.

Bob wanted me to answer the phones and take down the requests—despite my lousy penmanship. It was a *real* job with real pay for about 75 cents an hour. I agreed to be there every day knowing that I would have to fit this in with studies and my obligations as stage manager at John Marshall. I was still riding the bus every day to commute between home and downtown, except Saturdays when Kenneth Fleet helped with the Top 40 delivery.

Within a day or two of starting the request and dedications format, Bob discovered we both had to answer phones; the calls never stopped. I sat across from Bob at a second microphone in the studio, which he had used to interview guests. Bob had me read the dedications I fielded and he read the ones he took. Bob would say "Here is Frankie Avalon with *Venus*. It's going out to Johnny Schwartz from his girlfriend Molly... and who else, Gene-O?" My cue to read my names.

Bob nicknamed me *Gene-O* without asking how I liked it. He never said "I have this high school kid in here so I'm getting him to work cheap because he loves radio." Suddenly, I was Bob Joyce's sidekick—Gene-O, the dedication voice.

I worked the job two to five hours every afternoon from Monday to Saturday. A lot of people listened to WLLY; it seemed everybody at John Marshall High knew I was Gene-O, the radio dedications kid, including my teachers. One of my jobs at school was to read announcements in the school cafeteria at lunchtime, so students were hearing the same voice. I think my parents were more than surprised that their gangly mid-teen was becoming a local celebrity.

Bob treated me as his partner on the air, and took me to his record hops where we both talked to the crowd and took turns spinning vinyl. I went to his house for dinner, met his mother and his girlfriend, Joyce. I also sat next to him in the studio while he talked to his friends on the phone about all kinds of adult things—a real education for an impressionable teenager. Bob would let me drive his T-Bird convertible when we went to the hops, which I could not believe was happening.

**Bob Joyce and me throwing out free 45rpm records
at a hop WLLY staged in the basement of The Mosque auditorium.**

Looking back on it with less star-struck eyes, it might have been that Bob let me drive because he enjoyed sipping hard liquor from a silver flask and didn't want to drink and drive. Whatever his reason, accompanying him was a chance of a lifetime for me. Bob became a mentor and friend, teaching me the ropes and giving me an unvarnished view of the radio business.

Bob had been stationed in Europe while in armed forces radio before coming back to Richmond. I think Bob was about thirty when I met him, and he seemed mature and worldly to me. Bob talked about jazz clubs in New York and Paris, he subscribed to *Downbeat* and *Playboy* magazines, and would go to see any jazz band playing at one of Richmond's small clubs. I never understood the attraction of jazz, as it was so unlike the top hits we were playing on the radio.

• • •

It didn't take long for Gene-O, the dedications kid, to want his own radio show. The station had just hired a young college guy named Dave Van Horn to do weekend DJ work, which is what I really wanted to do. But I didn't want to seem ungrateful or pushy.

Dave turned out to be a great guy. On several occasions he brought me along to a college function he thought I'd be interested in. Dave was attending Richmond Professional Institute (RPI), an extension of the College of William and Mary. RPI would later become Virginia Commonwealth University.

I continued to look for opportunities and spotted one on Saturdays when WLLY did not have anyone at the station to read the news. During the week, a DJ who was not on-air doing a live show would read five-minute's worth of news copy under a different name, or under no name at all. Sometimes the station owner would do it. WLLY did not have many employees, so Bob asked me to start reading the news during his live Saturday show so he could take a five-minute break. I was more than happy to do it. It gave me a chance to be on the air more, but it was also a major challenge. I was nervous the first few times, but my year of practice at WBUG before becoming the dedication voice on WLLY helped. Most DJs hated reading news, but for me it was chance to establish credibility.

At the time it was called "rip and read" because you would go to the AP (Associated Press) machine, a non-stop typewriter with clanging bells for breaking stories. DJs would rip individual news items from a long roll of paper that had been spit out onto the floor. There were typically dozens of news items to choose from. Radio newscasts would be updated every hour by the AP. The DJ would rip new items to read while a record was playing, and then run back into the main studio and rehearse to avoid mistakes.

Many of the news items contained names of people or communities, or big words, that I did not know how to pronounce—even when they were spelled phonetically. Rather than risk flubbing a word or name, I would just skip them. If a foreign official was being quoted in a news story I would just give his title. Not one time in the years I skipped a name did anyone ask why. One name I didn't skip was my own. I was newscaster *Gene Loving*—not Gene-O.

I cringe when listening to some of the old recordings of me on WLLY promo disks. I had a Southern, distinctly Richmond accent at a time when *real* announcers were supposed to have perfect diction. Also, I sounded like the kid I was. Another embarrassment was that my vocabulary was limited, so I used the same words too often. I'm guessing I sounded perfectly normal to other young Richmonders listening in, but I also bet a lot of listeners must have thought that WLLY was desperate. At the time, I was oblivious to my "Richmond sound," thinking only that being a dedication reader was the first rung on the ladder to a full-time DJ show. If this had been 1961 or later, after WLLY had become established—not 1958 at a start-up station—I don't think I would even been hired to deliver their music charts.

The station had very little money and all of these new daytime stations were trying to figure out how they would compete with the established giants. Again, I was at the right place at the right time. I think the owner and Bob Joyce figured, "Let's put a teen on the air on a show aimed at teens. He's known at his high school where half the tenth-through-twelfth-graders in the city go. Maybe he can bring a few people over to listen." Who knows what their real motivation was; they didn't tell me. Now that I think about it, my high school teachers probably cringed, too, at my stunted vocabulary and accent. That may explain why they rushed me along with honors. They wanted to get me out of high school ASAP to prevent further embarrassment—and the feeling was mutual.

Bob and me guest hosting with Roy Lamont on Channel 12 TV.

• • •

Embarrassment was certainly not the goal. So, I practiced— a lot.

Since WLLY signed off at sundown, which was 5 p.m. in the winter, the studio was available to me to practice everything: running the control board, getting a record ready to play, and starting one of the four turntables used for commercials and jingles, or a live thirty-second tout about a sponsor's product. I had watched George Prescott and then Bob Joyce enough to grasp how it was really done. Finally, Bob gave me a chance to sign on WLLY Sunday mornings and do some DJing between church programs and other prerecorded shows, which most all stations aired early Sundays to take care of their FCC commitment to "public service." The station engineer did weekly maintenance early Sundays, so he covered the FCC license requirements because I had yet to obtain a permit to turn on the transmitter.

About the time I believed Bob was going to promote me to mid-days Saturday, I got a serious shock. I came in one afternoon to do our regular call-in show and Bob said he was moving to Las Vegas, leaving the next day. He did not think WLLY had a promising future and said that I should look for another job right away. Easier said than done. I had stumbled into the job I had at WLLY, and what we had been doing with the dedications still had limited appeal. WLLY felt like family to me and the idea of leaving my ever-so-slight fame was frightening.

Bob had known about the Vegas job for a couple of weeks and said he had been thinking about what to tell me. He said he had always wanted to work in Vegas because of the jazz scene there. Bob Joyce stayed in Las Vegas for the rest of his career, writing the jazz column for the main regional newspaper, and doing a weekend jazz show from studios at the Tropicana Hotel. I remained in touch, grateful to Bob for giving me my first real job in radio for pay. Decades later, our company, MAX Media, would own radio stations in Las Vegas. But by then, Bob had passed on to that big record hop in the sky.

It seemed likely the dedication show Bob had started with me would be scrapped after his departure. So the very next day I decided to walk a couple blocks down the street to visit a new daytime station that had just signed on a few months before.

· · ·

WEZL, pronounced *weasel*, was five times more powerful than WLLY—five thousand watts, like WLEE. The station had moved into an old three-story house on Grace Street and painted a giant weasel on the side. WEZL initially was going to position itself as Richmond's *EZ* listening station, but at the last minute they decided to go Top 40. WEZL jumped into the Richmond radio fray by hiring Jess DuBois, professionally known as Jess DuBoy, as program manager and afternoon DJ. Jess was a young, well-known Richmond music star with a 1957 hit single called *Beautiful Love* on ABC records, with his backup group, The Hitchhikers. Jess had made several appearances on Channel 12's local afternoon teen dance party hosted by Roy Lamont. Jess was about twenty-four years old, married to a former Miss Virginia, and now he was the lead DJ at WEZL. He was, in my eyes, a big-time personality and someone whom I desperately needed to meet.

I had never seen Jess in person, so I was nervous about going into the station and asking if I could visit him while he was on the air. WEZL encouraged visitors because, as a new station, they needed to promote their air talent and build listener loyalty. I was sent to the second floor studio. The receptionist thought I was just another fan. My plan was to see if I could connect with Jess the way I had with Bob Joyce. I introduced myself as Gene Loving, and was shocked beyond belief when Jess said, "The same Gene Loving on WLLY?" Turns out he had been listening to WLLY prior to signing on with WEZL and was very familiar with our request-dedication show. Jess complimented me on the speed at which I had been able to read off names and dedicate songs. I disclosed to Jess that Bob Joyce was leaving WLLY for Vegas and said "Bob didn't believe WLLY would continue the two-man show," so I might need a job.

I had just turned sixteen and had sprouted to a six-foot-three beanpole and must have looked older than my years. Jess never asked whether I was in school or any personal information. He treated me as a professional. Maybe it was because Jess himself was new to radio. Whatever the reason, I could tell he was sizing me up. I knew I had two things in my favor: my WLLY experience, and just days earlier I had obtained the FCC license I needed to work taking transmitter readings. I also had a car—finally.

I had convinced my father that I really needed transportation. My Sunday shift at WLLY started at 5 a.m. and I think my parents understood taking a bus that ran sporadically so early in the day might risk my job. I don't think the option of my father getting up at 4:30 a.m. to drive me to work was too appealing, either. Around December 1, a couple of weeks after my birthday, my dad bought me a used, hand-painted Hillman Minx—a small family car similar to the better-known Sunbeam. Almost no one in Richmond had a European car, and certainly no one had a Minx painted by hand with a paintbrush. The car was a four-door pale blue model and just outright strange looking. But since it was a gift and I needed wheels, I was not about to complain—but when I went on a date, my father let me use his Cadillac. Turns out, that wasn't much of an inconvenience for him: I was so busy with school and radio jobs I didn't have time to date much. My

Hillman eventually crapped out on a cold winter morning, so after I used my mother's car to get to work, my father traded in the Hillman on a black 1952 two-door Chevrolet. The car looked pretty good, but it, too, was also not 100 percent reliable.

My first car, a Hillman Minx.

• • •

In the summer of 1959 I had started to study to get a certificate from the FCC that I needed in order to operate certain broadcast equipment and record readings from the transmitter. I didn't need it for what I was doing at WLLY at the beginning, but I figured it would come in handy if I stayed in radio. The closest FCC office at the time was in Norfolk; so after studying a book for a few months I traveled the 90 miles southeast to take the test. I passed and was mailed a little card that looked like a driver's license—an official document from the agency that had brought the hammer down on me a couple of years earlier for being a pirate broadcaster on WBUG.

Jess didn't waste much time making up his mind about my skills and credentials because he gave me an immediate test. He handed me the five-minute newscast he had just ripped from the AP machine, which he was due to deliver shortly. "Go in the newsroom and read this when I point to you," he said. It was a live audition. I did it, and it must have sounded okay, because he started talking to me about a job—a DJ job—he'd call *The Gene Loving Show*, from 5 to 7 a.m. every morning before school. Jess needed to fill the slot quickly because the guy who had been doing it was staying on until 9 a.m., and four hours every morning while in college was too much for him. I immediately accepted the job, believing that my trusty but ugly Hillman Minx would get me there on time.

• • •

I went to WLLY the next day and nervously gave notice to the owner, Lou Adelman, who was always smoking a cigar. I don't think he cared or thought my departure unexpected; he knew Bob and I were close and my resignation most likely saved him from having to fire me. Quitting my first radio job was easier than I thought.

Jess DuBoy just as he looked when I first met him at WEZL.

CHAPTER 4

THE BIG WEASEL

When I started at WEZL, I learned from the college guy, Lou Brink who had been doing the 5-to-9-a.m. slot, how to get the station technically ready for the morning broadcast. The job included sifting through the reams of AP radio newscast updates that had piled up on the floor overnight. Carlton Shrieves, another RPI student, would be my relief at 9 a.m. It turned out that he and I would work at the same radio stations off and on for the next thirty-six years.

That night, after WEZL signed off, I returned to the control room, practicing on the control board, learning how WEZL played commercials off of tape recorders, getting comfortable with saying "WEZL" instead of "WLLY."

My days were packed, more so than ever. I'd be at the station by 4:30 a.m. and then bolt out of there at 7 a.m. I drove eight blocks to school, studied from 7:30 until 9 a.m., go to class, and afterwards head back to WEZL to hang out. I joined Jess, and others, many nights for dinner. I usually went to bed around 10 p.m. and was up again by 4 a.m. A couple of times after he got off the air, Jess came to my house for dinner. My mother was thrilled that such a big star was eating her cooking. She was very favorably impressed with Jess DuBois.

Between work and school I was also trying to foster a romantic relationship. Whenever possible I was seeing Susan Onyschuk for short dates, like going for a hamburger at a drive-in. My life was one mad dash of activity.

A couple of months into the job, Jess also assigned me the Sunday afternoon show he had been doing, which started at 2 p.m. Working six days a week was normal in radio. Jess had decided to take weekends off—the privilege of rank. I was wide-eyed and thrilled at the opportunity to work Sunday. I was building my résumé, and the Sunday audience was bigger than my early morning weekday shift. In those days of no FM competition, longtime on-air personalities dominated the morning ratings, and it was very hard for an upstart station to break listening habits. WEZL was knocking heads with the formidable Harvey Hudson on WLEE, and Alden Aaroe on WRVA, both of whom had been on-air since the mid-1940s.

Me doing my show at WEZL.

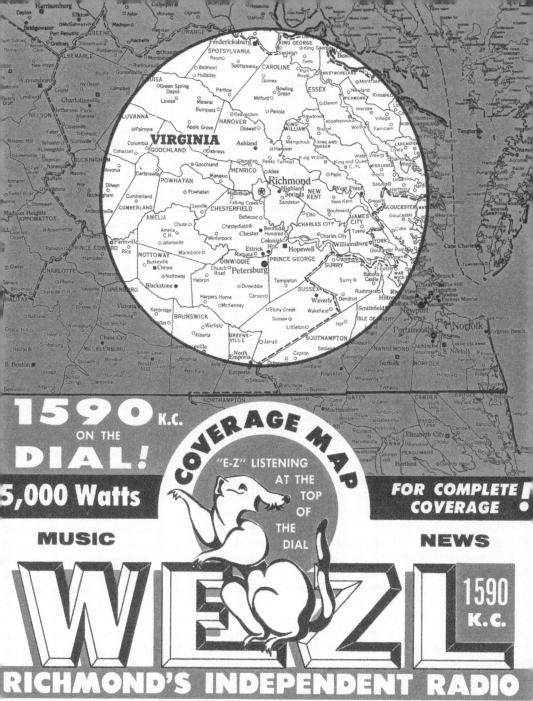

A copy of the coverage map from 1959 when I was on WEZL
doing Monday through Friday, and Sundays.

We were also competing against WRNL on Sundays. *The Richmond News Leader,* the city's afternoon daily newspaper, owned WRNL and had pumped a lot of money into it. WRNL had a top studio building and major on-air content. On Sunday afternoons WRNL aired network news shows, and a live local talent-scout program from its audience theater. Roger Mudd, who would later become a network star at CBS News, was one of the local talents discovered there.

• • •

Suprisingly, as the new kid on the block, The Big WEZL scored quickly in the ratings. We were very happy to be tied for second on Sundays with WLEE. I attribute the station's quick success to the vision and resources of its owner, William Benns.

Benns was a radio engineer, so he outfitted his stations with the latest equipment, which improved the air quality and flow of commercials, jingles, and music. Most notable was a rack of three Ampex tape recorders, plus a big one in the back of the studio which could be remotely operated by a DJ using the main control board. This meant we had high-quality jingles and commercials. In fact, our broadcast quality was superior to WLEE or WLLY in many respects. WEZL used tape for almost everything we produced at the station so it could be repeatedly played back without wearing out; WLEE and WLLY recorded their commercials and jingles on what was essentially a big plastic record. After a few dozen plays it got scratchy and everything on it had to be re-recorded.

WEZL was reinventing itself every month; management actually acted on one of my ideas. Since the station called itself *weasel,* like the rodent, I suggested we get a real weasel as a mascot that we could take for personal appearances on a leash. Within a few days someone found and bought a weasel, which was kept in a large cage. Guess who was assigned to take care of the weasel? What I didn't know, and I suspect no one else at the station knew either, is that weasels are dirty, smelly and vicious—or at least ours was. When I tried to clean its cage it bit me on my right index finger, severing the tendon and crippling my writing hand to this day. I had to go to the hospital to be bandaged, and the weasel had to be checked for rabies. The only time I recall using the little nipper was at the Virginia State Fair where WEZL had a broadcast booth. We invited folks to come by and name our weasel.

Requests for us to appear at record hops poured in. To fulfill the gigs, I teamed up with Carlton Shrieves, the college-student DJ. Maybe I was afraid that my '52 Chevy was unreliable and I needed someone else to drive, or maybe Carlton didn't want to lug all the equipment by himself. Whatever the reasons, we made a good on-the-road team.

Carlton was about twenty-one at the time. He had a two-door black 1949 Ford with a very good AM radio. We drove to locations that were often a couple of hours from Richmond due to the broad coverage of WEZL. On some of the narrow back roads we could only get the Ford up to 35 miles an hour. While driving, we often listened to the out of town fifty-thousand-watt stations fading in and out, borrowing ideas from the big name DJ's. Most notable was a guy out of Cincinnati who created a little character he called *the Fluke*. We found it fascinating that a radio personality was creating something out of nothing. It was pure theater.

• • •

One of my most memorable road trips was with Jess DeBois. He knew my mother had a station wagon, which was not that common in the 1950s. So Jess asked if I would drive him and his band to New York City for the Saturday night Dick Clark show. I had never driven farther than Norfolk, and I had never been to New York City. I jumped at the chance to go, but I would have to convince my parents to risk the car. It was not an easy sell. They agreed to let us use the station wagon, provided Jess drove. He had been to New York a few times and had lived in Washington with his parents, so he understood big-city traffic and how to get to New York. Like I said, my mom had been impressed with Jess.

Jess managed a local band called The Rock-A-Teens, which had released a song on Roulette Records titled *Woo Hoo*. Various versions of the song have stuck around for decades, and it was used by Quentin Tarantino in his 2003 movie, *Kill Bill Vol. 1*, starring Uma Thurman. At the time of its release in 1959, *Woo Hoo* climbed to sixteenth on the Billboard Hot 100. (If you're into music history, Roulette Records and its manager, Morris Levy, are worth Googling.)

Dick Clark's Saturday Night Beechnut Show, broadcast live from the Little Theater in New York, was the most important music program on TV at that time. And the Rock-A-Teens were invited to appear on Dick Clark's show. Dick had already become the king of hit music via his daily *American Bandstand* show from Philadelphia. Jess informed me, confidentially, that he was the actual voice on *Woo Hoo.* But Jess was signed to ABC records, so he had to keep this fact secret. The Rock-A-Teens' lead singer, Vic Mizel, would lip-sync the song on TV.

At about 2 a.m. as Jess and I came up out of the tunnel from New Jersey into New York, I saw steam rising from the subway grates and sensed the smell of the city. We found our hotel, got a few hours' sleep and then headed to the theater. I sat in one of the one hundred audience seats and watched as that night's acts rehearsed. After a few run-throughs with someone standing in for Dick Clark, *Mr. Magic* himself appeared. I was star-struck to be this close to one of the best known figures in broadcasting. But a couple of things went badly during the rehearsals and I was surprised to hear language from Dick Clark that he could not use on the air. At one point he dropped his mic on purpose and just walked off.

I went backstage to the Rock-A-Teens' dressing room on the third floor and ran right into Dick Clark standing in the hall talking to rock 'n roll star Freddy Cannon. I had planned to ask Dick for an autograph, so I did. He signed a piece of paper I handed him—I still have it. This was a big deal for me. Little did I know I would one day be in business with Dick Clark.

Actual Dick Clark autograph, which I obtained backstage at the *Saturday Night Beechnut Show* in New York. 1959

After the show, which seemed to go perfectly to me, Jess and I had to go get my mother's station wagon to pick up the band members. The entire block from Broadway to 8th Avenue was closed off due to a crush of teens surrounding the theater to get autographs. When the band members appeared and made their way to the station wagon, the kids were all over the hood of my mother's Buick. Thankfully, Jess got us out of there before any real damage was done. We left New York City and drove back to Richmond.

I had a mentor, guardian and friend in Jess DuBois. He continued to create opportunities for me at WEZL and taught me a lot about show business. What I lacked, however, was an education in office politics. As with so much in life and business, radio is a push-pull industry with winners and losers. I was about to see that firsthand.

• • •

Transistor radios were just getting popular, so I bought one. Mine was about the size of two packs of cigarettes, costing me a months-worth of record hop money. The transistor was a marvel for its time, a technological game-changer. Radio was now portable.

I arrived at WEZL and showed Jess my new radio. He took it, asked me to sit down and fill in for him on his show because he "had to do something." This was around three-thirty in the afternoon. Jess never came back. I finished his show, signed off the station and went looking for Jess. I was told he had quit. My first thought was *Where's my radio?* My second thought was *Now what?*

I knew each station had a general manager. And I had noticed that the ones at WLLY and WEZL barely said hello to the staff—and never to a lowly part-time student like me. I knew there were salespeople who brought in the ads and others who handled all the business stuff. What I didn't fully appreciate was the dynamic—and pecking order—of station owners, their general managers and the program directors. I knew that on-air and support staff came and went, but I didn't grasp why.

Jess' fate at WEZL had been sealed when William Benns fired the station's GM and the owner brought in a replacement from Washington, Sid Magaloff. From what I could gather, Jess and Magaloff clashed over the station's imaging—the so-called one-liners that described the station. Magaloff immediately wanted to start using the phrase *The New WEZL*, similar to what he had been doing at the Benns-owned station in Washington, WEAM. Jess wanted to stick with *The Big Weasel*, believing you can't become "new" when the station was only ninety days old.

Jess had been sitting in the studio fuming when I arrived that afternoon. He then had gone into the GM's office—and that was the end of that. When I left work that evening I found my new transistor radio in the front seat of my car. That evening, I reached Jess at his home and he told me what happened.

The next day I was temporarily plopped into Jess' old shift as the afternoon man. The station also had me still doing the two-hour show that started at 5 a.m. All of us DJs at that time, except Jess, were part-time and had other obligations, like school. I was the most available. Basically, I was working before school started and now several hours after it let out. The only time I wasn't on-air was when I was in classes, or sleeping, or sleeping in class.

A few weeks after Jess left, a new program director was hired. Earl Sherman was middle-aged with wavy gray hair and had a girlfriend who never left his side. Earl was gruff but soft-spoken when he told you off, usually addressing me as "hey, kid." I don't recall exactly how Earl rearranged the DJ schedule, but I went back to mornings pulling at least a five-hour shift on Sunday afternoon, until sign-off, which at times kept me on for seven hours straight. I was doing a lot of on-air work, taking care of the weasel and playing chauffeur. I also got to do my first star interview because Earl Sherman didn't want to waste his time on a "has-been" named Johnny Cash. I was sent to the Jefferson Hotel with a tape recorder to talk to this country music legend. At the time Sun Records was trying to relaunch Johnny's career following his time in jail. The local stations were invited for breakfast and a chat. Sadly, I was the only one there. I pre-scripted my questions and played the interview on my Sunday afternoon show.

· · ·

Several of WEZL's Richmond competitors were also in the local news business. So, they had logos painted on their cars, creating rolling billboards visible around the city. Harvey Hudson drove a Ford convertible with his name on the side, supplied to him by a Ford dealership—one of his main sponsors. WLEE personality Lud Sterling drove an old Chrysler painted silver with his name on the side. He was known as the station's "Silver Man," probably because of the color of his hair. I suggested to Earl Sherman that WEZL get a Cadillac limousine, so our station personalities could use it to drive to hops, or be in parades, and we could pick up recording stars at the airport. We would have something none of the others had. The station obtained a ten-year-old limo a few days later and turned the keys over to me.

I parked the car at John Marshall High during the day and drove it home at night. Why? There was no room at WEZL to keep it parked, and other potential chauffeurs were college kids who lived in dorms with no parking. The other reason: Earl did not have a driver's license; his girlfriend had to drive him everywhere, which is probably why she was always at his side.

She thought the limo was too big for her to handle. I was very happy working at WEZL, doing record hops, driving the limo, and trying to figure out how to get rid of that nasty weasel.

WLLY radio was sold about this time. Amazingly, the new ownership included my former mentor, Jess DuBois. The radio world, which seemed so vast to me as a young teen, now began to feel much smaller and interconnected. Radio stations, just like the people who worked in them, traded back and forth. Competitors often raided each other's staff. I had only been in the business two years—at the bottom rungs—and, at just seventeen years old, I was about to jump ship again.

• • •

In April 1960, my mother took a phone message for me to call George Prescott, my old friend from WLEE. I called George as soon as I heard, and he told me that Harvey Hudson wanted to see me right away. Harvey, my early DJ idol, was also the general manager of WLEE.

I was ushered into Harvey's office where we were joined by George and WLEE's program director, Dave Lyman. The trio said they had been monitoring my progress at WLLY and WEZL and they wanted me on their team. They offered me the biggest show for Top 40 in the Richmond market, *Music After Hours* from 9 p.m. to 2 a.m. Monday through Friday, plus a weekend shift. The pay was $75 a week. Neither WLLY nor WEZL was on the air at night, so WLEE had a monopoly when it came to playing the hits. The job was to start the day I graduated from John Marshall High, considering the late hours, but they wanted me at the station right away. I accepted the job.

WLEE's *Music After Hours* took requests and dedications by mail. Every teen in town listened to that show. *I listened to that show,* which had been hosted by Lud Sterling, who was around age fifty at the time. He created the persona "Uncle Lud" with the long white beard. I guessed that Harvey and Dave wanted a "teen" DJ to appeal to the *After Hours* teen audience. I found out later that Lud liked to drink and Harvey wanted his friend of twenty years on the air with him during the morning show so he could keep an eye on him. They ended up making a great team and became the No. 1-rated morning show.

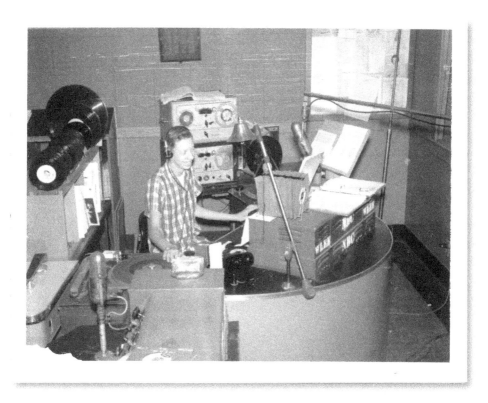

Me, age 17, hosting *Music After Hours* 9 p.m.-2 a.m. on WLEE. In those days WLEE was the No. 1 station in Richmond per the only survey taken for radio PULSE.

WLEE

1480 KC — 5000 WATTS
RICHMOND, VIRGINIA

NEWS

THOMAS TINSLEY, PRESIDENT
IRVIN G. ABELOFF, SENIOR VICE-PRESIDENT
HARVEY L. HUDSON,
VICE-PRESIDENT AND GENERAL MANAGER

HAVE YOU SEEN THE LATEST

RICHMOND AREA SURVEY★

BY PULSE, INC.

AVERAGE 1/4 HR. RATINGS DELIVERED BY EACH RICHMOND
RADIO STATION IN 9 COUNTY AREA DURING A TYPICAL BROAD-
CAST WEEK (6:00 A.M.-6:00 P.M. - MON.-FRI.)

WLEE	5.9
WANT	2.2
WEET	1.7
WEZL	.9
WMBG	.7
WRNL	2.2
WRVA	5.1
WXGI	1.3

NUMBER OF RADIO HOMES REACHED BY EACH STATION IN
9 COUNTY AREA DURING ANY AVERAGE 1/4 HOUR PERIOD

WLEE	8175
WANT	3145
WEET	2425
WEZL	1316
WMBG	1039
WRNL	3159
WRVA	7067
WXGI	1829

★ OFFICIAL AREA SURVEY BY PULSE, INC., CONDUCTED
FEBRUARY-MARCH 1961

National Representatives: **Select Station Representatives** · New York, Philadelphia, Baltimore, Washington.
Adam Young, Inc. · New England, Chicago, St. Louis, Detroit, Los Angeles, San Francisco.
James Ayers · For the South.

THESE RESULTS are based upon minimum sample of 3,080 homes by Pulse, Inc., and were made
as follows:

	Interviews %	Radio Families *
Charles City	1%	1,050
Chesterfield	13%	21,060
Goochland	1%	1,760
Hanover	5%	6,580
Henrico (including Richmond)	69%	94,410
Louisa	2%	3,100
New Kent	1%	980
Powhatan	1%	1,490
Prince George (including Hopewell)	7%	8,130

* U. S. Census adjusted to Jan. 1, 1961.　　　TOTAL.............................. 138,560

This area represents the Richmond Trading Area where many of the residents shop in Richmond for major pur-
chases and where the Richmond stations are dominant. Beyond the 9 county area measured by Pulse, the
local residents listen to stations located in other cities; for example, Norfolk, Newport News, Portsmouth, Washington, Arlington, Fredericksburg, Charlottesville, etc. This 9 county area measured by Pulse, therefore, represents the total effective listening area of the local Richmond stations and coverage beyond this point is of
negligible value.

• • •

After my meeting with Harvey, I went back to work and found Earl Sherman. I was very nervous telling Earl I was leaving. I was sure his first thought would be *Who's going to take care of that nasty little weasel?* It was much worse than that. *How could I leave after they bought the car I wanted? How could I leave him when he thought so much of me? How could I leave WEZL and go over to their biggest competitor? WLEE was just trying to get me off the air at WEZL and soon they would fire me.* No one had tried to keep me when I resigned from WLLY. So, I was shocked, a bit flattered and mostly intimidated by Earl's forceful response.

I was too embarrassed to call Harvey back to decline his offer, so I called George Prescott and told him I had changed my mind and I just couldn't leave WEZL. Lucky for me, George did not rush in to tell Harvey. Instead, he said he was doing a remote that night for the grand opening of a local hamburger store, Kelly's, and please come talk to him.

I drove the Cadillac limo over to the hamburger shop to speak face-to-face with George. He climbed in the limo and told me why I could not turn down the WLEE opportunity. Harvey Hudson had not offered me a job just to harm WEZL, George assured me. Harvey truly wanted me in his DJ lineup. I later learned that Nancy Moran, the record distributor from Allen Brothers who helped me out during my WBUG days, had been watching my professional progress. She told Harvey I had been moving up at WEZL. Nancy was highly respected within the Richmond radio community, and I am certain her endorsement carried a lot of weight with Harvey.

I flip-flopped again. I worked up the nerve and the next day I told Earl I was accepting WLEE's offer. Earl immediately took the limo keys; I collected my stuff and unceremoniously left. (I thought they might kill the weasel when I exited, but I never found out what happened to the vicious beast.)

Just before I started at WLEE, my father decided I was ready for another car. My '52 Chevy was unreliable and my dad was probably tired of loaning me his Caddy on mornings when my car didn't start. Sitting in the driveway was a used 1957 black Corvette—my dream car. I was blown away. I had been contributing to my car expenses with my radio pay, but a Corvette convertible with red leather interior was beyond anything I would have ever had the nerve to ask for. I always liked cars. My dad loved cars and had no other hobbies except washing the car. So I think he was almost as excited as I was to have a 'Vette in the Loving family. That Corvette began a lifetime of always wanting something special to drive. I was beyond joyous that summer of 1960, driving with the top down on those warm summer nights, and dating Susan. I had the ideal car and just landed the ideal job.

• • •

WLEE was much different than WLLY and WEZL. It had been on the air for years and was a financial juggernaut. And the ownership of WLEE had several of the same principal investors as WXEX-TV, which broadcast from nearby Petersburg, its city of license, but shared executive and sales offices at the WLEE building at 6200 West Broad Street in Richmond.

Because the radio and TV offices were in the same building, there were a lot of people coming to work there every day. WLEE had more salespeople than WLLY and WEZL's entire staffs put together. The station had three full-time newsmen with news cars and two-way radios, plus a news director. A couple of the salespeople also drove company cars with two-way radios so they could report on traffic and other newsworthy events. At WLEE, the news department believed it was the main driver of the station. The newsmen viewed music programs as filler between newscasts.

Dave Lyman did a mid-morning program until noon and was my direct boss as the station's Program Director. He also teamed with George Prescott as the second man on a 4-to-7 p.m. show called *Your Suppertime Hall of Hits*. As soon as I started, Dave assigned me to replace him as the second man on the 4-to-7 show with George Prescott. My job was to play the commercials off the giant discs on George's cue while he played the records. Here I was, working at WLEE with the man who recorded that tape of Ronald Peters and me three years earlier.

George was using my name, asking me to do the weather or say something else that did not require a lot of responsive thinking. WLEE had always aired a two-person format during drive-time periods, or at lunchtime from noon to 2 p.m. I soon eased into becoming a true co-host with George, often acting as straight man for his jokes. My job also included reading movie listings and live commercials. All of the DJs at WLEE—except top dog Harvey Hudson—did a split shift on the air as well as performing a variety of other off-air duties.

Recording "the book" for WXEX-TV Channel 8, Richmond's NBC station in 1960. This was one of my daily assignments at WLEE, whose owners were also the principals of WXEX. I'm recording the guest lineup for tonight's *Jack Paar Show*, after which the tape was driven to Petersburg to be broadcast on the WXEX-TV "Station Breaks."

CHAPTER 5

WLEE

The night in June 1960 that I graduated from John Marshall High, I took over as host of *Music After Hours*. I also learned I would continue as co-host of the *Suppertime Hall of Hits*, and do grunt work like opening the packages of records sent to the station, filing records, and changing the music boxes the DJ's used at record hops and on remote broadcast. If a record in the main studio was scratched and I hadn't replaced it, Harvey would send me a nasty note and a 50-cent fine. But I had a title printed on a WLEE business card for the first time: *Gene Loving, Assistant Music Director, WLEE.*

Harvey had owl ears, listening for any issue of any kind. He would often pick up the two-way radio in his Ford convertible and communicate his dismay to the DJ in the main studio. This was very unnerving the first few times it happened to me, and very different from my experiences at WLLY and WEZL. It almost made me wish I hadn't come to work at WLEE, but soon I realized I was learning things from someone who only wanted the best for the station.

Harvey was very enthusiastic about station branding. If you worked for WLEE, you *were* WLEE. In fact, he required all DJs to make *LEE* their on-air middle name. I was Gene *LEE* Loving.

At some point, Harvey thought WLLY was stirring up the ratings, so he decided we should call WLEE, *Wi*-LEE, a version of *Wiley*, which was the on-the-air name for WLLY. I thought this was silly and confusing, but Harvey did things his own way and few challenged him. He was teacher and a taskmaster, and if you wanted to benefit from his wisdom you had to toe the line.

WLEE personalities had long days due to their split shifts, which meant twelve hours of not being able to do much on personal missions. I came to work by at least 2 p.m. to do music department chores before going on air from 4 until 7 p.m. then again at 9 p.m. and finishing at 2 a.m. The half-hour commute each way added another hour daily to my six-day work schedule. When you included record hops, I was logging close to eighty hours a week.

If I recall correctly, in 1960 WLEE charged $25 for a DJ to do a record hop. The station got $5 for use of the equipment and the DJ made $20. If I did a couple of weekend events I made $40, which was more than half of my *weekly* WLEE salary of $75.

The DJs's pay was supplemented by reading live commercials on our shows for about 25 cents each (termed a "talent fee"), and doing remote broadcasts, which paid an extra two bucks. My work assignments eventually included recording station breaks for WXEX-TV. I did "the daily book" for Channel 8, the NBC station, which was their audio that went with pictures or video between or during network shows. In those days, many commercials were just color photographs on slides that were aired as the announcer (me) read a script. I also did some feature news stories on camera when regular WXEX-TV news reporters weren't available in Richmond.

Unfortunately, I never collected much "talent fee" income. Most of it went to pay *fines* issued by Harvey, or the program director Dave Lyman, for on-air mistakes. At 25 cents, 50 cents or $1 per fine, I wound up owing the station money by the end of the week. The same was true with most other DJs. With Harvey, you literally paid for your mistakes.

The pressure and long hours were unrelenting. It was radio boot camp, with Harvey Hudson as the drill instructor. In little less than the two years I worked at WLEE, about seven DJs quit. I went through four different co-hosts on the *Supper Time Hall of Hits* show. Among the causalities was the guy who recruited me to WLEE, George Prescott. He quit to go to work in Florida. And

WLEE's mid-day guy and music director Joe Murray left to join a new start-up FM classical music station.

While it made me anxious to know that Harvey could call on the two-way radio at any moment to voice an opinion, I had so little experience that all I wanted to do was please the man. Eventually, having been at WLEE six months, turning 18 years old in November 1960, I gained some confidence, protesting some of Harvey's fines, usually to no avail. What I soon discovered was that turnover created opportunity for those of us tough—or naïve—enough to survive the turmoil.

In the personnel shuffle I was moved to the main chair for the two-man 4-to-7 p.m. program. That meant I was the daily producer, saying what we would do between records. And I was given the job and title of music director. That meant I was screening all new records coming in to the station. For all of these new responsibilities I got a whopping $5-a-week raise. Still, success felt good. I had traded in the Corvette for a brand new red T Bird convertible.

sta-
)er."
ium-
iome   VITAL STATISTICS:
:tant   Dick Lawrence named new program
ying   director for WJJD-Chicago. Prior to
vell-   appointment he had been doing radio
been   work in the Empire State and at
:ey."   WCOP-Boston. . . . Robert Forward,
has   veep in charge of programs at KMPC-
ages   L.A., named exec veep and general
        manager of L.A.'s KLAC. . . . Milton
        H. Klein, general manager of KEWB-
        Oakland, has been elected to the San
        Francisco Radio Broadcasters Asso-
the   ciation for 1962. . . . Jim Gallagher,
ntist   formerly spinning for WADE-Tampa
start   in the 8-12 AM stanza, has taken
died   over the 10 AM-2 PM slot at Tampa's
e of   WINQ. . . . Gene Loving promoted to
        music director of WLEE-Richmond as
        Joe Murray, previous music topper,
        exits the station. . . . New personality
        at WROV-Roanoke is Jim Richmond,
Take   WIST-Charlotte DJ, who moves into
ional   the 9-12 AM slot opened by Dave
egon   Novak.

Cash Box—November 25, 1961

Cash Box Magazine's announcement that
I am now music director of WLEE.

• • •

The music director position meant I was dealing with all the promotion people trying to get WLEE to play their new record. Every day boxes of new releases came into the station addressed to me. And, almost every week I was meeting a new record promoter for dinner. I had learned: never assure them of airplay unless I knew beforehand that the song was going to be placed in our rotation. WLEE's program director made that decision, but it was based on what I presented to him as possible hits. Often we would listen to a record together and scan charts to see how a release was trending elsewhere.

One way for the promotion people to get a better shot at having their record played on the air was to give us an *exclusive* release over WLLY and WEZL. That allowed us to say WLEE was first to introduce new hits. I was never offered money to play a record on WLEE. However, I was courted; it was the job of the record promoters to befriend radio music directors. Dinners and free concert tickets were often given. If a recording star was appearing in Washington, a record promoter would invite me up for the show. I seldom went, though, because I just didn't have the time.

• • •

WLEE was also running promotions or some gimmick to keep the audience's attention. In one promotion, listeners voted on which DJ they'd like to send to Mars. It was a knockoff of the Jackie Gleason sitcom, *The Honeymooners*. The Gleason character, Ralph Kramden, would threaten to punch someone "bam, zoom, straight to the moon."

In this case *Mars* was Mars, Pennsylvania, and one lucky listener (and guest), whose name was drawn from a fishbowl, would join the DJ who was voted to be sent to Mars. The trip included a night in New York and a Broadway show. Dave Lyman, the station's program director, would usher everyone on the trip and Harvey Hudson would join the winner and DJ in New York for dinner and the show. I won, or lost, depending on your point of view. Listeners wanted to send me more than any other DJ, to Mars.

When we landed in Pittsburgh, about 50 miles from Mars, there was a major welcoming committee at the bottom of the ramp. About twenty citizens and the mayor handed us city memorabilia, including a Martian hat which I still have. When we got to town they had arranged a parade with bands and other attractions. A few hundred people came out to cheer as we rode in an open convertible. We got the key to the city, and dinner at the country club. The next, day we flew to New York. This was a first-class experience: The Plaza, dinner at Trader Vic's and a Broadway show—my first—*The Music Man*. I loved the New York City scene and was determined to come back soon to see more.

Tom Martin (left), the salesman at WLEE who showed up at his client's remote broadcast, and me at the famous Snake Pit Promotion at Southside Plaza. Yes, the snake is alive and heavy. I hold the snake in hopes it will say something as Tom keeps the microphone nearby.

Another crazy WLEE stunt. A tricyle race between myself (left), Art Lane, Dave Lyman and Mickey Kahn. Any listener that picked the winner in advance got a free pizza. Yes, it was about 35 degrees and live outdoor remotes happened no matter what the weather.

Miss Personality Pageant, 1961

The judge on the left is not known, but typically the station would invite the manager of Thalhimer's department store or the owner of a modeling agency. Next to the unknown judge is Harvey Hudson wearing one of the suits he just had shined. At the end is Bernie Wayne, down from NYC, to do locally what he does yearly in Atlantic City as a judge for the Miss America Pageant. This was fun live broadcasting at a time people really listened to these special shows. I am the one in the white coat.

• • •

Much of WLEE's appeal was personality-based and because of this the station did lots of live promotions and remote broadcasts. We did so many, in fact, that it was a treat to actually do a show from the studio. One of my biggest remote gigs came within my first month of taking over the evening DJ slot. I was told WLEE had just sold a live broadcast sponsorship of my show to the Beacon Drive-In restaurant on Broad Street. I would be doing the 9-to-11 p.m. segment of the show from the restaurant parking lot, broadcasting the prerecorded 11-to-11:30 p.m. segment to allow time to drive back to the station, and then finishing the show from the main studio. An engineer in the station's highly decorated WLEE Volkswagen van would play all the records and recorded commercials and I would roam around with the world's longest microphone cable and interview people in their cars who came out for a burger or pizza.

I just didn't feel experienced enough to do this, and interviewing people scared me. I was going to have to think on my feet and interact with the listeners face-to-face instead of the one-dimensional comfort of facing a microphone in a studio. I had done a little improvising with a Gillette razor commercial at WEZL, which I had to ad-lib every day from a fact sheet. But that was nothing like hosting what was essentially a never-ending live event, interacting with the people who may say who knows what.

Within a few days of starting the Beacon Drive-In night show at WLEE, Gillette decided to move their ads from WEZL to me at WLEE, doing the same ad-lib. I was still so young I didn't even shave, but Harvey asked his national sales company to hide that fact from Gillette, which had only heard me on tape. I have that memo.

The live nightly Beacon Broadcast ended up being the best education I could have ever gotten. It made me an entertainer— not a DJ doing planned patter. I soon got very comfortable doing the "man on the street" version of the show, and teens and their parents poured in to eat Beacon burgers in hopes I would come around, ask their names on the air, and chat with them.

Broadcasting from the Beacon Drive-In with recording star Johnny Tillotson who had a big hit at the time, *Poetry in Motion*. Johnny is just to the left of the poodle.

I interview a "man on the street," someone walking past Miller and Rhoads department store, most likely at Christmas based on the coats. These remotes from all over Richmond were a big part of WLEE's image at the time that the station was "everywhere."

• • •

Another of WLEE's hallmark remote broadcasts was a program from noon to 2 p.m. every day from Nick's House of Steaks, which was about 2 miles from the radio station at Staples Mill Road near Broad Street. WLEE kept a permanent broadcast line to Nick's and had a rather simple turntable-mic setup at the first table where patrons entered the dining room. Lud Sterling and Juanita Hove did the show most of the time weekdays and Harvey did a live two-hour show on Saturdays at 6 p.m.

Except for Harvey Hudson's show, no programs were named for the DJ on the air. Every show had its own institutional name, but the DJs came and went. It was the same concept as the *Tonight* or *Today* shows on NBC. There was no time limit on what you could say, as long as it was meaningful, entertaining or informative. If someone called in with something of interest, you could put them on the air over the phone and chat about it.

The Nick's restaurant programs set the standard, though, allowing DJs to ad lib with patrons, asking their names, where they lived, and about menu choices. Harvey encouraged—make that required—all of us to do remote broadcast, because that's how he grew up in radio. But not everybody wanted to know the name of another WLEE listener's pet dog or why someone was dining at Nick's, and WLEE's emphasis, I think, was one of the reasons WEZL, the competitor, got so far so fast in the ratings, as WEZL focused on Top 40 hits only.

Despite the stress, I enjoyed working in the freewheeling atmosphere of WLEE—much more so than with the heavily formatted music jukebox, which was essentially WLLY and WEZL. I was learning to communicate, and sell the clients' products on the air. Almost all Richmond business commercials were done live from a script or a fact sheet at WLEE: in contrast, half or more were prerecorded at WEZL on their fancy high-end tape equipment.

WLEE did have an orderly rotation of the records—but it was a system that seemed to change every few months. WLEE's format was fairly loose compared to the tight regimens of our competitors—except when it came to the news.

WLEE was a Mutual Radio Network affiliate, which ranked third behind NBC and CBS. That meant that every hour we joined the Mutual Network for its five-minute newscast. On the half hour, the WLEE newsmen did local Richmond or state news. A major Harvey Hudson fine was triggered when a DJ talked over a segue to a Mutual Network Newscast.

At 6 p.m., during our *Supper Time Hall of Hits,* Mutual had its marquee commentator on for fifteen minutes, a man named Fulton Lewis, Jr. Harvey knew Fulton and once he invited him to speak at a local club, so on the day Fulton came to Richmond his nationwide show originated from our newsroom during my program. So honored was Harvey Hudson that he had asked the WLEE janitor, Otha, to double-clean the building the day Fulton Lewis visited. The big opportunity for someone at WLEE would be to act as Mr. Lewis' announcer for the program, introducing him, and then reading the network commercial. Lud Sterling, whose legal name was Sterling Ludgate, was chosen for the honor. Lud did a perfect job. I watched Fulton and Lud, thinking *These guys are speaking to a nationwide audience. Wow!*

WLEE routinely sold a local sponsorship for the Mutual Network news. It was our job to read the local commercial while listening to the network announcer in our headphones. I had to pick up the cue to rejoin the network, saying "Now, back to the news," or the name of the newscaster, at just the exact right second. Listening to someone talk in your ear the whole time you're reading something different was not easy. I had to practice doing it in a production studio for days before I felt comfortable. Making everything seamless was fun, once you got the hang of it.

Typical WLEE remote broadcast for the grand opening of a business. Most of the time, two or three of the DJs were present as two-man shows were common on the station. Here, Lud Sterling (left) gives the sponsor's pitch while I look on, wearing an outfit I saved in case the style comes back: white belt, white shoes, pants two inches too short, and a very thin tie. WLEE salesman Mickey Kahn is behind me and the famous WLEE mobile VW studio rounds out the picture. This is the same mobile studio used every night when I did my program from the Beacon Drive-In.

• • •

On Sunday mornings WLEE featured classical music for an hour. I could pronounce only a few of the great conductors' names and knew little about their work. So, I mostly kept quite except to say the station's call letters and frequency on the dial—1480. The station also did sports. We had the rights to VPI football.

Harvey Hudson called the games and news director CB Bailey did "color." On occasion, the engineer, Tom Kita, also chimed in with comments on what was happening in the stadium. Most of these games were on Saturday afternoon, and for many of them I rode the board back at the studio and on cue from Harvey, did live inserts which could come at any moment depending on the action on the field, so I couldn't even go to the bathroom. I also had to read the scores of other games at other schools. It was another part of radio that I had not experienced at WLLY or WEZL.

We also broadcast big band music, just like stations did in the 1930s and 1940s. Whenever one of the name bands came to town to play at Tantilla Gardens, a venue from yesteryear, Harvey would usually emcee the event and WLEE would broadcast all of it, without regard to the drift from our Top 40 format. Harvey assigned me to join him a couple of times as co-emcee.

Harvey knew several big band stars, and was friends with trombonist and bandleader Buddy Morrow. Once, I had a chance to sit with Harvey and Buddy after the show. As they talked about touring during the big band heyday, I remained silent and star-struck, listening to stories about a time when I had been listening to these broadcasts on my bedroom radio.

Me with announcer John Wilson (L), live on WLEE, in front of Ray McKinley and the Glenn Miller Orchestra. We were doing an afternoon gig for the grand opening of a Ford dealership.

WLEE announcers on stage at Tantilla Gardens with the Buddy Morrow Night Train Orchestra, another live big band remote. (L-R:) Me, Harvey Hudson, Lud Sterling, Dave Lyman, and Joe Murray

• • •

One of my biggest thrills from that live-broadcast period was a late-night show from the Thunderbird Club with one of my original favorites—Fats Domino. The station engineers had set up mics around Fats' band, and added one mic at the piano. When I arrived I was very surprised that Fats, whom I had met the prior year when he appeared at the Mosque, had agreed that I would sit on the piano bench with him as he performed. We chatted between songs, teeing up the next one that Fats would sing. The club was packed, the band was terrific, and it was unbelievable I was there with one of the best artists ever in rock 'n' roll. I only wish they had taped that broadcast back at the station; it would have been a real treasure for me.

• • •

Being courted by record promoters, interviewing rock 'n' roll stars plus comped visits to Washington and New York widened my eighteen-year-old eyes. I had a glimpse of the *big time* and very much wanted to be a part of it. To get there I knew I would need more polish, just like my Ford Thunderbird.

John Wilson, whom I first met at WEZL, was still in college at RPI and filling in sometimes at WLEE. John, who was two years older than me, had become a friend by helping to expand my exposure to college life. On some evenings between my split shift, John and I would meet for a sandwich. John was very involved in the Drama Department at RPI and appeared in many of the school's plays and musicals. I went to several performances and heard him sing. I was very impressed, as he had the aura and sound of a star. I also thought his radio voice was much better than mine.

John, like me, was a Virginia boy. He had worked at his hometown station in Big Stone Gap before moving to Richmond to go to school. And, like me, John said he had a bit of an accent before starting college. John pointed out that my *local speech* could hurt me if I wanted to move to another market, like New York. So, he suggested I start classes at RPI in voice and diction under the tutelage of Raymond Hodges, the famous head of the Drama Department. Actor Warren Beatty and his sister, Shirley MacLaine, had been taught by him when they went to college in Richmond.

Classes were in the morning, so this meant little sleep for a couple of semesters, but it was one of the best things I could have done. I shed my Southern sound. To this day, my diction remains generic. Plus, speech classes also helped me to project, enunciate and have more confidence when I was reporting on a newscast.

My voice went out across the country one night late after the regular newsmen at WLEE had gone home. There was a major plane crash at Richmond's Byrd airport. During this tragedy, as our regular newsman was on the way to the scene I did two live feeds on the story for the Mutual Network—without the Virginia twang. The next day I expected job offers to pour in from around the country. None came.

· · ·

John Wilson and I continued to pal around and even took a couple of road trips together, including three days in New York. We rode the Greyhound bus to the city and, once there, we were treated like royalty. Our boss, Harvey, called on some friends to show us around, and I had some record company contacts who were happy to get us great Broadway show tickets. John and I lapped it up. We saw a matinee of *Camelot*, starring Richard Burton and Julie Andrews. We also saw a performance of *The Fantasticks*, a musical with lyrics by Tom Jones. We were in the audience during the broadcast of the popular TV game show *What's My Line?* We attended a private movie showing in a living room setup at one of the major studio offices, and went to WABC to watch Howard Cosell do a sports broadcast. He did so without notes or a teleprompter; he had a photographic memory. After seeing Howard, I was wishing I had that kind of retention, too. A few months later I made another New York sojourn with my old neighborhood buddy and WLLY chart delivery mate Kenneth Fleet. New York was getting in my blood.

(L-R:) Kenneth Fleet, myself, special guest, Bernie Wayne, writer of *Blue on Blue*, a hit for Bobby Vinton, and *There She Is,* the theme song for the Miss America pageant. Bernie sent roses to Angie Loving in 1982 with a note saying "she was his Miss America," inviting us to dinner at the Dunes Hotel in Vegas.

• • •

One day Harvey came to my cluttered music desk and said he wanted me to go on an agency call with him in New York. I was floored to be invited by the boss to go anywhere, especially to the international advertising agency J. Walter Thompson to discuss a Ford Motors account. I think Harvey wanted to say the two of us were both driving Fords. Some of my peers at WLEE were jealous; Harvey never had taken a mere DJ on such a trip.

Harvey was a bachelor and lived with his mother whom he called Aunt Lill. Often he would broadcast from home, talking about Aunt Lill's flowers. She would appear on the program and became one of his oft-referenced characters. One of the things I later discovered about Harvey and the radio business in general was the amount of things he *traded* for airtime. A car dealer might give Harvey a car to use, and in exchange Harvey would offer the dealership advertising. Apparently, WLEE owners let Harvey barter in lieu of raising his pay. Since WLEE didn't have any commercial limits, trading really didn't cost the station cash income. Harvey ate well, dressed well and rode in style. Harvey traded air time for meals, air travel—domestic and overseas. Even his home was partially paid for via a trade deal with local builders. While vowing not to marry, Harvey had a different beautiful woman with him every time I saw him at some event. Late in life, in his sixties after his mother died, he married Bobbie, a college sweetheart who was divorced and had recently returned to Richmond.

Harvey was the spokesman for Rockingham Clothes, which gave him suits. He also strongly suggested to me and others that we buy our duds from there, too. After a few months at WLEE, a small local men's shop named Swatty's asked me to do commercials live on my nighttime radio show. They also wanted me to wear clothes from the store during these ad-lib radio spots. I dealt primarily with Joe Goldman, who had recently left his traveling job selling ties to clothing stores with his cohort, Ralph Lifshitz. Later, when Ralph founded Polo, he changed his last name to Lauren and gave Joe the nationwide exclusive for all Polo's leather goods. Joe now lives in Virginia Beach and has done as much for the homeless through the Christian Outreach Organization as anyone I know.

When I went to New York with Harvey for the sales call to national advertising buyers, I met a woman to whom he had been engaged. She brought a date for me, too. She was a producer of TV game shows. At dinner I learned the woman had offered Harvey a spot as a host on one of the ABC daytime game shows. Harvey decided to remain a big fish in a smaller pond rather than risk a TV show being canceled after a year or so in New York. That night after dinner, the four of us took a carriage ride through Central Park.

My job the next morning at J. Walter Thompson was to literally say nothing, and let Harvey do the pitch. I think Harvey just wanted me to see him in action and to understand that the radio business was much more than playing records or speaking into a mic. The life's blood of radio was landing sponsors, selling advertisements and doing promotions for clients. Ford did commit to additional commercials on WLEE, so the trip to New York was a great experience all around. Harvey may have been a tough boss, but he knew how to live well and he certainly understood the importance of image in broadcasting.

CHAPTER 6

BOWLING TO WGH

Ome of WLEE's regular sponsors was a bowling lane owned by Ned Grossberg. Grossberg's nephew, Fred Weiss, managed the business, so I interacted with Fred when we did all-night remotes from the bowling alley. Fred knew I was the WLEE music director, and on occasion I would give him a record album, as we did for a lot of our best clients. Fred asked if I could book a national recording star for one of the late-night bowling promotions.

So I called Tony Mammarella, president of Swan Records in Philadelphia. One of his artists was Freddy Cannon. Tony was happy to help set me up with Freddy, who agreed to do the bowling lanes event for a reduced fee. When Fred Weiss anted the deposit to pay Freddy Cannon, I then became an official promoter, having just booked my first artist for a live show.

I picked up Freddy Cannon at the airport. Fred Weiss, his girlfriend, I and my future wife, took Freddy to dinner before the show. Freddy Cannon was happy with his appearance and became one of my friends in the record business, appearing for me several more times in the years ahead. Most important, both Fred Weiss and I got a taste for staging a show, selling tickets, and seeing a profit. WLEE made out too, receiving ad money from the bowling alley for the on-air promotion of the show. I got a talent fee, as usual, from the station for doing the live broadcast. The poster for the event was headed "Cannon Balls"—Freddy *Cannon* and bowling *balls*. Pretty clever, don't you think? The event sold out.

Fred Weiss and I were ready to try something bigger, like renting The Mosque and producing a show similar to the traveling *Dick Clark Caravan of Stars,* or one of the shows produced by Irving Feld. Ned Grossberg, "Mr. Ten Pin," agreed to back the venture with Fred and me by sharing a slice of the profits with us—if there were any. I started calling talent agencies because I knew this show was going to take more effort than simply calling in a favor from a record company. We wanted a big name and a few other well-known acts.

Our star ended up being Gary U.S. Bonds, the R&B performer who had the No. 1 record at that time, *Quarter to Three,* which followed his mega hit, *New Orleans.* Bryan Hyland, Bobby Lewis and others rounded out the show. This was going to be a *WLEE presents* promotion, so a lot of the commercials advertising the show were aired at no charge to us.

My buddy John Wilson and I hosted the show. We typed up index cards to keep our introductions straight. The show was a success. We didn't sell out the two performances, but everyone made money. So now we envisioned doing concerts on a regular basis.

John Wilson and me preparing to host my first concert promotion at The Mosque in Richmond. Backstage we are typing up our introductions.

**Dagmara and Patrick Wilson at their
wedding reception with me and Angie.**

Of all the people I encountered over my early years, few have remained as close to me as John and his wife, Mary K. Their son, Patrick, is my godson and a great success, singing, acting and starring in Broadway shows like *The Full Monty* and *Oklahoma,* and going on to have a major career in motion pictures and TV. You can see him as the star of *The Conjuring* on the big screen, *Fargo* on TV, and singing a duet with Barbara Streisand.

Shortly after the Mosque concert, Fred and Ned offered me a job. They wanted me to sign on as promotion manager for their chain of bowling alleys located all over Virginia. They would guarantee me twice what I was making at WLEE. Plus, I would go to the various towns, stay in nice hotels, and entertain local people who helped us to promote local events by buying the newspaper and radio advertising to support what we did. They also wanted me to host a local TV bowling show. Most important, we would continue to produce concerts.

It was about August 1962 when the offer was made—and I took it. When I told my mother and father I was leaving WLEE and leaving town most of the week to travel the state, my mom was shocked and disappointed. No one thought I would quit my dream job at WLEE, especially Harvey Hudson. He took it personally and tried to persuade me to stay. Once it was clear I was leaving, he asked me not to work out my two-week notice. It was sort of a "get out, you ungrateful SOB" moment.

Within an hour or so, Dave Lyman called to say Harvey had acted too hastily. He asked if I could work out some kind of transition to remain at WLEE until they hired my replacement. We reached an agreement and I slowly started to turn over duties to others at WLEE while reporting to Bowling Headquarters at 9 a.m. I was still doing 4 to 7 p.m. and 9 p.m. until 2 a.m., on the air. I think now that Harvey may have changed his mind about the transition because my new employer was a major advertiser on WLEE, and so I was now going to be in charge of buying radio ads. After about three weeks, the transition was complete.

• • •

Shortly after I started full time with Grossberg and Weiss, Fred informed me I needed to go to Hampton, Virginia and check in to the Holiday Inn. He would call me about some things they needed to have done at their West Lanes bowling alley in Buckroe Beach. I knew the area well; the bowling alley was not far from my parents' cottages. The Holiday Inn was about three blocks from WGH's studios on Mercury Boulevard. Before he left WGH in 1957, station manager Dan Hydrick changed WGH from a Frank Sinatra-style station to a Top 40. The man who had first talked to me at WLLY when I visited as a kid, Gene Creasy, now did mid-days on WGH and was the program director. Keith James, another DJ I knew, was doing a night show. Keith had attended that first show Fred and I produced at The Mosque and I had driven down once for a show Keith promoted at the Virginia Beach Dome when it first opened.

The Holiday Inn was new, my job was new, and just before leaving WLEE I traded in the T-Bird for a white 1962 Corvette Convertible, so my car was new. I was nineteen years old.

Fred called and gave me my assignment. "Gene, we want you to go over to West Lanes, fire the manager, and be sure she takes nothing out of the office." I was flabbergasted. Why me, a complete stranger with zero experience dealing with personnel issues? I protested, but Fred insisted I do the deed. Then he added, "You will have to take over as manager of West Lanes until we find someone." I didn't know anything about managing a bowling alley, which included food service, coordination with bowling leagues and supervising several employees—all adults.

Plus, I could barely bowl.

For a couple of hours, I rehearsed what I was going to say, and then drove over to the brand new alley on Pembroke Avenue and asked to see the manager. I introduced myself, and then explained that I had been sent from Richmond to tell her she was fired. I told her to make a list for me of the personal items she took, and that a severance check would be sent. I sat there while she collected her things. It was one of the worst experiences of my life; I was physically sick. Shortly after I canned the manager, I called a staff meeting and announced that I was temporarily the new boss.

By the next day, the worst was over. Fortunately, everyone else at the Alley did their jobs without asking me for instructions, and I learned a lot about the food and bar business listening to the restaurant manager and reading her daily reports. I pretended I knew what I was doing, and the staff cooperated, probably because they feared for their jobs.

I was anxious to start my real job of promoting the bowling alleys, so I did. I called WGH, talked to Gene Creasy, explained I had left WLEE and that I was in town to set up some advertising. The next day a WGH salesman came to my office and we discussed buying ads promoting our weekend all-night bowl. I also met with a salesperson from the *Daily Press* newspaper and bought some space in that publication.

Grossberg had two other bowling alleys in Hampton Roads, one in downtown Norfolk and another in the Hidenwood section of Newport News. Fred Weiss came down to check on these two operations and dropped in to see me for a visit. He assured me that soon things would be finished in Hampton and I would be on the road, doing promotions statewide. A month later I was still at West Lanes, being well paid, and having at least a day or so off to drive back to Richmond to attend my church, where I was involved with the youth ministry, and to see my girlfriend and my parents. Another week passed and I was still at West Lanes.

One day I got a call from Gene Creasy saying he had a problem: all of the WGH staff was committed to be at the Center Theater that Saturday in Norfolk for the Miss Teenage Tidewater pageant, and their star announcer, Bob Calvert, had just resigned to go to the competition WNOR. WGH was stuck and needed someone to do the 7-to-11 p.m. show Saturday night, and would I please fill in so they didn't have to pull anyone out of the live stage show? It would be my day off, so I agreed.

Gene asked me to meet him at the station around 2 p.m. to allow plenty of time for him to explain what had to be done. When I got there, my first visit to the WGH studios, I found out that I had to drive to Newport News to go on live at 10 p.m. from Skateland for the final hour of the 7-11 p.m. show, recording 30 minutes to allow enough time to get to the rink. When the live show ended at 11 p.m. I was to stay there until midnight, doing what amounted to a record hop. Somehow Gene had not mentioned any of this when he asked me to fill in. He even asked I change all the stickers on the records for the next days Top 30 Countdown. The owner at Skateland, Mable Gordon, and the crowd were expecting Bob Calvert and seemed disappointed. But after a while they got into the music, ignored me, and the place stayed packed. Bob Calvert or Gene Loving—it didn't really matter to those on the dance floor having a good time.

I took the records back to WGH, never expecting to hear from them again. On Monday morning Gene Creasey called. He said Ambert Dail, the station manager, wanted to meet to offer me the afternoon show from 3 until 7 p.m. that had been hosted for years by Bob Calvert. I was beyond surprised. Bob had been one of my radio heroes when I vacationed with my parents in Buckroe Beach. I immediately thought about how big a void Calvert's absence would create for WGH. Big shoes to fill, no doubt. I had cold feet and explained it was way too soon to consider changing jobs—again. Gene convinced me to come over to at least meet with them.

Unlike the flamboyant Harvey Hudson, Ambert was very distinguished in appearance and demeanor. I did not know that at one time he had been the station's morning man in the 1950's. He explained that he had heard me Saturday night, that Gene Creasey had told him that I worked at WLEE doing afternoons in Richmond, and that he wanted to fill Bob Calvert's spot quickly. How much money did I want to come to work? I figured I would name a number they would never pay, saving face for me. Ambert agreed to my salary request and asked when I could start. I told him I would call Gene back with an answer the next day.

Gene invited me to his home that night for dinner and we discussed the offer. He suggested I simply tell Fred and Ned I wasn't doing what I was hired to do and a great opportunity had dropped from the sky at a salary I would be silly to pass up. It sounded good, so the next day I called Fred and told him that very thing. Ned got on the line and made a fuss. What about the concert business? Just like at WLEE, I agreed to transition to WGH while Fred found a replacement. I was just doing the on-air 3-to-7 p.m. show at the start. After about month, Ned and Fred stopped paying for the Holiday Inn, so I had to find another place to live. It was time for me to leave bowling and focus on radio only.

. . .

It only took me a couple of days to overcome my guilt about leaving the bowling alley promotions job. My parents were about the only people close to me who seemed disappointed. I was still technically living at home while working for Ned and Fred, so now I would be working full-time, 80 miles away in Hampton. It meant I would have to move—permanently. My parents understood and offered me one of their vacation cottages in Buckroe Beach until I found my own place. The Loving cottages had no heat and in late fall it would be very chilly, so finding something I could afford, paying rent for the first time, became a priority.

Accepting the WGH job also taxed my personal romantic relationship. I had been seeing Susan since high school and we had planned to keep dating while I worked for the bowling company in Richmond and she attended James Madison University in Harrisonburg. It became quickly apparent that we now lived too far away from each other to keep the relationship exclusive, so we decided to date others. We were still both very young and far from settled.

. . .

I think WGH employees were surprised that the station hired me to replace one of its big stars, Bob Calvert. And I don't mean because Bob weighed about three hundred pounds. I, a skinny nineteen-year-old, was taking over the prestigious afternoon drive-time program from 3 to 7 p.m. Apparently, Gene Creasy was impressed with how well the afternoon show at WLEE had scored in the ratings with teens. Even so, replacing his big-name star seemed risky. It would have made more sense for Gene to take that slot himself with me doing his mid-day show.

Bob was a very talented radio personality and had become the voice of WGH, recording most of the station's promos and ID's, plus a good percentage of the commercials. But apparently, Bob had a temper and could sometimes be a handful to manage—or so I was told. I don't really know if he quit or was fired, but a day or so after I went to work at WGH, Bob showed up opposite me on the only other real local radio competitor, Top 40 WNOR.

The same set of problems Bob had dealing with management at WGH apparently surfaced at WNOR. Bob would eventually be brought back to WGH as a mid-afternoon DJ and I would see, first-hand, his extraordinary talent and mercurial temper.

I suspect one reason for Bob's unhappiness at WNOR was his ratings. Bob and WNOR had expected him to carry his listeners with him and crush his replacement's audience on WGH. That didn't happen, but when I started at WGH I was certainly intimidated by Bob and worried he would beat me in the 3-to-7 p.m. ratings.

I didn't really grasp WGH's competitive advantage during the first week; I was too busy trying to get oriented to station policy, pick up on my additional assignment as assistant music director, and get station publicity photos taken. I also had to get measured for a red coat and black pants—the station uniform for all public appearances. As with the other stations where I had worked, there was much more to my WGH job than hosting a show six days a week. If you are on the air four hours at WGH you will spend another four hours recording commercials or, in my case, working in the music department.

Within the first few days at WGH I learned that Betty Blinco, the station receptionist, knew everybody in town and everything important to know. She was a one-woman community news department. Her big focus was lost pets; she recorded one-minute features every hour on missing animals. Her roots ran deep in the Virginia Peninsula and she helped me find a place to live—with heat. Her pharmacist, Russell Davis, was looking for someone to share expenses at a beach house he had recently rented in Grandview. She called him, the same night we met, and the next day I moved in with Russ at $60 a month.

Unbelievably, the house was in the same community where,

as a kid driving around with my parents, I had seen the homes with boats and docks in the backyard. It was more a cottage than a house, with a wraparound screened-in porch and a fireplace in the living room. A separate small building behind the main structure contained the washer and dryer. One of the two bedrooms had a potbelly stove. It was the only heat for the entire place, other than the fireplace. My bedroom was literally a pantry converted from an enclosed back porch, with just enough space for a single bed. When cold weather set in I needed an electric blanket to stay warm, and Russ was happy to sell me one at the drugstore.

The cottage was across the street from a vacant lot on the beach, so we could see the Chesapeake Bay from our porch and front window. It was a true bachelor pad with a view. I often had the place to myself. Russ worked from 3 until 11 p.m. most days, and on weekend days when I was off. By the time he'd get home I would be asleep.

Glenda, an artist, lived next door along with her sometimes-employed husband, their four-year-old son, and a golden retriever who spent most of its time on our porch or in our cottage. We didn't have air conditioning, so our doors and windows were left open. In time, I became somewhat of a neighborhood celebrity. Neighbors saw me come and go in my Corvette, and sometimes I was dressed in my bright red WGH jacket. Soon I was invited to weekend cookouts on the beach or other parties. Many of my neighbors were in the military and stationed at Langley Air Force Base, which was about fifteen minutes away. Some of these single jet-jockeys shared houses. The only thing missing—a boat. Time to see Betty Blinco again.

Betty knew Bob Winstead, a salesman at Tysinger Motors who just happened to be selling an overpowered ski boat. My dad had a cabin cruiser for a couple of years when I was really young, but I didn't know much about boats except that they were fun and I wanted one. So I met Bob at a boat ramp on the Hampton River and we went for a test run. The thing was a rocket ship—basically a triangle-shaped flat-bottom boat that bounced off waves and then nose-dived, drenching its passengers. Being soaked was no fun in December, so I bought a tarp and put the boat to bed for the rest of the winter. I remained friends with Bob who helped me satisfy my real fetish—hot cars. Bob found me an almost-new Corvette Stingray—bright red with a white top.

**My WGH publicity pictures,
November 1962**

Here is WGH receptionist Betty Blinco who was so much a part of my early days at WGH and very helpful finding me a place to live and a boat. She was the voice of the station if you called to report a lost pet or request a song.

Launching my second boat in 1964, at Grand View, Hampton, Virginia. My neighborhood, in the background, fronted on the Chesapeake Bay.

• • •

WGH was owned by the *Daily Press*, the main newspaper serving Newport News and Hampton. The principals were the Bottom family and the Van Burens. They also owned Virginia Color Print, which published the comics and Sunday advertising sections for many papers in Virginia; plus they owned Muzak, which provided commercial-free background music for businesses, elevators, doctors' offices and such. They were to soon launch a cable TV operation for Newport News and Danville, Virginia.

Ray Bottom had an office at WGH. At the time I went to work there, Ray was about thirty years old and had just gotten out of active Air Force duty. As the son of Captain and Mrs. Dorothy Bottom, he looked the part of well-bred, well-educated sophistication. He drove an Austin Healy and ran WGH-FM, the classical music station. Other than Ray and his mother (his father had died many years earlier), I never heard anyone mention they listened to the classical FM station. Once in a while Ray would nod to me, probably mistaking me for a food-delivery boy. We were making money playing rock n' roll on the AM station and the FM station was losing some of it. Neither the Bottoms nor the Van Burens seemed to care. Radio was a hobby compared to the newspaper, which practically printed money in those days. WGH was financially healthy and formidable.

WGH was a big station compared to WLEE. Even though Richmond was the state capital with lots of history and prestige, and both stations were 5,000 watts day and night, WGH's market contained about twice as many people spread over the six cities known as Hampton Roads. Due to the region's flat terrain, WGH's signal traveled much farther than WLEE's. The station claimed to serve twenty-eight counties in Virginia, North Carolina, and Maryland. Some of my record hop requests came from as far north as Salisbury, Maryland and well into northeastern North Carolina. WGH boasted that it ranked among the ten highest-rated stations in the country.

When my first ratings from the fourth quarter of 1962 were published by the only ratings service at that time, Pulse, I had a 50 percent share. That meant that of all the people who tuned in to the radio in our primary market between 3 and 7 p.m., half were listening to WGH. Eleven other stations divided the other half of the listening pool. In the early 1960s, just about everybody listened to the radio, and there were fewer stations to share the audience.

I attribute some of that early success to a persona I decided to exploit as soon as I started at WGH. I was really skinny. I was teased and heard all of the skinny-kid jokes. So on the air I started calling myself *Lean Gene,* the world's thinnest portable record player . . . etc. There was an old Bill Haley & the Comets hit, *Lean Gene (Jean)* which I edited to just the title lyric, and a *ump de bump bump* beat. I was making fun of myself, and it worked.

• • •

After a couple of months on the job I was happy, comfortable and settled in. WGH was so dominant that I was starting to get recognized just about everywhere I went: my picture was on the station's music chart or I was seen live broadcasting from clients' locations and shopping centers. All was good, and then, just like in the past, a bomb hit from out of nowhere. Gene Creasy, my boss, quit WGH to take a job back at his small hometown of Lynchburg, Virginia.

Roger Clark, who had been the all-night man at WGH, was now named program director. I had yet to meet Roger and was concerned that he might change the station rotation and knock me from my afternoon spot. Fortunately, that didn't happen. Roger didn't make any changes at WGH in the programing lineup. I was now age twenty and I settled into a weekly routine that was more like a normal job: no double shifts or getting up at 4:30 a.m. or taking care of a rodent.

One thing in my favor was that Gene Creasey's secretary, Sandy, stayed on to assist Roger, and she seemed to like me. Among her jobs was booking record hops at schools, community centers, or even birthday parties. Sandy was assigning me some very good appearances, partly because the other DJs didn't want to do them. At that time, WGH was charging $75 for a hop, of which $25 went to the station for the equipment and the on-air promotion. One problem I had—a big one—was that the station's turntable, microphone and speakers did not fit into my Corvette. I asked if I could obtain my own equipment and keep more of the money. So the station offered something that would keep us all happy.

Roger, who also did some hops, knew the portable equipment was not as good as the equipment he used for his live on-the-air hops at Mercury roller rink at Norfolk's Ward Corner on Saturday nights. Additionally, I had become friends with two technicians who worked in the Muzak garage behind the main WGH building. Four of these garages had been built because more space was needed for employees. The buildings also housed the WGH-AM music library, a little-used lounge for DJs, another garage for writing and recording commercials, and one more for junk.

So we came up with a scheme whereby one of the Muzak technicians would drive separately to my record hops, and help set up the equipment that he carried in his car. He liked going to the hops and didn't charge for helping. I had described what

I needed: the kind of two-turntable, self-contained setup with high-end small speakers, something that would fit easily into my Corvette. The technician nailed it, building me a state-of-the-art portable system that could quickly switch records and tempos for dance contests. It was the first in the market and a forerunner to today's big-club DJ equipment.

Hosting live events weeknights was good for my pocketbook and my popularity.

• • •

It didn't take long to meet girls, especially with the help of Keith James, who introduced me to several young women. Among them was Sharon Kaye Potter, who had just returned to Hampton from a stint with the Rockettes in New York City. She had won a Miss Teenage Tidewater pageant staged by WGH, and was involved in a promotion with Keith James to break the world's roller coaster riding record at Norfolk's Ocean View Amusement Park.

A few weeks after my arrival at WGH, Keith approached me about being his partner in producing a concert in December 1962 at the Norfolk City Arena. He wanted to sponsor a multiple-act show, similar to what Fred and I did at The Mosque but Keith didn't have enough money, and didn't want to take all the risk alone. Keith proposed an equal partnership. The problem was I didn't have money, either. I was spending all of my pay on rent, a car, a boat and eating out. So, I called my mother who agreed to loan me the cash I needed to invest in my half of the show. Our star was Roy Orbison, plus Ray Stevens, the comedian Cousin Minnie Pearl, and a few other newer acts sent by record companies at no charge.

Keith James and I co-promote Roy Orbison in concert. 1962

Ray Stevens, whose hit *Ahab The Arab* was top 10, with me and
my new partner in concert promotion, WGH night DJ Keith James.

The show was a moderate success; we sold 85 percent of the tickets, enough for me to pocket some profit and repay my mother. Keith and I could see the potential, so we quickly started looking at doing another show in the spring at the Virginia Beach Dome.

Keith was dating the receptionist from Casey Chevrolet, who also worked nights like Keith. Casey was one of the major WGH clients, and I had been doing some broadcasts from the dealership's Warwick Boulevard location in Newport News. The son of the Casey service manager started hanging around these broadcasts, similar to my hanging around George Prescott at WLEE. In the years ahead, Dale Parsons would work at WGH, WTAR, and WNBC in New York City as program director supervising guys like Howard Stern and Don Imus. Today Dale is retired in Hawaii and is the keeper of the golden era WGH flame. See his website http://www.alohanews.com/wgh_history.htm I am still working. Is something wrong with this picture?

Keith and his girlfriend often invited me to dinner at Pappa D's after his evening radio show. I loved the spaghetti with white clam sauce and the Liebfraumilch Riesling wine they served, so it was an easy sell. Other nights Keith wanted me to come with them to the couple of nightclubs in Norfolk where he had a regular job as an emcee of live bands. These places largely catered to Navy sailors, and they were interested in being promoted on the radio. Keith would plug these events on-air by saying where he would be appearing, similar to the record hop mentions.

Since Keith and his girlfriend could not fit into my two-seater, we took his white Chevrolet Corvair convertible. We walked in, Keith went on stage for thirty seconds, introduced the band, picked up his $50 appearance fee, and we then drove to the next club to repeat his "performance." No records or equipment to set up—same net money. Most nights I drove back because Keith liked to sample the beverages. These kinds of *appearances* interested me more than the hops; you didn't really have to do much. You could make a hundred bucks a night by simply showing up at two places.

I came to understand more about why I got a lot of good record hop assignments: The other DJ's at the station really did not like doing record hops, or night appearances. These gigs were time-consuming and my co-workers had families who wanted them home. Suddenly, I was flooded with live-appearance requests, which was entirely my own fault. I had let Sandy in Roger's office know I would take every appearance she could book. After a couple of months of establishing my name on the air, people specifically requested me to make appearances. I was young and single and off after 7 p.m. most nights, so I had the time and realized I could make as much money from concerts, hops, and emcee work as I was earning at WGH.

• • •

Keith James had been renting a house on an obscure road, almost in the woods, in Hampton. One night he invited me over to watch a movie that was coming on TV. When I arrived I found that Keith had a new roommate, David Carradine, who had just gotten out of the Army at Fort Eustis. David would later become the lead actor in the TV show *Kung Fu*. His father was actor John Carradine, who was starring in a 1940s movie broadcast that night on TV. We all watched it together. Also about this time, Keith changed girlfriends and was losing his lease. So, he suggested we look for a place together. I needed to move anyway because my roommate was getting married soon and needed my space.

Keith James and I rented a white cinderblock cottage with a big screened-in porch on the beach overlooking the Chesapeake Bay. Compared to the place I was leaving, this was a mansion. I now had a real bedroom and a place with central heat and air conditioning. The place was so big, Keith's girlfriend also moved in. Now, this was the ultimate party place for WGH. Instead of going out to Pappa D's, we were grilling steaks on the porch late at night.

Just before our concert at the Virginia Beach Dome in 1963, Keith shocked me and the rest of the WGH staff by announcing he was taking a job in Canada. Now I would have the whole cottage—along with the entire rent—to myself. Keith's departure was going to leave a big hole in the WGH lineup. Roger Clark had just two weeks to fill Keith's 7-to-11 p.m. slot. He would do so with a guy who would become my main business partner and closest colleague to this day, fifty-three years later.

I was only twenty and had been at WGH just eight months when Roger promoted me to music director of WGH replacing

Keith James—no one was named as my assistant. Somehow, what had been a two-person job at WLEE and WGH became one person after I inherited the position. There was a small pay increase for taking on the extra responsibility, but the truth is I would have done it even without a raise. I loved working with the record promotion people, the record shop managers, and going through all the new releases to see what I believed could be a breakout record in the Norfolk market. That dovetailed nicely with my concert promotion ambitions.

• • •

I did not know much about Dick Lamb other than he had worked at WGH in 1958 for a short time. Roger informed us that he had called Dick and offered him his old job doing nights at WGH, and Dick had accepted. Dick first worked at WGH the same year I started at WLLY. He had worked in the Alexandria, Virginia market when he started.

Dick's given name was Norman Beasley. But when he arrived at WGH in 1958 the station told him that they had just bought a jingle for a DJ named Dick Lamb, who had only lasted a week. So they asked Norman if he would change his name so they could use the jingle, and he agreed. In the 1970s Norman legally changed his name to Dick Lamb.

A year or so into the 1958 WGH job, Dick visited his hometown of Baltimore and, on a whim, auditioned for WJZ-TV and was offered a job. Dick then quit WGH and moved back to Baltimore. While waiting to start his promised position, Dick was assigned to host a kiddie cartoon show where he wore a space suit, including the helmet with glass faceplate. He was known on the air as "Space Cadet Norm." (Pictures of him in this outfit are still locked in his safety deposit box.) Dick didn't stay in Baltimore long, accepting a morning show and sports announcer opportunity in Dayton, Ohio. He left Baltimore just in time to avoid being typecast as a kiddie-emcee for birthday parties and fast-food openings.

By now Dick and his wife, Donna, had three children. He had married the daughter of Jack Rowzie, one of Washington D.C.'s best known WWDC radio personalities. They had met at church just before Norm realized he also wanted to be on the

radio like Donna's dad. Roger Clark must have offered Dick the
job at WGH on a day when it had just snowed again in Dayton—
in May: Dick always knew when it was time to get out of town,
until now.

• • •

I had just gotten off the air at WGH, put away my jokes, my ad
libs, headphones and other support material we used to create four
hours of entertainment in the 1960s. I went out to the parking lot
to get into my car when I saw something I still remember vividly
to this day. There was a guy getting out of a 1960 Black Ford
Fairlane two-door coupe. His pants were about five inches too
short, showing the tops of his white socks. Thinking he was lost,
I said, "May I help you?" Dick introduced himself. *This could not
possibly be the person WGH was counting on to be the new teen
heartthrob, replacing the ever-popular Keith James?* I thought.
Dick said he was looking for the program director, Roger Clark.
I pointed out that it was 7:30 p.m. and Roger worked from 9
a.m. to 5 p.m. like most executives. (Roger taped his all night 11
p.m.-5 a.m. show during the day.) Out of sympathy, I may have
offered to buy Dick a drink or dinner, or both. It has proven to
be the most expensive evening of my life, if you add it to the cost
of my association with Dick over the years, like the time I took a
significant discount to sell Dick my guitar, which he desperately
wanted.

Even though Dick was married, he rarely rushed home when
he got off at 11 p.m. His wife and young children were asleep
by then, anyway. So, Dick accepted my invitation to continue
occasional late dinners at Pappa D's, with me usually meeting
him there and pre-ordering.

Dick, like me, was also much younger than the other WGH
DJs. In fact, WGH's on-air staff, known as the Swingin' Six,
were in their forties or older. Dick and I, in our 20s, were
compatible—at least agewise. And our youth played well with the
teen audience. In those years we had lots of local and national
sponsors who wanted to sell to our young demographic.

Local high schools let out around 3 p.m., just as I went on the
air, so in addition to teenaged listeners, young adults working
staggered shifts at the Navy and the Newport News shipyard

became listeners. Afternoon drive-time started around 3:30 p.m. and stretched to 6:30 p.m. because the two largest employers released their people every fifteen minutes. The afternoon WGH cumulative audience was almost equal to morning drive-time, which is a little unusual in radio, but could be attributed to the young military market, service guys tuning in to a Top 40 station during or after work.

Dick Lamb had a major lock on the teens from 7 until 11 p.m. Basically, I had them from after school until dinner, and then Dick grabbed the baton and carried it until their bedtime. They'd listen to Dick while doing their homework. Our main competitor was WNOR, a 1,000-watt station that had to cut its power at night thus significantly limiting its reach. In contrast, WGH remained a full-power station twenty-four hours a day, but did go to what was called a *pattern* at sunset. That meant that our signal had to be shaped to avoid interference with stations in other markets. At night WGH lost coverage in Williamsburg and York County.

Dick was limited to what he could do in the record-hop world because he worked six nights a week. His "hops" were mostly limited to some roller rink live broadcasts on Saturday nights. The demand for WGH DJs was more than we could fill, so I pushed Roger and Sandy to raise the rate to $100, which they did, and we got it easily.

After a few months, I explained to Dick my dabbling in the concert-promotion business, and he seemed intrigued. Anyone who wants to be on the radio has an ego—and I was no exception. After Keith James left, the name on the commercial radio ads as concert producer changed from "James-Loving" to "AGL Productions," which stood for A Gene Loving Production. I told Dick I still wanted to use the AGL name because it was established, but that was only based on the one concert staring Leslie Gore I had promoted after Keith left. But Dick was agreeable. We then became equal partners in the concert business, which would continue for almost thirty years. Dick also agreed that we would split up the duties; I booked the entertainment and handled the logistics of the on-stage production, and Dick took care of the tickets, kept the checkbook and settled the shows with the acts agents. He didn't have that much to do during the day, so he had time to distribute concert tickets to businesses that agreed to sell them. Dick also went back to school, pursuing a degree from William and Mary. To me, the only degree of interest was the temperature in the WGH big portable trailer studio, which was either too hot or too cold.

Dick needed to work on his image—the car and the clothes. I convinced him that a teen DJ star should not drive up to personal appearances in a 1960 Ford Fairlane. So Dick bought a maroon Oldsmobile Cutlass convertible. We used it for the Oyster Bowl Parade and the Portsmouth Christmas Parade. And the WGH uniform requirement solved Dick's short pants problem.

station breaks

Vol. 2 - No. 7, May, 1968   A MONTHLY PUBLICATION OF WGH RADIO   Tidewater, Virginia

Why are these men smiling? (See story inside)

Each year WGH won something from the Associated Press for its local news coverage. WGH News Director Jim Moore is on the left, next to WGH General Manager Ambert Dail.

TV **RADIO** **MIRROR**

two magazines in one

MARCH, 1968   ATLANTIC EDITION   VOL. 68, NO. 4

SPECIAL
ATLANTIC
STORIES

SHIRLEY REINARD
Regional Editor

That LOVING Man

● Radio's one and only child prodigy—Gene Loving built his own radio station in the attic when he was 13—now lives his "dream come true." That first station had a one-block range, but it got him a write-up in the local paper and his idol, the Richmond, Virginia, DJ actually offered him a job. "That was the start of my career," Gene confesses, "and things like that just don't happen, but it did to me!"

He is now the host of his own show, known to the Newport News, Virginia, audience as *The Gene Loving Show* heard Monday through Saturday from 3:00 to 7:00 P.M. over WGH-Radio. Gene features current popular hits, old favorites and spotlights a new song each day. During the show, he presents the "Loving Cup" to a promising new record.

Gene was born in Richmond, Virginia, on November 18, 1942, and went to public school and studied voice and diction at R.P.I. College, both in Richmond. He says, "One day after receiving a tape recorder for Christmas, I made my own version of a local radio show. After telling the announcer what I had done, he invited me down to the station to listen to the tape. From that point on I wanted to be in radio."

A highpoint of his career was his exclusive interview with Beatle George Harrison in England. He visited the family and stayed with them at their home in Liverpool. Gene also joined them while they were in Nassau filming *Help*. He fed his exclusive interviews back to 16 radio and television stations in the U.S. and foreign countries. Most important of all, Gene pulls number one ratings with his show, and has for the past 4½ years.

Gene's home is a ranch style located near a sandy beach on the Chesapeake. His leisure time is spent out on the bay in his motorboat, crabbing. He enjoys many pleasant hours viewing the Bay from his living room window—it's his way of relaxing. Gene says, "I want to live without worry and have a free mind to think about new and exciting projects."

TV Radio Mirror, a major monthly magazine, featured a different DJ in each issue from markets around the nation. In this issue, the picture was taken backstage at The Dome. Posing with me, (L-R:) Gary Lewis, Bobby Goldsboro, Gene Pitney, and Brian Hyland.

The Virginian-Pilot

action

the magazine for young moderns

Saturday, Sept. 2, 1967

Lean Gene of WGH:
Hit Picker

By Joseph V. Phillips, Action Editor

A DJ SKETCH

Lean Gene's radio shows stay ahead of the hit records, but he also digs into the files to spring surprises on listeners.

Tidewater swingers gather 'round 'the world's skinniest portable record player' wherever he appears in the area.

The Norfolk newspaper, *The Virginian-Pilot*, published a weekly entertainment magazine where they often featured WGH DJs.

For several years, I raced a soap box car against the mayor or other local celebrities from the top of a bridge into downtown Newport News. It was actually pretty frightening. The car is named for the daily "Loving Cup" I presented for the record I would feature that day.

Once a month, I did a big hop at the Virginia Beach Dome, playing records and featuring a live local band. Here is a marquee from one of those events. Often we would fill it with 2,000 young people. No drinking, just cokes and popcorn.

WGH had the DJs rob a bank every two weeks to meet payroll.
I'm driving the getaway car.

Somehow, when the DJ staff was asked to pose for a picture
their idea seemed to always include getting rid of me.

WGH DJs 1965 (L-R:) George Crawford, Glen Lewis, Dave Cummins, Dick Lamb, Bob Calvert, Roger Clark, and "Lean" Gene.

(L-R:) Jack Whitehead, Wayne Combs, me and Pete Glazer, of WGH. We had been the third car, after two carrying the builders of the brand new Chesapeake Bay Bridge Tunnel. The interior of the tunnel was unfinished, complete with hanging bulbs and a sandy floor, as they had just connected the last section of the bridge the day before.

WGH

HAMPTON ROADS BROADCASTING CORPORATION

711 BOUSH STREET
NORFOLK, VIRGINIA
23510

P. O. BOX 98
NEWPORT NEWS, VIRGINIA
23607

April 20, 1965

This letter, Gene...

    ...will serve as a "one hour leave" during
working hours for you to visit the local public
library to read books on "How to Play Basketball"!
Please study carefully the chapter on "Scoring
Points -- The Object of the Game".

        Cordially,

        AMBERT DAIL
        MANAGER

AD/mc

Mr. Gene Loving
WGH RADIO
Hampton, Virginia

THE "SOUND OF PROGRESS" IN TIDEWATER VIRGINIA

Typical letter from managment during my early years
telling me I'm terrible, gently.

Listeners considered the WGH DJs popular enough to seek autographs whenever we made an appearance. Here, fans ask me to sign their program at one of the Micro-Phonie games.

Here, as part of the WGH Micro-Phonies,
I'm making my famous half-court jump shot.

station breaks

Vol. 3 - Special Souvenir Issue   A PUBLICATION OF WGH RADIO   Tidewater, Virginia

EVERYBODY LISTENS TO
THE MEN OF MUSIC

Larry O'Brien
Bob Calvert
J. J. Bowman
George Crawford
John Garry
Roger Clark
Tom Scott
Gene Loving

wghradio1310

Over the years the staff evolved at WGH from the basic same six guys who worked together for about seven years to a larger group. This picture was taken shortly after Dick Lamb left for TV full time.

Every year WGH recruited local guys to join the Army and stay together for most of their service as the Tiger Platoon. Here I am with them at basic training in Ft. Jackson, near Columbia, South Carolina. I was out on maneuvers with them during the day, but I slept at the Holiday Inn.

One of many trips to NYC to meet new groups that were being introduced to America. Two other DJs pose with me and Herman's Hermits, above.

Me and The Animals in NYC during their first trip to the USA. Eric Burdon is in the sunglasses. On the far right is Chas Chandler, who left The Animals to manage the career of Jimi Hendix, whom he discovered.

Fabian, who had several hits in the late '50s, flew to Norfolk to promote his new movie, *Thunder Alley*. WGH hosted a welcome event, typical of the never-ending promotions the station did every week.

Me, in the main WGH studio with Doug McClure who was well known from the hit TV show, *The Virginian*. If any name entertainer was in town they usually primarily visited WGH as the size of our audience was well known to the music and movie companies.

In my WGH music department office, there were stacks of new releases which had just arrived in that day's mail. I tried to open all of them and review each for about 15 seconds before going on the air. In those days I wore a coat and tie to work every day.

WGH remembered

WGH RADIO

AM 131   WGH TIME / WGH TEMP   FM 97.3

MICROPHONIES WILL MAKE $5000 FOR AREA SCHOOLS IN 68

Mighty WGH sign once rose beside Military Highway.

Continued from E-4

Golden age of rock

When DJs were kings

Goodbye to an era

Disc jockeys Lamb and Loving helped WGH reach top.

Ms. Webb built WGH's large classical record library.

Derring-do

The 1960s were a golden age for WGH-AM, which fueled listener excitement through zany and daring promotions. Good-natured announcers took pies in the face (left); fans donned WGH T-shirts to enjoy station-sponsored surfing championships at Virginia Beach (above, left); the Microphonies took to the basketball court to raise money for area schools (above); and the Tidewater Tigers platoon was recruited, with the station's help, to head for the war in Vietnam (below).

See related story on E-8.

Lamb transmitter building sat near Small Boat Harbor.

In 1983, for the WGH 50th anniversary, *The Daily Press* featured a story about the station. Under the heading "When DJs Were Kings," I was mentioned—first due to the international publicity the station received from my Beatles syndication, next for the *Disc-O-Ten* TV show with Dick Lamb and finally for the "Micro-Phonies" basketball team. By the time this feature was published I had been gone from the station for thirteen years.

• • •

WGH hired newsman Ira Hull, who had been on one of the national networks. Ira replaced Wayne Combs, the afternoon news voice during my show, when Wayne moved back to Kentucky. Another WGH newsman who often was on during the hours I worked was Carlton Shrieves, who I first met when we worked together at WEZL.

Ira needed a place to live so he replaced Keith James as my new housemate. Ira was in his mid-fifties and had some great radio stories from the 1940s—and he liked to drink. He fit right in when record promotion guys bought a bunch of steaks and beer for our regular parties on the beach house porch. Lots of WGH staffers attended those cookouts, cementing some of my best memories from 1963. Even station owner Ray Bottom and sales manager Howard Jernigan occasionally attended.

Things at WGH were good and our concert-productions became steady. We even developed a teen dance in a Hampton school cafeteria every Friday night, which featured a different local popular band each week. Dick and I produced these dances under the AGL banner, hiring one of WGH's accounting people to take the money at the door. The school sold the soft drinks and received a small rent payment. These dances became very popular because there wasn't much else for kids to do on the Peninsula in those days. Dick and I started to make some serious money promoting these dances, dividing up $500 to $600 a week after expenses. This was in addition to the hops, concerts and radio pay. Making this kind of money in 1963 was beyond my wildest dreams, especially because I was doing something I really loved.

• • •

My high school sweetheart, Susan, called me one day in June 1963 to ask if she and some of her family members could stay at the beach house. They were coming to Hampton for a meeting. That weekend stay led to our engagement. She decided she would leave school in Harrisonburg after we were married, because at that point she would have enough education to become a substitute teacher. The wedding was set for the following April

1964. During the engagement, I traveled to James Madison University about once a month to see her. On the Sundays I wasn't on the road visiting Susan, I was on the water. Several of my friends from Richmond would visit and we would use the boat to venture onto empty beaches around the Chesapeake Bay. I could now afford a bigger boat so I traded in the single-bench-seat ski boat for a seventeen footer that would seat six. I still launched at a ramp two blocks from the Grandview cottage, pulling it with my red 'Vette. Once, Dick came over on a Sunday, his day off too, to help me wax the car and boat.

My new housemate did not last long in the WGH news department. Jim Moore, the station's news director, quickly decided that Ira just could not transition into a newsroom where one guy had to do everything himself to prepare a five-minute newscast. The WGH job involved pushing buttons and prerecording inserts from reporters or the network, and Ira was used to someone else doing all of that while he just read the news. So Ira moved to Charlottesville to live with his girlfriend Kitty, who had a good job and supported him the rest of his life. We remained in touch until he died.

After Ira, I had two other housemates for about three months each. One was Bob Winstead, who had sold me the ski boat and the Stingray. He was between marriages and needed a place. The other was Kenny Rossi, a real teen heartthrob who had been the most popular regular dancer on *American Bandstand*. Google Kenny Rossi to see his history.

Kenny had signed a recording contract, had a semi-hit, and had been booked to appear at the Jolly Roger in Norfolk for three months in the fall of '63 with the house band. I had met him once before when he came through promoting his record. His stories from his *Bandstand* days about the girls chasing him were beyond entertaining—and had me wondering if I really wanted to get married. It seemed like he was bringing home a different girl every night. Our cottage, already *the* party spot on Grandview Beach, increased in popularity after Kenny moved in—1963 was one of the best years of my life, but it would end on a tragic note.

The artist lady, Glenda, who lived across the street on Lighthouse Drive, took her son to school each morning and then bought me a dozen powdered-sugar donuts on her way home. I paid her for the donuts and took them to the studio every day to eat while I was on the air, along with several bottles of Pepsi. I never gained an ounce. This was a daily ritual. On this particular morning, November 22, I decided to walk a boxer dog given to me by my fiancée's aunt. We were on the beach near an old lighthouse ruin about half a mile away. Basically, it was just a pile of rocks a couple hundred feet offshore that you could wade to at low tide. The dog loved the water and it was a perfect day to be outside. Suddenly, Glenda came running down the shoreline screaming something, so I ran toward her. "The President's been shot," she yelled.

We went back to the cottage and turned on the TV. We sat there, stunned. I left Glenda and the dog to drive to WGH, listening to the station as I drove. They had joined the national network. All our local programing stopped for the next few days— no music, just the news coverage, through the funeral. Everyone was sent home. I went to the apartment of one of our revolving midday guys, who lived about a block from the station with his wife. I stayed there through dinner watching TV and then went home. WGH slowly crept back into regular programming, without commercials, starting the day after the funeral.

· · ·

Although the country was emotionally traumatized, we all fell quickly back into our routines. I was doing my regular radio show, serving as music director, making personal appearances at hops, hosting bands at local dances and promoting concerts. Most of our events were in Virginia Beach at the Dome, which was a landmark in the oceanfront resort. It was during that period in 1963 that I met a couple of people who would become connected to a part of my life in the future. One was Richard Levin. You may have heard of Levin's of Virginia, famous for its brass beds. That chapter of Richard's life was still a couple of decades away. Back then, Richard was promoting high school dances along with his partner Tommy Herman. Tommy was destined to be an entertainment lawyer in California and eventually retire to Virginia Beach. (I'm still working.) Tommy's brother Steve gained fame as a DC-based attorney at Kirkland

& Ellis LLP, a law firm specializing in SEC work. Steve and his firm would help us take our company public in 1985. Tommy's other brother, Robert, took a small hotdog stand with picnic tables, then started selling crabs you cracked on newspapers, and developed it into one of the best restaurants in Virginia Beach, The Lighthouse at Rudee Inlet.

When I met Richard Levin and Tommy Herman, they were high-schoolers promoting some of the first dances featuring black bands at the Monticello Hotel in Norfolk and the old Nansemond Hotel in the Ocean View section of the city. Richard and Tommy hired me to emcee and promote their dances on WGH. Soon we were co-promoting events at larger venues in the Norfolk-Virginia Beach region, like New Year's Eve at the Golden Triangle Hotel in downtown Norfolk. I was able to land some acts through agencies in New York that agreed to play two forty-five minute sets at our dance promotions. That entertainment was the precursor to what has come to be known as "Beach Music."

Bill Deal and the Rhondels, which had been a house band for the Peppermint Beach Club and the Top Hat at the Oceanfront, started to back up some of our concerts at the Virginia Beach Dome. Bill and his band also was the opening act for the Beach Boys when we brought them here for the first time. Bill Deal and I went on to become friends and business partners. Instead of just being paid a fee to perform at local events, Bill agreed to become a partner in the event itself . That partnership arrangement was more lucrative for Bill and led to him doing a lot of dances for us in conjunction with Richard Levin and Tommy Herman. We had especially high demand in small towns in the WGH coverage area where entertainment was scarce. These relationships ultimately led to me helping the Rhondels secure a recording contract in the late 1960s. I was managing the band when its popularity exploded. I also assisted Richard with getting recording contracts for a couple of bands he managed—Bob Marshall & the Crystals, and Charlie McClendon & the Magnificents. We were young and energetic at just the right time. Our paths would stay linked for years to come and ultimately lead to even bigger things.

After establishing his brass beds business in a store on 21st Street in Norfolk, Richard Levin started investing in Ghent real estate. In the late '90s Richard invited me to co-invest with him in a couple of new properties on Monticello Avenue. For more than twenty years we have bought, renovated, and sold a lot of commercial properties throughout Ghent and still own some of the classic buildings that were a big part of Norfolk's history, all due to Richard's dedication to a first-class approach to whatever he does. Who could have guessed when this high school kid walked into WGH in 1963 wanting to promote a dance that we would still be "promoting" together.

**For fifty years I have been associated with Richard Levin (left)
seen here with me in 2015 on 21st Street, Ghent, Norfolk.**

CHAPTER 7

YEAH, YEAH, YEAH

One of the most enjoyable parts of my job as music director at WGH was selecting singles that I thought could become hits, or might score on the charts. In many ways, finding great music is the essence of great radio. My hope was to discover something I thought could be popular and bring it to the attention of my audience— before other radio stations found it. If it sold a million copies, I might also get a gold record for the station wall for being the first to introduce it, or a mention in a national publication. Such a mention, in turn, would influence other DJs to check out the record. In the 1960s there were no instant tweets or social media.

The Gavin Report was a weekly newsletter based in San Francisco and founded in 1958 by Bill Gavin. It was distributed nationally, and its Top 40 listings were used by radio stations to see if they had missed something that was breaking elsewhere. Bill was considered the leading music guru in the '60's because he had a good track record for predicting hit songs. He had one DJ for each region of the country, and I was his Mid-Atlantic guy.

It was no surprise that record promoters swamped me with new releases. Getting a plug in *The Gavin Report* was like striking gold. Each day I'd come to work to review stacks of newly minted

45 RPMs. I routinely received one hundred to one hundred and fifty releases a week, and maybe two or three calls a day from record company promoters. Some promoters even stopped by to see me in person and take me to lunch or dinner after my show. Despite the flood, I tried to give each release its due: I would listen to about 25 percent of each disc. If a song didn't grab me in the first minute, it went into the reject pile.

One of the record company executives I got to know in Richmond when I was at WLEE was Tony Mammarella, co-owner of Swan Records. In the late 1950s, Tony was the producer of Dick Clark's *American Bandstand,* which was broadcast from Philadelphia. Tony and Bernie Binnick started the Swan label and Dick Clark came in as an investor. When *Bandstand* started nationally broadcasting from Philly, Dick Clark, of course, became the voice and face of teen music, and he routinely featured the biggest talent of the era on his afternoon dance party. After the payola hearings in Washington, Tony left *Bandstand* and Clark divested his interest in Swan.

Tony had first invited me up to visit Swan in 1961, taking me to a great Italian restaurant for lunch. I had booked Freddy Cannon, a Swan artist, through Tony for the bowling alley promotion, which ultimately led to the concert business for me. Tony regularly called me—and about a dozen other DJs—when he had a new release, asking that I listen and let him know what I thought. That's how the music business operated back then.

• • •

In September 1963, Tony called to say he had just mailed me a release by a group from England, a band named the Beatles. The group's song, *She Loves You,* was climbing the British charts. Tony was in England when he heard the record and saw a picture of the band. Dubbed "The Fab Four," John, Paul, George and Ringo already had one hit in the UK, *Love Me Do,* and were becoming a sensation there.

Tony saw the enormous reaction to the group's music and look—mop-top haircuts and matching uniforms. Tony bought the American rights to *She Loves You* from a record company in the UK called EMI. He asked me to call him with my opinion after I reviewed the record.

I never pretended to have any musical talent myself, but I had developed an ear for what young people liked, and what I thought would sell. These boys from Liverpool had a different sound, very upbeat with catchy lyrics, great harmony and a heavy dose of rock 'n' roll. This was no cover band. I was convinced, as was Tony, that this band and this song could be a hit in the US. I really believed *She Loves You* had Top 10 potential—maybe even No. 1 possibilities. Tony had real street credibility. He saw some of the best musicians up close while working on *American Bandstand*, so when he asked me to listen to a record, I did so seriously.

 I featured *She Loves You* that week on my WGH radio show. By doing so, I was the first DJ in the US to nationally get credit for picking a Beatles song, per my report to Bill Gavin's weekly newsletter.

Committing to play a record wasn't something to be done half-heartedly. Once you told the record company you were going to start playing its release, they rushed copies to local record stores so they could get enough sales to have it reported back to local radio stations. Top Hits lists were formulated, in part, calling the shops every week to get a report of their best sellers. Also, when people called the station asking for a record to be played, it would be written down by the receptionist or the night DJ, and those calls became part of our calculation of the most popular records of that week.

Sounds corny now, but on my show every afternoon I presented the "Loving Cup" to a new record that I believed had potential. Once in a while, our WGH weekly music chart referred to a former "Loving Cup" winner as a song that had made it to No. 1. The whole idea was to create an image that WGH was the leading music station introducing the hits first. I gave the Loving Cup to the Beatles that day, continued to play the song every day for a few more weeks, and reported it as a hit prospect to the Bill Gavin newsletter.

•   •   •

During that initial week, when I first believed *She Loves You* was going to be a big hit, I was talking to Nat Weiss, an agent at General Artist Corporation (GAC), about a concert we wanted to do at the Virginia Beach Dome in the spring of 1964. Beatles manager Brian Epstein, laying the foundation to promote his band in America, hired GAC to book TV appearances and concerts at about the time when he believed a couple of Beatles songs would have gotten on US charts.

By then, I had booked acts a few times and knew enough to sign rising stars early and dovetail their growing popularity with our concert date. When Nat and I spoke, Nat mentioned the Beatles as a possibility to play the Dome in May 1964. The timing for me was perfect. I needed acts for my spring concert, and the Beatles, still being largely unknown in the US, were affordable. I don't know how many other promoters said they would book the Beatles. But most were professional promoters who did not have radio shows to stir interest in a concert. I was one of the very few—if not the only actual DJ promoter—who put up a deposit to book this group of British rockers. Several big-name DJs in New York and other cities often "fronted" concerts, but very few actually risked the money to book a talent.

There were several such professionals booking events in the Norfolk and Richmond markets at the time, but apparently none were familiar with the Beatles or their song, *She Loves You*. So, Nate and GAC booked a date with me. It's possible I was the only "promoter" who immediately said "yes" to the Beatles. I have never heard or read anything to the contrary.

• • •

September 1963 came and went and the song *She Loves You* was a flop. Record sales and play requests were weak—which, in truth, wasn't all that unusual. Most of the time, only one out of four new releases that made it to the radio became a Top 40 hit. The market was flooded with new releases and known talent. Unfortunately, I had not seen anything in the trade papers about the Beatles in the fall of 1963, other than my own recommendation in the *Gavin* report. For whatever reasons, the record had no traction. In fact, I later learned that Indiana-based Vee-Jay Records had acquired rights to *Love Me Do* but chose not to release it until 1964.

Despite their underwhelming radio debut in America, I wasn't concerned at that time about the Beatles flopping because our spring show at the Dome was still half a year away. The band was prolific, had a great sound and had some powerful names behind it, like Tony and GAC and the British-owned record label EMI, with subsidiaries in America and Canada. The Beatles were a sensation in the UK, so I figured the band was just slow catching on. I figured their next release would catch fire by the time they were to perform at the Dome.

My hunch paid off. In late fall of 1963, the American behemoth Capitol Records decided to release the Beatles in the US. Capitol was one of EMI's subsidiaries. A lot has been written about what Capitol Records did for the Beatles, initially refusing to distribute the band because it didn't like the Beatles' sound. Capitol had been around since 1942 and its managers thought they had a pretty solid grasp of American musical tastes. After all, The Beach Boys were on Capitol. Once they committed to a new artist, Capitol knew how to gin up publicity.

On December 10, 1963, CBS did a five-minute news report about the Beatles' popularity in England. NBC's top-rated nightly news show, The Huntley-Brinkley Report, also did a news feature on the band. Teenagers in the UK were hysterical over the Fab Four. Teenage girls screamed and fainted like they once had for Frank Sinatra and Elvis in the US. It was very rare for Huntley-Brinkley to do this kind of report. Network news in those days was very serious business. But the swell of popularity over the double-sided hit *I Saw Her Standing There* and *I Want to Hold Your Hand* signaled a cultural shift. It was the start of Beatlemania.

My AGL Productions concert partner, Dick Lamb, and I were ecstatic. There was no doubt now that our spring concert at the Virginia Beach Dome, featuring the Beatles, would sell out. Capitol had also released a whole album of Beatles tracks. Unlike most LPs, which have only a couple of really good songs, *Introducing . . . the Beatles* received across-the-board airplay on almost every track. Several of the songs made it to the Top 40 chart, even though they were not out as singles. Tony Mammerela at Swan re-released *She Loves You,* which went straight to No. 1. Vee-Jay released *Please Please Me.* Almost overnight, the Beatles had Top 40 hits on three different record labels simultaneously—another first in the music industry.

• • •

In those days, most long-distance business calls were "person to person." Around late January 1964, WGH's receptionist paged me on the house PA system. "Gene, long distance on line three." The operator asked if I was Gene Loving and then connected me to Nate Weiss.

I had sort of expected to be hearing from Nate. We had signed the Beatles to play the Virginia Beach Dome for $500, which was standard for new acts in the early '60s. With the Beatles' exploding popularity, I figured he may ask for seven hundred and fifty as a favor. Unfortunately, the news was worse. Nate was calling to cancel the show. Beatles manager Brian Epstein had decided to abandon the entire spring tour—including our date.

Nate quickly put salve on the wound. He said that the band appreciated me booking them when they were still unknowns in the US. To ease the cancellation news, they wanted me to be their guest on February 11, at the Shoreham Hotel in Washington, DC. The band would be performing its first US concert at the Washington Coliseum sports arena as part of a multi-act event, similar to what Dick and I had planned for the Dome. I accepted Nate's invitation, wondering how many other angry concert promoters would be there. I didn't ask.

The Washington Coliseum had already sold out because of the other acts on the February 11, 1964 date, before the Beatles were even announced. The Beatles were an add-on. So, eight thousand lucky ticketholders got to see the Beatles—essentially for free. Tickets sold for between $2.00 and $5.00 in those days.

At least I had a consolation prize to see the band, and maybe meet them and tape an interview. But I knew everyone at WGH would be very disappointed. WGH banners would have been on stage during the Dome show and Dick and I would have emceed the event, giving us a connection to the Beatles' erupting success in the US.

Then, of course, there was the matter of my relationship with the folks who ran the Dome. In those days we seldom had a signed contract for entertainers many weeks before the show. Typically, I would send a Western Union wire confirming a band's date, and I would get a wire confirmation back. I would then send a deposit to the concert venue and the entertainers' agents. Unfortunately, I had not received a contract by February from the Beatles, so I have nothing in writing that helps me recall specifics about the Beatles' agreement. And I also had only a verbal invitation to come up to Washington.

• • •

A couple of days before I drove to DC, I got a call from Bill Turner, the Capitol Records promotion man based in Baltimore who handled our territory. I knew Bill and spoke with him often, and he would come to see me about once every two months to chat about the next release from their recording stars. Until now, the big focus at Capitol was on The Beach Boys. Bill said he understood I was coming up to the Shoreham and he would see me there. This was reassuring, since I figured the invitation to meet the band had some kind of structure beyond just me fending for myself.

By now, like everyone, I knew the Beatles were coming to the US primarily to appear on *The Ed Sullivan Show* on February 9. I expected to watch the show from home and drive to Washington two days later. I figured that if I got to interview band members, I would ask some questions about their experience in New York. The weather forecast for Washington predicted a foot or more of snow. I thought the concert might be canceled, especially since it was in a downtown sports arena. Knowing it was going to be a long, cold and possibly icy and dangerous drive in my Corvette Stingray, I decided to look for a companion to make the trip with me. Dave Cummins, a WGH mid-day DJ, agreed to tag along. Dick Lamb may have been invited, but my guess is the station didn't want to have its two back-to-back teen DJs gone at the same time—or frozen to death together in some roadside ditch.

Dave and I decided to leave very early and drive on the less-traveled Route 17 north through Fredericksburg on to DC. It took eight agonizing hours to make the normally four-hour trip. Dave was a recent hire and he was married and therefore not a regular at my cottage parties. We really didn't know each other that well, socially, but he seemed like a decent enough guy. Dave and I each brought our WGH red jackets just in case we had a chance to have a photo taken with the Beatles.

• • •

When we finally arrived in Washington, we tried to navigate the streets, which were mostly closed due to the heavy snow. We had no idea if the Beatles had yet arrived in Washington—or even would. Finally, we found a Washington radio station that said the Beatles made it to town and the concert was going to be played—snow or no snow. Turns out the band's flight from New York had been cancelled because of the bad weather. So they traveled by train instead. According to at least one eyewitness account, nearly ten thousand teens were waiting at the Union Station and broke through the barriers. The band escaped the crush of frenzied fans, which by then had become routine for the Fab Four.

Dave and I found the Shoreham and recognized immediately that we were in the right place, as evidenced by the teenagers packed along the sidewalk in the driving snow. Some news organization reported that thousands of fans braved the cold and eight inches of new snowfall to get a glimpse of the Beatles. Security was at every door, keeping the kids outside.

Once inside the Shoreham, we went to a house phone and asked to be connected with the Beatles' room, but the operator was not persuaded when I told her that the band's managers were expecting us. We then found a bellman to carry a message up to the room. Soon, Bill Turner of Capitol Records appeared and escorted us up to a secure floor with guards at every exit and elevator. Bill took us into an empty hotel room and said he would be back soon. After about fifteen minutes, Bill returned with John Lennon.

He stuck out his hand saying, "Hello, I'm John Lennon." I was looking at the founder and leader of what would become the world's most popular band. He had just walked into one of the bedrooms of Suite 305. I introduced myself and my traveling companion. Before we sat down to talk, John agreed to a few pictures, which Bill Turner of Capitol Records took with my Polaroid camera. As John posed with us, he was easygoing, funny, and self-deprecating.

Our chat lasted about fifteen minutes and John had as many questions as we did. He was curious about US radio, and how it worked compared to what he had known his whole life. It was amazing to him that we had so many stations playing rock 'n' roll twenty-four hours a day. The British Broadcasting Corporation (BBC) was owned by the government and was mostly "block programmed." It did an hour of news, followed by a game show, followed by a soap opera. Once or twice a day for about an hour, a formal announcer would play a few popular records—very little of which was rock 'n' roll. Like an earlier time in America, teens in England heard new music in listening booths at record shops.

John did not mention "pirate radio," which was starting to broadcast illegally from ships anchored off the English coast. Those floating radio stations mimicked US-style stations, providing an alternative to the stuffy BBC. The British government did all it could to shut down the pirate broadcasters polluting their children's mind with anarchistic rock 'n' roll. *The Boat That Rocked*, a movie starring the late Philip Seymour Hoffman, illustrates those wily days.

John asked about my favorite US singers and groups. In almost every case he said he had records by those I mentioned. John told me he hoped to visit some record shops during his time in the US to acquire some new music not yet available back home. I recall John saying how much he liked The Beach Boys. But I doubt that John had a chance to visit any record shops during his first US visit.

While talking to John, I was wondering whether Paul, George or Ringo would be stopping by. I thought that maybe John, as bandleader, was checking me out before further admission to the inner circle. John hadn't said anything about my being first with *She Loves You* or booking his band at the Dome. So I wondered what he knew about why I was there.

I did some name-dropping and I'm guessing that John was impressed that I had met a lot of his favorite US artists over the years. Next thing I know, he says "Let's go see who's next door." We went to the adjacent living room of the suite. Ringo, George and Paul were there along with several other people I didn't recognize.

Curiously absent was the Beatles' notoriously protective manager, Brian Epstein. Brian, I later learned, did not accompany the Beatles on their trip to America because he was fearful of being outed as a homosexual and arrested under the laws of many US states at that time. Had Brian been with the Beatles, I doubt I would have been invited to spend the day with them in Washington. Brian died about four years later of a drug overdose, but I was to meet him before that tragedy.

I had on a red WGH coat with my name above the station logo. I don't know if John Lennon remembered my name or was rechecking it on the tag when I wasn't looking, but he used my full name each time he introduced me to people in the room.

Those in the inner sanctum included John's wife, Cynthia, and Louise, George Harrison's sister living in America. Little did I know that at that moment I had just met someone who would later connect me to the Beatles in a big way, giving me national and international recognition I had never dreamed possible.

As I began to feel welcomed into the Beatles' fold, I no longer felt comfortable asking for the band or its entourage to pose for pictures or to record interviews. It felt invasive. I thought it better to keep things casual and see what might be offered next—if anything. Dave Cummins was chilling out, mostly sitting on a couch across the room, observing.

Food was brought to the room and we all had something to eat. I could hear the four band members talking about the show they would perform in about four hours; they seemed nervous. They kept reviewing which songs they would sing and in what order. When they finally decided how the set would go, a playlist was given to an aide who would take it to the arena and glue it to Ringo's drums.

• • •

About an hour before the scheduled departure the band members went to their individual rooms to get dressed. While they were getting ready I spoke with Louise Harrison Caldwell, George's sister who was now living in Benton, Illinois. She was about thirty at the time. I did not ask her about George or the band. We mostly chatted about her time in the Midwest, and her previous life with her husband in South America after they left England, about ten years earlier. She did tell me that George and his bandmates held most of their rehearsals at the Harrison house in Liverpool.

The band members reappeared about 6:30, ready for the trip through the snow-covered streets to the arena. I took a photo of George and John in the suite and all four Beatles getting on the hotel elevator on their way to the car. They were wearing matching topcoats and were in a joking mood. When we all got downstairs, I really didn't know what to expect. I wondered how

Dave and I were going to get to the arena to see the show. I wasn't about to retrieve the Corvette and drive through the icy streets. Maybe a cab? Everyone went to a freight loading area of the hotel where two Cadillac limos were sitting inside. The band, George's sister and Cynthia Lennon got in the first car. To my surprise, Bill Turner waved the rest of us into car number two. When we pulled out to the street, a police car was there to escort us.

Another Polaroid yellowing picture taken when I first met John Lennon at the Shoreham Hotel in Washington, DC, in February 1964. John did this pose on his own just before Bill Turner of Capitol Records snapped the shutter.

Some of the pictures I took were with a Polaroid camera, which gave you an instant print, but the chemical you had to apply right away has yellowed over the years. I took this picture in the suite at the Shoreham Hotel in Washington right after George Harrison and John Lennon put on their top coats to head to perform their first US concert.

"Look this way guys!" One of my favorite pictures of the Beatles that I took, again on a Polaroid instant camera, just as they were about to get into the elevator to go to the Washington Arena for their very first concert in America. They were wearing matching top coats and suits and ties. I had listened to them decide on which songs they would play as we sat in the suite of the hotel.

Once at the arena, the Beatles disappeared into a dressing room, leaving the rest of us to roam the sold-out sports complex. The arena had been set up to host boxing matches, so there was a ring in the center. The show started, moving along with the performances by Jay and the Americans, The Righteous Brothers and Tommy Roe. Each did two or three songs, supported by a house band. About three-quarters of the way into the show, the Beatles were introduced, and the crowd of eight thousand ninety-two—mostly girls—went wild.

I found a phone booth and called WGH to go live on the Dick Lamb show with a report. Girls were screaming in the background. The band went on around 8:30 p.m. and played thirty-five minutes. They did twelve songs: *Roll Over Beethoven; From Me to You; I Saw Her Standing There; This Boy; All My Loving; I Wanna Be Your Man; Please Please Me; Till There was You; She Loves You; I Want to Hold Your Hand; Twist and Shout;* and *Long Tall Sally.*

We had been told to be at the car when they came offstage. Another act would close the show, so the Beatles were expected to be gone before the crowd broke. We made it back to the Shoreham unscathed and all went up on the elevator together. Each of the guys was really upbeat and enthusiastic about the reception they had just received at their first true concert appearance in the US. *The Ed Sullivan Show* was played in a small theater studio where most of the audience was probably hand-picked.

The band members went straight for the beer and started to peel off to their assigned rooms. They would be flying to Miami in the morning to perform for a TV show taping. Before they turned in, each member came around and said good night to about ten of us in the suite. Before leaving, I told Louise Harrison that I was intrigued by the early days in Liverpool and asked if I could call her to interview her on my radio show, and she gave me her telephone number.

• • •

After collapsing for a few hours' sleep in rooms at the Shoreham, the next day Dave and I made the still very slow drive back to Hampton and our jobs at WGH. I talked about the Washington experience on my radio show, and we published the photos taken with my Polaroid on the next WGH music chart.

It didn't take long for the phone to start ringing. Girls started calling the station wanting to talk to someone who had actually met the Beatles. I sensed that the Fab Four would not fade after a few months. They were real musicians, real songwriters, live performers who ignite crowds. They created and recorded their own material—no backup band.

The Beatles completed a taping in Miami for another Ed Sullivan show, and after playing around on the Florida beach for a couple of days went home to England. Soon afterward, I called Louise, George's sister. Originally I had intended to interview her just once, so I recorded the interview and promoted it on my show before airing it. Louise really knew a lot about the band, much more than what fans were reading in magazines. She agreed that I could call her again. We would do a Q&A that I would edit into about a one-minute segment, and I could stretch out airing the Beatles' tidbits over a few days. The interest from the listeners was overwhelming. I told Louise what kind of response we were getting and suggested she could be paid for giving an exclusive to one radio station in every city, even though she never asked me or WGH to pay her. We sent Louise a tape showing how we edited the interview into short segments, providing her with a one-minute format she could syndicate. She started doing so right away and soon she was paid a fee to be on radio stations all over the US.

Louise continued as my guest on WGH, and our interviews about the Beatles landed an official sponsor—Pepsi Cola. One day Louise called with an idea. She hadn't been home to the UK in twelve years and thought going there could provide great fodder for the radio if she and I went to England. She asked if I could help find a sponsor to pay for airfare, hotels and other expenses. I knew it was a very good idea and I told her I would look into it.

Taking off a week from work for an unplanned trip, however, was not easy. It meant other DJs would have to fill in for me and handle my various other responsibilities. And, no one was allowed to have time off during ratings periods when the listening audience was measured. However, meeting the Beatles in England and providing the station with exclusive interviews from there could be a coup for WGH. Fortunately, station management and Pepsi liked the idea and agreed to sponsor the trip.

CHAPTER 8

A HARD DAY'S NIGHT

I did not have a passport, and it typically took a month to get one. The trip with Louise was going to happen in a couple of days, so I would have to go to the State Department in Washington to beg for a one-day process. But who would go with me to be sure I wasn't kidnapped and could tell the officials at the passport office that I was legit? Dick Lamb was the first name to pop into my head. Dick quickly agreed and the station gave its blessing when he promised not miss his 7-to-11 p.m. radio show. When he got off that night, we left for Washington with no suitcases or plans. We put the top down on the Corvette and turned up the radio.

We arrived in the Washington area about 3 a.m., having discussed on the way that I needed a passport picture. I had to be ready when the State Department opened in the morning. So we went to Washington National Airport and found a photo booth. By now, both Dick and I were pretty tired and in a silly mood. As soon as the photo machine started warming up, we started cracking up. The booth did not wait for the perfect pose and the first round of photos were unusable. We found another set of quarters and the second time around I made Dick stay far away so I wouldn't be laughing and twitching. We finally got one usable picture out of five. We found a cheap motel, got about three hours sleep, and I was the first in line when the passport window opened. The clerk took one look at the photo and said it wouldn't work—wrong size. We were given an address for a professional photographer (most likely the brother of the clerk) and we drove over, had the picture done and got back to the line around noon. By now I was really worried there wasn't enough time to get the passport that same day. Fortunately they took pity on me, and possibly checked out my airline reservation to be sure I was telling the truth. Around five we left with the passport, but we didn't make it back for Dick's 7 p.m. show! That week WGH published my passport picture on the station's music chart.

Had I planned better, I would have taken my stuff with me, had Dick leave me in Washington for the night and drive my car back. But I didn't. So, the next day, on just a few hours of rest, I took a plane back to the DC airport. Louise was flying in from Illinois and we'd be taking a TWA jet from Washington National to London. International flights were very expensive back then, so thank goodness Pepsi paid for the tickets. It was daylight for almost the entire nine-hour trip, so I still didn't get much sleep. It was the first time I had seen Louise since the Shoreham Hotel two months earlier. She was excited and talkative. She told me that her brother had visited her about eighteen months earlier at her home in Benton. George talked about the band's popularity in England, but Louise was not impressed. She reminded George he had been in a band for years and maybe it was time to get a real job. During his visit she had filmed some home movies. She had them with her to show her parents back in the UK. Enroute to London we agreed that any interviews I got from the Beatles would be shared for her syndicated radio show.

Mrs. Harrison, George and Louise's mom, was traveling from Liverpool and would meet us at the airport. Louise told me that it would be her mother's first trip to London. Mrs. Harrison had lived her whole life and never had made the 178-mile trip from Liverpool to see her country's capital. Mrs. Harrison, whose first name was also Louise, had raised George, his brothers Harry and Peter, and sister Louise. In 1962, George had moved away from home in Liverpool to London.

After clearing customs and immigration, Louise spotted her mother. They had the kind of warm long greeting you would expect for a mother and daughter who had not seen each other in years. Soon a tall, distinguished-looking gentleman in a formal black suit and tie arrived—Bill Corbett, the Beatles' driver. We took our luggage to the big Bentley limousine that George had sent. "I understand you have been taking care of my daughter," Mrs. Harrison said to me. She was a smiling, outgoing lady, and very easy to talk to.

Bill Corbett drove us to Mrs. Harrison's hotel, and after we checked in we each said goodnight and went to our rooms. It was about 9 p.m. and I was ready to try to get some sleep, so Louise said she would call me in the morning. But before I could get undressed, Louise phoned to say come to her room. When she opened the door, there was George Harrison and his girlfriend Patti Boyd, and Mrs. Harrison. George had come to welcome his sister. George remembered me from Washington, and I assume Louise had briefed him on my reason for being with her on the trip. I sat quietly and listened to the family chat. Patti said almost nothing. Finally, when it seemed the visit was about to end, I asked George if he would accept a fan letter I had brought from Virginia. He was gracious and also agreed that I could do a short interview. I went to my room got my stuff, including my camera.

Louise Harrison Caldwell, George's sister, and I board our flight for England.

Our first picture after getting off the flight to London. Bill Corbett (who was both security and a driver for the Beatles), Louise, and the Beatles' limo.

Right after we checked into a London hotel, George Harrison and Pattie Boyd came over to see his mother and sister. I was invited to join them. Here I give George a fan letter from someone in Tidewater who asked for it to be delivered personally.

I also took a photo of Louise, George and Mrs. Harrison, and handed George the Polaroid picture to keep. I got out my small battery-powered tape recorder and did the interview, which I transmitted back to WGH over a long-distance phone line in the morning. During the interview George mentioned they had just finished filming that very day the movie *A Hard Day's Night*.

As we walked out of the room, George asked if I wanted to go down to the bar for a drink, and I immediately accepted. Apparently this was a London hotel favored by recording artists, and nobody seemed to pay special attention to George and Patti, even though they were both in the English tabloids. When we got to the bar, George introduced me to Billy J. Kramer, a pop singer managed by Brian Epstein. George and Patti chatted with Billy J. for a while as I listened and drank an English "pint." Around 1 a.m. I excused myself and went upstairs. Musicians often didn't go out until midnight, so it was still early for them, but I couldn't keep my eyes open.

The next morning Louise called to say George had arranged for the limo to take his three "visitors" on a tour of London. So I ate a full English breakfast that was included as part of the room cost, delivered to me by room service, after which we spent several hours seeing all the sights.

George arranged for the Beatles' driver and car to take his sister, his mother, and me on a tour of London the morning before we joined the Beatles at the *New Musical Express Show.*

Here is a picture I took of Mrs. Harrison, her daughter Louise and two others.

Brian Epstein backstage at Wembley Stadium shortly after I arrived with Louise Harrison and her mother for the Musical Express awards show. On the right, Gerry Marsden of Gerry and The Pacemakers who had signed with Brian for management, also performing at the awards show. They were soon to release a new single in the US, *Don't Let the Sun Catch You Crying* which went Top 10.

Louise and me on stage at the Cavern Club
where the Beatles started to gain success in England.

Here I am in the home in Liverpool where George Harrison grew up
and the Beatles practiced. Next to me is Harold, George's father.

I took this picture of Louise and her mother sorting through
fan mail for the Beatles at the Harrison home in Liverpool.

Mr. and Mrs. Harrison had arranged for the Cavern Club to be opened for a tour for their daughter and me. Here we are going down the steps into the basement of an old warehouse where the club was located.

George Harrison's mother was so excited to be in London to see the band perform. It was her first trip there since they had become a giant success after all those rehearsals in her home. My WGH tape recorder and mic can be seen to her left.

After a late lunch the car headed to Wembley Stadium so we could attend an awards program staged by the New Musical Express, which was the principal British trade paper for records, singers, bands and concerts. Our timing for the trip to England could not have been better, because every major music star or band in the UK would be performing there . After the performances, the pre-determined awards would be announced, just like the American Grammy Awards.

The building was surrounded by kids held back with barricades. As soon as we pulled onto the street in front of the arena the crowd started going crazy because our car was widely recognized as the Beatles' limo. As we headed down the drive leading to a secure area, several teenagers broke through the police lines and started jumping on the car, banging their fists, and screaming the names of the band members. We eventually got through and parked next to Brian Epstein's car, an Aston Martin.

As soon as we got inside backstage we learned the Beatles hadn't yet arrived. So I stood around, having just been introduced to the Beatles' manager by Mrs. Harrison. Brian Epstein was welcoming and introduced me to other acts he managed, including Gerry and the Pacemakers, who were about to release a record in the US, *Ferry Cross the Mersey*. There were members of other British bands, like the Searchers and the Hollies who walked by and stopped to say hello to Brian.

Soon word was passed that the Beatles were in an assigned dressing room, and the three of us were escorted up to join them. It was a very simple room with maybe one full-length mirror and a couple of chairs painted white. We all spent an hour together in this confined space, waiting for the Beatles' turn to perform.

Ringo took an avid interest in my Polaroid camera. I had just taken a picture of the Beatles looking through a hole in the wall, watching the Rolling Stones perform on stage. The Fab Four were impressed and speculated that the Stones would win music awards at next year's event.

In the dressing room at Wembley Stadium, George's mother is the one on the left. The Beatles are staring through a hole watching The Rolling Stones perform.

Ringo took a picture of me and Paul McCartney, and Mrs. Harrison and Louise. I interviewed Ringo and Paul on my little tape recorder while we waited. Ringo informed me that the Beatles had arrived in a plumber's van to avoid the kind of experience we had in their limo.

The band seemed surprisingly nervous about performing in front of other musicians at the awards event. Nonetheless, they would play flawlessly. When it was time for the Beatles to do their three songs, Louise, Mrs. Harrison and I went to an area where the managers and guests of the bands could watch. After they finished, they left immediately. Bill Corbett drove us to a restaurant for dinner, then to the hotel to check out, and then to the station for the late train to Liverpool. When we arrived in Liverpool at sunup, George Harrison's father was there to pick us up in their family car. We went to 12 Arnold Grove, a small terraced home on a cul-de-sac in the Liverpool suburb of Wavertree. This modest house was where George had grown up, and where the Beatles had practiced in their formative days.

• • •

I learned that Harold Hargreaves Harrison, George's dad, was a bus driver in Liverpool. He, like his wife, was very talkative and outgoing, so I didn't have to ask much to learn about the band's days in Liverpool. The dining room was stacked with Beatles fan mail and letters to George. I guessed the Harrisons' home address was known by early fans. Mrs. Harrison said she opened every letter and tried to respond to many.

Hanging on the wall was the gold record for *Please Please Me*, the band's first top ten hit in England. Mrs. Harrison explained the band wanted to hang this symbol of success in the Harrison abode because that's where the boys melded and often practiced.

Here, Mr. and Mrs. Harrison pose with their daughter, Louise, and the Beatles' first gold record for *Please Please Me*. The group asked the Harrisons to keep it safe for them at the house where they so often rehearsed when first starting.

I bought this Beatles picture at a stand in Wembley Stadium, took it into the dressing room to have all four sign it for fans in Tidewater. George Harrison wrote the inscription.

• • •

Harold Harrison expressed his appreciation to me for helping make it possible for their daughter to visit. He offered to take me to Liverpool's main shopping street so I could gather some souvenirs. We visited several stores, and everyone knew Mr. Harrison. I bought a very English sports jacket as my evidence that I was really in Liverpool. Believe me, nothing like it was for sale in the US at that time. I had lunch with Mr. Harrison in a classic English pub where he seemed to be a regular. Next, we toured Liverpool with Louise and her mother, which included a stop at the school attended by John Lennon and Paul McCartney.

Next was a visit to the Cavern Club where the Beatles really broke through in England and attracted the attention of Brian Epstein, who would become their manager. The club opened that afternoon, just for the Harrisons.

The evolution of the band has been thoroughly documented. As the story goes, the band had mostly matured while working in Germany, returning to the Cavern where they were discovered by locals who frequented the basement club. And it was as rough and dirty a public place as I have ever seen. The Harrisons had called ahead so the club manager met us. The entrance was off a back alley. The entire place was cement and brick. The acoustics there are terrible. The now-world-famous Cavern was a dive. We took some pictures, I interviewed the manager and we left.

That night the Harrisons took us to the bus drivers' private club. I learned that most "trades" in England were unionized and each had a meeting house, or clubhouse where they socialized. We went for dinner and I felt welcomed, relaxed, and even danced with a couple of the girls who were sitting at our table.

Later that night, George's brother Peter came over with his wife to watch the 8mm home movies Louise had recorded of George's visit to her American house a couple of summers earlier. It was fascinating seeing George looking and acting like a typical nineteen-year-old, hanging out by the swimming pool and having fun. I have never seen these films again—not in the many specials about the band or the documentary about him released shortly after he died in November 29, 2001.

Peter Harrison was working as a mechanic at the Liverpool Jaguar dealer and he had a green four-door Jag. It was about 11 p.m., but Peter wanted to drive me through the Mersey Tunnel so I could see Liverpool from the other side. During the excursion, we just talked, and I didn't interview Peter about George. It felt inappropriate, because his brother George had gone on to fame and fortune while Peter remained at home. Just like the other Harrisons, Peter treated me like someone special and went out of his way to see I had a good time. I was so impressed with the entire family. They were fun, gracious and accommodating.

After my first good night's sleep in days and then another big English breakfast, Louise and I were taken to the train station for the trip back to London. Mrs. Harrison stayed behind. When we arrived in town, Bill, the Beatles' driver, was there with a different car to take us to the Rediffusion TV studios where the Beatles were taping a special, along with a couple of Brian Epstein's other acts, including Cilla Black. We were taken into a sponsor's booth overlooking the studio. Afterward there was a "wrap" party in the same building.

At the party Paul McCartney decided that my status as an American DJ should be known to everyone: he made me sound like a big deal, and I must admit that I didn't dissuade him. He also made sure I had plenty to eat and drink. I was surprised he didn't tire of me, and of the round of introductions. At some point, however, Louise and I said goodbye to them, and checked back into the same hotel where we first stayed. The next day we flew back to the States.

Gene Loving With Paul McCartney

The picture published in the The Virginian-Pilot after my return from England.

• • •

All during the trip, I was calling in to the station with reports that aired on WGH and on about twenty other radio stations around the country. I had syndicated the reports to subscribing stations. Before leaving for England I had given the WGH morning man's son, George Crawford, Jr., a list of stations to call to see if they wanted my Beatle reports. Just about every station he called accepted. I provided a custom introduction for each station by phone from London. George Crawford, Jr. would splice in the custom intro for each station, which preceded the generic report of an interview I did or experience I had. Example: *"This is Gene Loving in London, reporting exclusively for the Tommy Shannon show on WKBW."* My associate had been able to create about ten one-minute reports, which mostly included something from one of the Beatles or Louise or Mrs. Harrison. When I got back we were able to put together about another ten reports. The entire syndication lasted about two weeks.

My now-popular daily interview with Louise Harrison picked up the day after we got back, and we had a lot to talk about on the air. She was feeding her own station clients with her reports on the trip, too. WGH started to sell remote broadcasts for my show, enabling listeners to come by and get an autographed copy of the pictures I took on the trip. This got us another month's mileage out of what had been a magical experience for me. Once I got home and could reflect on everything, and experienced the response from those who came out to get the pictures, I started to appreciate the significance of my trip to England, the Harrison home, and mingling with the band. And, of course, WGH loved it. We became *The Beatles station* in our market, riding the band's swelling wave of popularity.

• • •

Susan on the day of our marriage.

Somehow, in the midst of all of this, I got married in April, 1964. Susan and I had a full church ceremony and reception in Richmond. Dick Lamb, my very close friend and steadfast business partner, was one of the ushers.

After a two-week honeymoon at a mountain resort and in New York City , including the world's fair, we moved into the Grandview Beach cottage and I bought her a used blue four-door Cadillac as a wedding present. A gray cat and boxer dog already lived there. A year later we had to find another place when the owner of the cottage decided to stop renting it, so the day we got the call, I opened the newspaper and found a beach house for sale in Poquoson, at 104 Sandy Bay Drive, facing the Chesapeake Bay. I didn't know anything about Poquoson, only that it was about the same driving distance for me to get to work. We bought it a few days later for $27,500. My parents helped out with the down payment and chipped in some furniture. We rented a U-Haul and my buddy Dick Lamb and WGH newsman Gene Galusha helped move us in. My only complaint after a few nights was the mosquitos. Poquoson was plagued with them. We fixed that by installing central air conditioning so we could keep the windows closed and the bloodsuckers out. And, we kept the house stocked with OFF.

The other surprise was our doorbell constantly ringing. Turns out the guy we bought the house from was the town doctor and locals were used to stopping by day and night to see him. After a few months, word got around that "the doctor was out" permanently. Despite the early interruptions, we were happy with our fishing village life in Poquoson. We kept a small boat and went crabbing and fishing. I was making enough money from WGH and the promotion business to pay our bills and take Susan out to nice restaurants. We also got a second cat when the boxer was adopted by the WGH business manager after a few incidents with other Poquoson pooches.

View of the Chesapeake Bay from our home in Poquoson on a cold winter day. The Hobie Cat on the right liked to sail in warmer weather.

• • •

The Beatles were in huge demand and soon they booked their first full US tour. The venue closest to Hampton was Baltimore. I was able to buy fifty good tickets through Nate Weiss at GAC. WGH chartered a bus and held a promotion to give away tickets to the show. This may have been the biggest ticket giveaway in the history of radio. Callers inundated the station and sponsors lined up.

Dick and Donna Lamb, and Susan and I followed the bus in Susan's Cadillac. This was the third time in a year I had seen the Beatles perform. Dusty Springfield opened the show and the Beatles played all their hits to date in about an hour. The crowd noise was ear-shattering. In fact, one of the reasons the band ultimately stopped touring was because their music couldn't be heard over the screams of hysterical fans. After the Baltimore show, Susan and I were allowed backstage for a short press conference. The band members recognized me among the thirty or so press people sitting in attendance, pointed to me smiling and gave me a shout-out. I felt very connected to these guys, but as with so many things, life moves on. The Beatles were now the biggest band—perhaps even the biggest entertainment act—in the world.

A picture I took backstage at the Baltimore concert.

When the Beatles came back to the USA to play a few concerts, WGH organized a bus to transport ticket winners to Baltimore. After the show, the Beatles held a press conference attended by about 30 people. It made me feel very special when they all shouted out a hello when they saw me. My wife in the light colored outfit is seated next to someone, just behind Ringo.

The daily calls from Louise faded. We had exhausted the topic and the media was saturated with Beatles coverage. Also, every US market had a bunch of radio stations with local star DJs who all wanted to ask questions on their own as the band toured. And their stations wanted to be positioned just as WGH was—as the Beatles station in their market. Many of the biggest names in radio, people like Murray the K in New York, and Larry Caine in Miami, tried to attach themselves to the Beatles by following every date of the tour in person, always attending the press conferences, and possibly connecting with one or two of the band members to hang out. Murray the K started to call himself the *Fifth Beatle*.

It was clear I'd had my day in the sun, and I was grateful for it but ready for something new. But I just couldn't get out of the way of Beatles-related things. The Gordon family, which owned Skateland, the site of part of my first night at WGH, also owned several local movie theaters. The Gordons were involved in boating and helped stage the annual WGH Water Ski show off Fort Monroe in Hampton every year. Jerry Gordon was an officer in the motion picture theater owners' association and had some influence in Hollywood with the movie companies.

Jerry had just arranged for the East Coast premiere of the Beatles' new movie, *A Hard Day's Night*. He knew of my connection to the Beatles and wanted WGH to promote and help stage the first showings of the movie with special souvenir tickets. And he wanted me to introduce each showing of the movie at the Palace in downtown Newport News, which was a fully functioning and vibrant town in those days. Jerry had arranged for a theater operator in Virginia Beach to duplicate the premier the next day in a theater more convenient to people living on the southside of Hampton Roads. Kids camped out on the sidewalks overnight to be sure they got tickets.

Herbert Morewitz, Sally Marshall and me starting to sell tickets for the Virginia premier of *A Hard Day's Night* at the Palace Theatre in Newport News. The next day at a theater on Atlantic Avenue in Virginia Beach, it was a repeat performance as people lined up for tickets to the first Beatles movie. It was my job to keep the crowd orderly before going in to introduce the film.

By now, my hand was getting tired after weeks
of appearances signing Beatles pictures.

After I returned from the trip to England with photos and interviews, WGH sold "remotes" in the Showmobile at shopping centers all around Hampton Roads. Listeners came out by the hundreds to get a signed copy of our Beatles photos. For most of these appearances, Sally Marshall in the WGH jacket helped keep things organized.

• • •

Paul McCartney just before he started singing (off key on purpose) to answer a question about *Help!*

By 1965, I was happy just to be playing Beatles music on the radio. But it was not to be. The phone rang and Bill Turner of Capitol Records told me the band was going to film some scenes for the next movie, *Help!*, in the Bahamas and suggested I go down. Bill was always trying to promote the next product, even for the Beatles. I had never been to the Bahamas, so it sounded like a good idea to me. It would also be a nice trip for Susan, since she had never met the band members. Once again, without any plan of how it was going to work once I got there, WGH supported the trip and we flew to Nassau.

There was a convention on the island that took up every room of the two or three decent hotels. The band, we learned, was coming in that evening and would be staying at the Balmoral Club on Cable Beach. The only place we could find to stay was at the opposite end of the island, about a forty-five minute drive on very bad roads. We checked into a cottage at the Blue Moon Club. This was different from being part of the Beatles' first trip to Washington or hanging out in England with the band and members of Harrison's family.

By the time we got back to a meeting room at the Balmoral Club, two or three other radio guys had arrived there too. I recall one of them was Larry Caine from Miami. The Beatles and their *entourage* arrived. There were far more people traveling with them than when I went to the Shoreham Hotel in February. Since there were just three of us media types at the "press conference," we just walked up to where the Beatles sat and interviewed each guy separately. Susan took some photos with a little brownie camera while I chatted with George, John, Paul and Ringo.

They each remembered me by name and were very warm and friendly, especially Paul. One thing had changed though; the band's innocent naiveté. The past year had hardened them to the press, especially John. He seemed cynical, saying he had gotten stoned during the flight over. After a little while, Richard Lester, the director of the movie who had come over with the group, announced the band was going to bed, and they all left. I managed to speak with Richard and asked what was happening the next day. He told me they were filming near the Airport Road and I was welcome to come out to watch.

After a good night's sleep, I showed up for a scene where they filmed the guys riding bicycles down a remote road. They were just hanging out and waiting, as you do when you're making a movie: two hours of doing nothing, just to shoot about one minute of film. I got a few comments on my tape recorder from each of the band members, and I shot a few pictures. Since there was nothing else to do, I started interviewing the Beatles' hairdresser, Leslie Cavendish, along with Richard Lester and other actors in the movie. Eventually I realized that I had gotten as much as I could get without repeating questions.

The next day I went to another filming location out on a cement pier. It was more of the same. So that afternoon we flew back to Norfolk. That was my last contact with the Beatles. In 1965, after I married, Susan and I visited George Harrison's parents in a Liverpool suburb, Appleton. George had bought his mother and father a large secluded country house to give them privacy. I brought them one of the sheets of pictures we printed after my 1964 visit to their home. Below is a letter from George's mother sent to my Poquoson address asking for the bigger copies of the pictures I took of her and the "boys." Amazing that George Harrison's mother was asking me for photos of her with the Beatles.

Gene Loving.
104, Sandy Bay Dr.
Poquoson.
Virginia
U.S.A.

The Harrisons invited me to come back any time to see them. They sent me a new address about a year after my first visit to Liverpool, so I knew the invitation was sincere. My wife, Susan, and I spent a pleasant afternoon catching up on Harrison life, having tea, learning that George had made it possible for his father to retire. This is a letter sent by George's mother asking for some of my Beatles pictures, taken with her during our time in London.

31st DEC! 1965.

Dear Gene.

I was pleased to hear from you.

I had wanted to write, but of course, I'm still snowed under with mail.

What I want you to do for me is to send a few of the pictures you took, in London & home. I only recieved the paper with tiny ones on. & I would love some big copies, if you can manage. Those of our family & Boys. Every one sends good wishes on your marriage & for 1966. Louise.

Harrison

Years later, Angie and I went to see Paul McCartney & Wings perform at Madison Square Garden, but made no effort to contact him. I believe that if I ran into the two living Beatles today, both would remember me. I knew the band early in their career at a time nobody else was there. I can only imagine the thousands of people over the years who have met the Beatles. I had a unique opportunity to be up close and personal with them in the US, England and the Bahamas. Few of the thousands that passed through their life got to experience what I did, and I am forever grateful.

In Nassau right after the Beatles arrived to start filming their new movie _Help!_ John Lennon listens as I talk to Paul McCartney. Brian Epstein stands behind George Harrison while Ringo gets his drink order. A reporter from a TV station in Miami is on the right.

The Beatles became the No. 1 creators of music of all time so far, and the memories resonate with me almost every time I hear one of their songs—even now, when it's background music on elevators or in restaurants. Every once in a while I drift back, ever so briefly, into Beatlemania.

Someone called me from Texas in the mid-1980s saying they wanted to make an album of all my Beatles interviews. I agreed. The record is called *All My Loving*. It seems that about every five years, someone who's writing a book about the band will call to interview me about my Beatles' experiences. Local TV stations and newspapers do anniversary features and want an interview.

Friends, and people I meet for the first time, always ask about the band. I have never met anyone who doesn't know of, or doesn't like, the Beatles. They are iconic, much more than any musical group; their music and movies are part of American culture—world culture for that matter.

Until 2015, I had put all of my Beatles material in storage and had not looked at it for decades. Going back now—seeing the pictures again, listening to the interviews, recalling my conversations with George, his sister, their parents, remembering the scenes in Washington and England with Paul from fifty years ago —those times seem surreal. Sometimes, when history is happening, you don't realize you're part of it. I didn't fully appreciate what was happening then—but I do now.

CHAPTER 9

DISC-O-TEN

Booking big talent for concerts was good for Dick Lamb and me as DJs. Our radio shows continued to score very well in ratings. (Dick still insists he had more listeners than me. Not so.) Undisputed is that the symbiotic relationship between our concert promotions company and WGH grew our brands as on-air personalities and show promoters. That success would soon breed new opportunity.

I was spending a lot of time traveling between Hampton and the Norfolk-Virginia Beach area, mostly for remote broadcasts or personal appearances. Hampton Roads is a confluence of rivers and tributaries of the Chesapeake Bay and Atlantic Ocean. But traveling in the beautiful "tidewater" area meant driving over bridges, through tunnels or taking a ferry. For me, in the '60s, it meant paying a $1.25 toll to cross the Hampton Roads Bridge-Tunnel, which connects Hampton with Norfolk. And, it usually meant at least an hour in each direction. Traffic bottlenecked at the HRBT and other crossings, especially around commuting time. The region has added tunnels and bridges over many decades to relieve the crush of cars, but traffic worsens as the population swells. The region has grown from about 1 million people in 1970 to more than 1.6 million in 2010, according to US Census data.

A significant portion of WGH's audience was in the Norfolk-Virginia Beach community, the region's biggest population block. And that's where we were in highest demand to do live events. To make us mobile, WGH converted a small house trailer into a fully equipped radio studio. Station engineers outfitted the rig and had it towed to wherever we needed it. It was an impressive setup which we called the *Showmobile*. From it we could play music, jingles, commercials, do interviews out over the air on 1310 AM, and also communicate with the home office semi-privately on a two-way radio frequency, the same frequency used in WGH news cars. We had to haul duplicates of taped advertisements and the records to each Showmobile broadcast and then take it all back to the main office in Hampton afterward. Doing live events also meant we needed cash for tolls and gas and incidentals. Back then, company credit cards were rare. Instead, we paid in cash and submitted expense reports to get reimbursed. Keeping track of mileage and other costs was a pain, and I often failed to do the paperwork required, feeling too busy. I figured a few dollars here and there didn't matter. *Wrong!* I'll bet WGH owed me $30,000 in unreimbursed expenses by the time I left. (Now that I think of it, as chairman and CEO of the company that now owns WGH, I should find my old receipts and get my money.) Dick and I would have never envisioned back then that we would actually own the iconic WGH.

• • •

One of our staple promotions at WGH that lasted years was the WGH *Micro-Phonies* basketball team. The station's DJs, along with a couple of good players to keep it competitive, challenged teachers at junior high and high schools throughout the market. Fifty years later it's difficult to explain how big an event this was back then. Every game was beyond sold out. It was most schools' biggest annual fundraiser. We were playing two games a week. The games created some real cheering and booing opportunities for favorite or despised teachers; school bands played and each team even had cheerleaders. At six foot three, I was perceived as a former star basketball player who now happened to be on the radio. But I had zero sports talent, no hand-eye coordination and couldn't jump very high.

One of the bits we did was a halftime showstopper, promoting that I would make my famous half-court shot. With each attempt, the crowd had to go silent, which didn't help—ever. I never hit the basket from half court, or from anywhere on the court for that matter. When I missed, the response from the stands was boos, taunts and laughs. My teammates sometimes took pity and came to center court to escort me back to the bench. Yes, we were bad, but famous. So famous, in fact, that once we played the original Harlem Globetrotters in front of ten thousand spectators at the Hampton Coliseum in 1970.

One of the early events at the Hampton Coliseum featured the WGH Micro-Phonies against the Harlem Globetrotters. This was the era of Meadowlark Lemon, Curly Neal, Geese Ausbie, among others. I'm in the center listening to 10,000 cheering fans. It's amazing how the WGH Micro-Phonies could fill an arena.

• • •

One morning, before heading in to work at my WGH office, I got a call at home from Roger Clark who said to meet him at the station right away. When I arrived Dick was there and the three of us went into the general manager's office. Ambert Dail explained that he had received a call from WAVY. The station wanted to create a weekly dance party show on TV, a local version of *American Bandstand*, and they wanted a WGH DJ to host it. Since Dick and I both had the largest teen audiences, Ambert thought it would be a good idea for both of us to go over to WAVY the next morning to meet with Van Camfort, WAVY's program director. Van would choose between Dick and me—an easy decision in my mind. I couldn't believe they were going to embarrass Dick Lamb by telling him that Gene Loving would be the show's host so he shouldn't bother with an audition. In truth, I knew Dick was better looking than me and had TV experience, but I figured I might have a chance if I showed Van the pictures I had kept of Dick wearing those hideous pants that were five inches too short.

I don't remember much about the meeting, other than another WAVY executive was also there smoking a big cigar. We kicked around some ideas for the show and its name, which was a play on *Disk-O* and Channel 10, and then we left. On the drive back to Hampton from WAVY's station in downtown Portsmouth, I tried to be magnanimous, telling Dick I wouldn't accept the job unless we co-hosted it, that the program would be better with both of us because we had the promotional opportunity to talk up the show on WGH from the time I went on at 3 p.m. until Dick's show finished at 11 p.m. That would be eight hours when we could mention *Disc-O-Ten*.

I was half kidding, as I didn't feel I had any chance of being picked as host over Dick. Nevertheless, Dick agreed to the co-host concept—even though he probably knew he was better suited for TV, and that he would get the job. When we got back to the radio station we told Roger about our plan. Roger passed it up the chain. To my surprise, we didn't get any pushback from the big boys at WAVY or WGH. The plan worked well and WAVY quickly sold out all sponsorships for the first season of the half-hour dance program.

Disco music was just emerging in the mid-1960s and exploded a few years later with the release of *Saturday Night Fever* starring John Travolta and scored by the Bee Gees. One thing that had caught on was teens dancing to R&B and rock n' roll. Dick Clark fueled that fad with *American Bandstand*. Now, local stations wanted a piece of the action. Back in those days local TV network affiliates had almost no competition, so just about any decent content had pretty good odds of scoring well with audiences, advertisers and sponsors.

Our show, *Disc-O-Ten,* was scheduled for 7 p.m. Mondays, but we taped on Saturday morning. It would normally take us about three hours to cull twenty-five minutes of content. The actual taping was usually aired without much editing. We even kept slight mistakes, fixing only major problems. Most of the time was spent explaining to show participants—teenaged students—what to do. We also had to get the stage prepared for the performing local band, and let them rehearse once.

WAVY did newscast from the studio we were using, so a crew had to cover the newscast set with our background and stage props. WAVY really got into the spirit and energy of *Disc-O-Ten.* Many staffers started coming in on Saturdays to help with the shows. We had "producers" standing by every camera. Dick Paul, WAVY's promotion director, became the floor manager, and WAVY's Van Camfort always came in to be sure the technical director and sound engineer understood this was not a static news program. Even WAVY's master control room people chipped in, racking up tapes of a music video or commercials on giant two-inch reels. At the beginning, *Disc-O-Ten* was in black-and-white. But when WAVY bought three new color cameras, which took an hour to tune every time before they were used, the station promoted for weeks that *Disc-O-Ten* was going color.

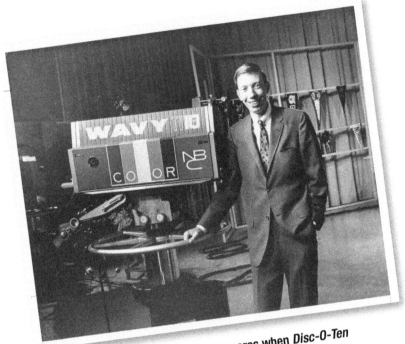

Me with one of the new cameras when *Disc-O-Ten* went from black and white to color.

Disc-O-Ten became the top show in its time period and Dick and I became the best-known radio broadcasters in the market. We couldn't go anywhere without comments about *Disc-O-Ten*. I still hear from people, fifty years later, who say they danced on that show. Pictures taken with us at the TV studio became part of area high school yearbooks. Students were selected to represent their school on the show. WAVY coordinated which school would be on when, and each school had a different process of selecting students. Soon Dick and I started to have some say about who appeared. In fact, one of the girls we decided to put on would eventually become Mrs. Dick Lamb.

Student body presidents were often tapped by the schools. They would bring pictures of school events, which we showed while interviewing them. But what soon became apparent to Dick and me was that often the criteria was academics—not dancing ability.

We wanted great dancers for our show. Dancers are integral to the program. Dick Clark had figured that out with *American*

Bandstand. Dick Lamb had called Dick Clark for tips when we started, and Clark suggested that we have some regular "ringers" to appear each week on *Disc-O-Ten.* Our talented regulars would mix with the students and give the show zest. The TV show *Hullabaloo* had a similar concept; it had girls dancing on caged platforms to add movement in the background. We borrowed from that idea; we assigned some dancers to bounce and groove on raised squares, each wearing *Disc-O-Ten* outfits like cheerleaders. The production of the show was getting bigger and more complicated, but along with that effort came rising ratings.

Dick and I didn't wear WGH uniforms on the TV show. Instead, WAVY arranged for us to get a clothing trade at a local men's store in Newport News. Each week we exchanged our duds for something new. Often they let us keep the clothes, which was a very nice benefit, especially for Dick who was stylistically challenged. I remember one week I went to pick up what they selected and for me. It was an all-black Nehru suit, which they let me keep. I wore it to WGH's 50th anniversary party.

• • •

Dick Lamb and me with the *Disc-O-Ten* platform dancers who were featured each week along with the students from the guest high school on WAVY-TV 10.

Dick Lamb and I had quite a run together. We were getting so popular so fast that we never quite knew what might happen next. One rare opportunity fell in our laps when we were tapped to help promote a real estate development. WGH saleswoman Kaye Foulkes (married to Channel 13 weatherman Joe Foulkes) was friendly with a Virginia Beach resident who got the rights to develop Grand Bahama Island, a British possession also referred to as Freeport or Lucaya. The scheme was to sell property for home sites in a developed community which would be a retirement destination, similar to what GAC had done through Florida.

Dick Lamb and I were selected as the test commercial spokespeople for the project, and we recruited listeners to fly on a charter with us periodically to the island for a tour. It went great; we loved the trips, lying on the beach, doing almost nothing, while people bought lots. Then, out of nowhere, Great Britain gave the islands back to the Bahamian people. Queen Elizabeth even showed up to hand over the keys. The very next week, the new Bahamian government passed a law that non-natives could no longer work there. So Dick and I were booted out. I go to Lucaya now on my boat as a tourist, often recalling those glory years.

• • •

One of the things that increased Dick and my profiles, more than the TV dance show itself, were the twenty—to thirty-second promos previewing next week's *Disc-O-Ten* show. "Hi! This is Gene Loving of WGH, and this is Dick Lamb! This coming Monday night at 7 p.m. on *Disc-O-Ten* we have . . . right here on WAVY-TV 10." The promos played on WAVY all day and night, including inside NBC network shows, like the *Tonight Show* with Johnny Carson. There was Johnny, and next up was Dick and me, promoting *Disc-O-Ten*. Dick and I leveraged our newfound stardom by plugging our upcoming concerts. If we had scheduled recording stars to perform at the Dome, WAVY would haul its portable eighteen-wheeler TV truck—the one it used for sporting events—and tape those stars lip-synching a couple of their hit songs. The *Disc-O-Ten* logo hung on a wall in a dome conference room where the acts recorded. Dick or I would step into the shot to shake hands with members of the group. We were able to clip those recordings into our TV show so viewers thought the acts were actually visiting with us in the studio.

Once we did a show from a flatbed truck parked on the street in downtown Norfolk. *Our Disc-O-Ten* guest was Neil Diamond who was so late to the taping that the crowd had left by the time he got there, and he sang to an empty parking lot. Monty Hall *of Let's Make a Deal* co-hosted the show with us one week. *Disc-O-Ten* had become so popular that we taped it twice at the Virginia Beach Dome, charging admission, and both times the shows sold out. Our company, AGL, was the producer and we had paid some small fees to WAVY to haul their equipment out to the Beach.

Me introducing the next song on *Disc-O-Ten*.

The back of WAVY-TV promotion manager, Dick Paul, who floor
managed *Disc-O-Ten* ready to give a cue to Lamb and me as
we clown on stage during the opening segment.

• • •

Disc-O-Ten lasted five seasons, which was a decent run for
a local TV program. One of our guests for the show was The
Hollies. The English band had several big hits in the late 1960s.
The group was led by Alan Clarke and Graham Nash. We booked
them twice at the Virginia Beach Dome, and both times their
concerts sold out. Promoting the Hollies' show gave me a chance
to get to know members of the band. I spent a few days hanging
out with them in Hampton Roads between dates of the tour. They
wanted to stay busy, so their manager mentioned a show for the
military. I got in touch with one of our contacts at the Navy and
the Hollies ended up doing a concert on the hangar deck of the
USS John F. Kennedy in front of about five thousand sailors. The

band was given a tour of the aircraft carrier, complimentary hats and a lot of pictures with the officers and crew.

Then they came to WAVY to record a segment for our *Disc-O-Ten* TV show. And Alan Clark and Graham Nash wanted to come to the WGH studio for my entire four-hour program. At that time I had a red Jaguar XKE with cream colored leather seats that held four people, tightly. Graham had a Jag in England, so I let him drive from the hotel to the station, which was a fun challenge for him and a little scary for me: in England they drive from the opposite side of the car on the opposite side of the road. We made it safely, which was a good thing for the music world, too. As you probably know, Graham eventually left the Hollies to help create one of the biggest rock legends of all time—Crosby Stills and Nash.

Graham Nash, me, and Allan Clarke in the WGH studio. Their band, The Hollies, played to a sell-out crowd the next evening. Graham Nash drove my Jag to the studio to hang out for four hours before we all went to dinner.

Dick did such a good job on *Disc-O-Ten* that WAVY offered him a spot as the host of its morning *Compass* show. That was great for Dick, but not so good for WGH. He left his daily radio show to move into TV full time. I was sad but fully supported Dick's move. It was a great opportunity. We were still the best of friends, and still partners in the concert business.

Dick would eventually join WAVY's direct competitor, WTAR-TV (later named WTKR-TV), and do a morning show that carried his name, *The Dick Lamb Show*. He became very popular, beating the national names that ran opposite him on WAVY and WVEC.

I stuck with WGH and continued working with WAVY-TV on occasion, doing things like hosting the local inserts of the *Jerry Lewis Telethon*, a program that broadcast for eighteen hours straight, from Military Circle. I was usually given a hotel room and when the program ended I would go collapse in the room and sleep for two days.

Me hosting the *Jerry Lewis Telethon*, live at Military Circle Shopping Center on WAVY-TV 10. 1974

Remaining with WGH continued to create some wonderful opportunities and relationships. I especially liked raising money for good causes. One of the most rewarding fund-raising efforts came when WGH General Manager Ambert Dail introduced me to Norfolk attorney Peter Decker. Danny Thomas was of Lebanese ancestry just like Pete, and he had called Pete for help with fund-raising for his new children's hospital, St. Jude's, in Memphis, Tennessee. Ambert had an idea based on a successful charity campaign in another market: he asked me to promote the fund-raising effort for a month on my afternoon show by asking listeners to "pitch in just a penny" for Saint Jude's. People started bringing jars of pennies to the station and to my live broadcast client locations. The Saint Jude's "penny pitch" became an annual event, and I became friends with Pete and Bess Decker as their dedication to Saint Jude's grew over the years, leading to telethons and other major fundraising events for the hospital. Pete's family has continued his good work, which has helped thousands of kids. Today, our company, Max Media, does an annual Radio-Thon on our country station, EAGLE.

CHAPTER 10

THE BEAT GOES ON

The concert promotions business kept chugging along. We routinely booked bands not only at the Virginia Beach Dome, but also at the Mosque in Richmond. WGH gave us the on-air promotion in exchange for tying the station closely to the shows. Often a show was billed as *"WGH Presents . . ."* in newspaper ads and window cards. My fellow DJs loved coming to the shows in their WGH uniforms to introduce some acts, or just to be introduced themselves. We worked with WLEE when we staged events in Richmond.

At our main concert venue, the Dome, we divided two-thousand seats into three sections based on ticket price, designated by colors. We typically did one show at 7 p.m. and another at 10 p.m. To pull this off we had to hustle out the early show attendees by 9 p.m. before the late show ticket-holders entered. That process usually went smoothly. Late-show attendees often stood in line, calmly, on each side of the building and well out into the parking lot. There were no reserved seats, just sections, so if you had a green ticket for the green chairs and you were first in line, you could sit on the front row. That seating concept is similar to the way Southwest Airlines first admitted travelers to its flights.

The Dome, the site of so many great shows, held 2,000 people seated.

AGL Productions staged probably four big-name events a year at the Dome. And we did many smaller events, which we called "Show Dances," where we took out all the seats, resulting in a giant live hop with name bands like Jr. Walker & the All Stars, and Question Mark & the Mysterians, who had the hit *96 Tears*.

When the Dome was already booked, we sometimes did shows at the thirty-five hundred-seat Norfolk City Arena. Our Norfolk shows included concerts by Tom Jones, Sonny & Cher, and The Righteous Brothers, all in the early stages of their musical careers.

The Righteous Brothers with me at the Norfolk City Arena. Following an unusual afternoon concert, Bobby Hatfield and Bill Medley rode with me to WAVY-TV to tape a segment for *Disc-O-Ten*, then to Fort Eustis to do a free show for the military.

At the height of CBS's *Sonny & Cher Show*, we promoted their local appearance twice: once at SCOPE and once the following year at the Hampton Coliseum. Sonny, who managed everything, remained loyal to us over the years as we hired them for a show at the very start (pictured below) when *I Got You Babe* was in the Top 10.

In those days we often picked up the performers at the airport and drove them to their hotels. Later, we'd chauffeur them to the concert hall and then dinner after the show. It was a great way to make personal connections with the stars, and to see them in moods other than "on." I remember when Sonny Bono wanted to come over early from the Golden Triangle, a hotel in Norfolk, to inspect the stage and sound system before the show at the Norfolk Arena. After dropping him off, I went back to the hotel to fetch Cher and her sister. Cher would have been around nineteen at the time and she seemed very nervous; she almost had to be talked into actually going on stage. The Norfolk City Arena was one of her first live shows.

Fifteen years later I would escort Cher to the stage in the dark with a flashlight at Norfolk's new Scope facility, during the height of the *Sonny & Cher Comedy Hour*. She had developed into a very confident performer by then, and that show was among the biggest moneymakers in our concert career.

Sonny was always the professional businessman, and he treated us like we were best friends. He understood what we did and grasped the importance of radio: he'd been in the record promotion business himself. He had called on DJs to get them to play Phil Spector releases. Denis Pregnolato, Sonny and Cher's road manager, was also very loyal to us, always asking the booking agents to give Norfolk or Hampton dates to Dick and me.

For one tour, Sonny had rented Hugh Hefner's black Playboy jet, the one with the white bunny on the tail. When I went out to pick up Sonny and Cher at the Norfolk airport, they invited me on the plane to see it, and to have Kentucky Fried Chicken. Sonny usually did most of the talking, asking about various artists I had seen or booked, and what new records I liked.

I recall a spat between the two performers as I was driving them to the hotel; it was over a new house they were looking at in Beverly Hills. Their argument became so heated I worried they wouldn't appear together on stage. Most big-name acts of Sonny and Cher's caliber were chauffeured by limo. Although Sonny liked to schmooze with promoters, I'm pretty sure Cher would have preferred a private car.

• • •

AGL productions would eventually bring just about every big name recording star—minus the Beatles—to Virginia. Some of our most successful shows included The Beach Boys, The Who, James Brown, The Rolling Stones, Jimi Hendrix, Eric Clapton, David Bowie, Glen Campbell, The Jackson Five, Liza Minnelli, The 5th Dimension, Three Dog Night, The Bee Gees, The Osmonds, The Monkees, Diana Ross and the Supremes, Al Green, Chicago, The Four Seasons, Led Zeppelin, The Hollies, Donnie & Marie Osmond, The Turtles, and The Carpenters. We also brought in some of the stars that I had listened to on my bedroom record player, when I became hooked on rock n' roll, most notably Chuck Berry, Little Richard, and even Bill Haley and the Comets.

One of my favorite stars of that early to mid-1960's period was Gene Pitney who headlined at least three different years at Dome shows. Gene and I became friends. We spoke often and I would meet him for dinner when I went to New York. When his tours started he would book Virginia Beach first, bringing in all the stars a day early for rehearsal. Google Gene's hits, and you will be surprised at how many you know.

One of the things that became a regular event for Dick and me, and something the acts looked forward to as well, especially those who were back for a second or third time, was dinner after the concerts. We'd take them to the Isle of Capri and sit in the back room. The Arcese family would stay open just for us, and around midnight we would bring the stars for the kind of Italian cuisine they seldom got on the road or in hotels.

Here is Al Green, mega star at the time of his appearance at the Hampton Coliseum. What I recall is Al wanted to be paid the balance of his fee in cash, about $25,000. When I went back to the dressing room after the show with the money, he drew a gun, laid it on the table, and proceeded to count the stacks of mostly hundred dollar bills, which he then stuffed into his pockets.

ASHLEY FAMOUS AGENCY, INC.

April 29, 1968

Mr. Gene Loving
WGH Radio
P.O. Box 98
Newport News, Va.

Dear Gene:

Herewith enclosed are the contracts covering the
engagement of THE FOUR SEASONS at The Dome,
Virginia Beach, Va. on July 5, 1968.

Please sign all the contracts, initial all copies
of the attached rider and return to me, at your
earliest convenience, in the enclosed, self-addressed,
stamped envelope; together with check in the amount
of $3,750.00 which represents deposit.

Also enclosed are photographs and biographical
material.

Sincerely,

Ed Rubin
Concert Department

ER:mr
encl.

1301 Avenue of the Americas · New York, N.Y. 10019 · Tele.: (212) 956-5800 · California · London · Paris · Rome
· Cable: Ashfame New York ·

The Four Seasons at The Dome. When we brought them to Tidewater in the late '60s, I don't think that even Frankie Valli would have predicted the success of *Jersey Boys* on Broadway.

Dick "Sideburns" Lamb, Anne Murray, and Scott "If You're Going to San Francisco Wear Some Flowers in Your Hair" McKenzie with "Lean" Gene. The picture was taken at Chrysler Hall for Azalea Queen Susan Ford's Coronation Concert. Dick had helped rehabilitate Scott and this was his first live appearance in about ten years.

Engelbert Humperdinck with me prior to a Hampton Coliseum sold out show. It was Engelbert's birthday. We had cake and ice cream in the dressing room after his performance.

The Carpenters

Among my favorite entertainers who we brought to Virginia several times, Karen and Richard Carpenter. For a soft music act their in-person show never failed to fill in the big halls.

A very unusual singer, Tiny Tim, chats with me. I spent three days with Tiny driving around and sharing meals. At the time he was one of the best known entertainers on the planet.

ARTISTS' MANAGER-AGENCY
CABLE: CREMANASSO

CREATIVE MANAGEMENT ASSOCIATES

SIX HUNDRED MADISON AVENUE · NEW YORK, NEW YORK 10022 · (212) 935-4000

April 11, 1974

Mr Gene Loving
AGL Productions
252 W. Brambleton Avenue
Norfolk, Virginia 23510

Dear Gene:

Please be advised that the following is the correct billing for
the forthcoming DAVID BOWIE Tour:

MAINMAN PRESENTS	25%
DAVID BOWIE	100%
IN ASSOCIATION WITH	10%
(Promoter's name)	25%
PRODUCTION SUPERVISED BY	10%
JULES FISHER	20%

Regards

RICHARD J ROGER
:ljb
cc: N. Weiss

NEW YORK · LOS ANGELES · CHICAGO · LAS VEGAS · MIAMI · LONDON · PARIS · ROME

Typical requirements or instructions from agents after you booked one of their
entertainers. In all ads, or on the marquee, font size was specified.
"Mainman" was David Bowie's managment company.

station breaks

Vol. 4 - No. 1 May, 1970   **A BIMONTHLY PUBLICATION OF WGH RADIO**   Tidewater, Virginia

WGH, Tidewater's top entertainment station, helps make history in the new Hampton Roads Coliseum.

Jack Benny and Hampton Mayor Ann Kilgore at opening night festivities.

WGH published a quarterly newsletter, which was sent to all its advertisers.
This edition featured the grand opening of the Hampton Coliseum in 1970.

Bob Calvert joins me and Dick Lamb with The Beach Boys
(L-R:) Al, Mike, Carl, Dennis, and Glen.

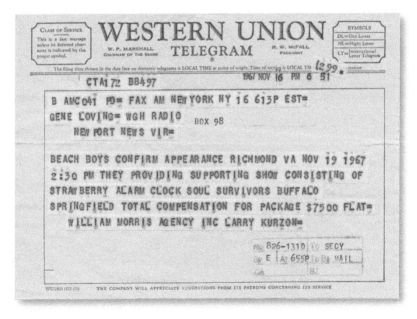

Typical way we did business in the 1960s—an exchange of telegrams.
This one is for the second time we promoted The Beach Boys in Richmond.

Glen Campbell, Mike Love, and Carl Wilson with Dennis Wilson in the background at the Dome, Virginia Beach 1965. The next day Dick Lamb and I drove The Beach Boys to Richmond for their concert at the Mosque.

• • •

Our interaction with the Beach Boys is especially memorable. We played many dates over the years at the Dome, Scope, outside at Virginia Beach Junior High stadium, the Hampton Coliseum, and in Richmond. After two sold-out shows at the Dome, and dinner at the Isle of Capri, the next day Dick and I picked up the Beach Boys and drove them to the Mosque in Richmond. The band rode in two cars. Mike Love, Dennis Wilson and Glen Campbell were in my car, while Carl Wilson and Al Jardine were with Dick.

On the drive, Mike got my tape recorder and interviewed Glen Campbell, who talked about releasing a record in the near future. He then sang and played some of *Universal Soldier* on the guitar with him in the back seat. We stopped at Stuckey's for a bathroom break and the Beach Boys were recognized by patrons, causing an unplanned delay while they signed autographs and posed for photos. Dennis bought some fireworks and set them off in the parking lot, which was quickly followed by Stuckey's manager asking us to leave.

Al Jardine's wife, Lynda, was with him on the tour. I stood with her in the wings while Al thrilled the crowd as lead singer on *Help me Rhonda*. Susan and I sat with the Jardines at dinner, in the backroom of the *Isle of Capri,* discussing our mutual interest in chess. I sent them a chess set. Her thank you letter is below.

Letter from Lynda Jardine thanking us.

• • •

Me and The Bee Gees

The Bee Gees was another band that remained loyal to us after they reached mega-stardom. Their shows sold out, sometimes within minutes, so they really didn't need a local promoter. Yet, they continued to work with us. Brothers Barry, Maurice and Robin Gibb were among the most personable and talented in the business. We brought them to Scope at the height of *Saturday Night Fever,* the mid-1970s movie that featured their songs. Ticket demand from our friends and clients was overwhelming.

• • •

The Kingsmen

In the '60s touring groups—even those with hits—pretty much took care of themselves on the road. There was no traveling entourage, equipment truck, or assistants to run errands. The guitar amps were checked luggage and hauled around in the trunks of cars. As local promoters, we took care of the logistics, making hotel reservations, arranging meals and transportation. And, we dealt with the band leader most of the time. The entertainers responded in kind and treated us well, hoping they would be invited back to perform again.

The Kingsmen from Oregon personified that collegial spirit. We were delighted when they reached the top of the musical charts with *Louie Louie*. The song became the most requested at record hops in the late '60s. We brought The Kingsmen to the Dome on at least three occasions. We did just one big show dance rather than a seated concert, taking out all the chairs, which increased audience. Below is the kind of personal letter that I would receive from acts following an appearance in those simpler days.

TELEPHONE 838-0200
TELETYPE 703 722-2993

Holiday Inn® OF HAMPTON-NEWPORT NEWS

INTERSECTION OF INTERSTATE 64 (TUNNEL ROAD) AND RT. 258 (MERCURY BLVD.)

HAMPTON, VIRGINIA

Dear Susan & Gene,

It is always fun for us to work with and for you people.

THANKS for ANOTHER GOOD DATE, WE HOPE you KNOW THE DOME IS ONE THAT WE LIKE to REPLAY.

Hope to see you BOTH again this year.

AGAIN THANK YOU.

(KEEP SMILES)
(ON THOSE FACES)

THE KINGSMEN

(P.S. Susan Keep up THE GOOD WORK, you LOOK GREAT)

Lynn Easton

Mike Mitchell

Dick PETERSON

YOUR HOST FROM COAST TO COAST

Letter from The Kingsmen following one of their sold-out dates at The Dome.

As rock 'n roll became big business, we started dealing with the well-known agents from big-time talent representation firms, like William Morris, was an education and a challenge. Some became friends. Many would accompany the entertainers to their date in Virginia Beach. One of those was Wally Amos, who was with William Morris for many years. Wally liked to fly down from New York City when his acts played the Dome, and we'd have a late-night dinner following each show. He created and marketed his own chocolate-chip cookies, becoming a worldwide celebrity in his own right, "Famous Amos." Wally also wrote several books and devoted a great deal of his time to literacy. He stayed with Angie and me whenever he came to town, which was often. Once Wally and his wife, Christine, baked chocolate chip cookies in our kitchen, allowing us to invite friends to enjoy his original recipe straight from the oven, still warm.

• • •

Some of our most successful Dome shows were Motown acts. The audience for those acts was 90 percent white. Bands like the Temptations, led by David Ruffin, had a string of big hits including all-time beach favorite *My Girl*. I remember standing outside the stage entrance of the Dome getting some fresh air between performances by The Four Tops. A big black Cadillac limo pulled up and out stepped David Ruffin. "I've come to see my boys," meaning The Four Tops. I went over, introduced myself, and mentioned that his group, The Temptations, would be playing the Dome in a couple of months. As I looked in the car I saw, sitting on the mink carpets, a white bulldog, which Ruffin led out on a silver chain. I asked David if he would come on stage with me to announce the Labor Day Temptations show, and he agreed. I introduced "Mr. David Ruffin" and his bulldog. The place went totally wild; fans were on their feet, screaming. It gave me flashbacks to the Beatlemania I had seen firsthand. When we announced the Temptations were coming for Labor Day weekend, the place erupted again.

With Smokey Robinson and the Miracles just before their Norfolk City Arena concert for AGL Productions. Starting with *Shop Around* in 1962, Smokey wrote, produced, and sang more hits for Motown than anyone.

Dick and me with Diana Ross and the Supremes, another of the acts we brought to town more than once. Over the years they played the Dome twice, outside at Virginia Beach Jr. High stadium, and Diana Ross alone at the Hampton Coliseum.

• • •

By then, the R&B sound had been ingrained in Tidewater Virginia, so it was no surprise to me that the acts were so well received here. Promoter Joe Murnick had a lot to do with that. He had been booking James Brown at the Norfolk City Arena for years. Black teens packed those shows and the girls screamed and swooned for James.

Joe and I became business friends, and once in a while I would have lunch at the Golden Key Club at the Golden Triangle, where Joe was a member. We did not see each other as competitors because his main promotion focus was staging professional wrestling events.

I had started booking dates for Chuck Berry, Otis Redding and many other great black performers at the Dome. By the mid-'60s I was also playing lots of James Brown on the radio. The "hardest working man in show business" scored well in our region—and nationally—with songs like *Poppa's Got a Brand New Bag* and *I Feel Good*. We decided that James could fill the Dome and it was time to book him. James had an upcoming concert in Norfolk via his agent Jack Bart and had agreed to come over to WAVY to tape a song and promote the Dome event on our *Disc-O-Ten* show. At this point in his career, James wanted to expand his audience and was anxious to build white fan support.

I had not met James Brown before that night. I went to the Norfolk arena with my tape recorder and watched his show from the wings. Afterward he went to his dressing room soaking wet from working the audience and dancing his special steps. His road manager told me James wanted to take a shower and dress before I went in. James' band stayed on stage behind the curtain, which I thought was very unusual. After about a half hour of waiting, I started getting antsy: it was getting late and we had to get to WAVY before they closed the station for the night.

Finally James came out from the dressing room, but he went straight to the stage where he asked all the band members to take a seat. He then started critiquing the night's performance. He really humiliated some of his players and then had them replay one of the songs. I found out later this was a nightly ritual with James: he was a perfectionist. I also discovered that everyone in his band addressed him as "Mr. Brown."

Since I was the only white person waiting around, James must have known I was his local contact for the Dome promos and TV show. "Mr. Loving, let's go," he said. I was impressed that he knew my name. When we got into the dressing room, James introduced me to a woman from one of the big-name black magazines. I also got a look at his wardrobe where there were racks and racks of clothes, and hundreds of shoes stacked against the wall. His selection depended on his mood. The dressing table reminded me of a hair salon, complete with a giant hair dryer, ironing board, and furniture that I knew was not normally there.

I got out the script for him to read, expecting the whole thing to take about five minutes, after which we would be off to WAVY. James continued an interview with the magazine writer, and when her article was printed, it mentioned the white DJ in the room and what had occurred.

James ignored my script and grilled me about the Dome and how his records were doing on our station chart. Apparently his music was not as popular in some parts of the country as others, and he wasn't always getting heavy airplay. Some stations had refused to play *Poppa's Got a Brand New Bag* due to the innuendo of the lyrics. I assured James that if we didn't believe the Dome shows would sell out, we would not have booked the date: we knew that no artist wants to play to half a house, even if they are paid their full fee.

Next, James started asking racially slanted questions like, if the white kids like him why didn't they come to the show that night at the Norfolk City Arena?

I told him the probable reason was that Norfolk City Arena had catered to the black audience for years and was located in the center of the area's largest black population. In the 1960's Norfolk still had mostly segregated neighborhoods. Redevelopment in downtown Norfolk and some of the now-trendy surrounding neighborhoods like Ghent was decades away.

James started to get testy, raising his voice, and I was thinking that I needed to leave, worried that James wasn't going to record the promos or do *Disc-O-Ten*. But finally he stopped grilling me and picked up my script. He read the pitch for the show, and tweaked it to fit better with his style and personality. By now it was well after midnight, so I wanted to get to a phone to see if the WAVY crew had stayed, having heard nothing from me. I told him he looked great just like he was dressed. He asked me to give him a minute and he would be right out, so the reporter and I left the dressing room. I made a call to let WAVY know we were still coming. Then James emerged, now in a skin-tight orange jumpsuit. He got into one of his own cars and he and his driver followed me through the tunnel to WAVY in Portsmouth. We did the segment, and I asked him a couple of questions on camera. He was very friendly, and never told me to call him Mr. Brown; we were on a first-name basis.

When he came for the Dome show, the dressing room was set up just like in Norfolk, and when I arrived about two hours before show time, he was getting his hair done, and asked me to take a seat. James was warm and welcoming as we casually chatted. We promoted James a couple more times after that, including an outdoor show in the Dome parking lot with bleachers to increase the number of seats.

Years later in New York, I saw a car pull up to a club and someone said James Brown was coming. I waited in the crowd to see him get out. He spotted me and came over saying, "Gene, my man. So good to see you." James Brown was a great showman.

• • •

One of the challenges at the Dome and other venues in those days was the technical system. Back then, few bands hauled around sound equipment—not even amplifiers for their instruments. As concert promoters, we had to either use what was available at the venue, or we had to supply something else. There were no concert sound and lights rental companies in those days, at least not locally. Dick and I would learn it was getting very expensive to find equipment specified by the artist. When acts became bigger they became pickier. They started to list in the contracts their specifications for sound and lighting. Companies providing that equipment started springing up in larger cities, but not in Tidewater. We'd get a list of what a band wanted and then have to see what it would cost to rent the equipment for a night, and if it had to be trucked in from out of town.

A lot of the performers we booked were up-and-comers and, as such, didn't have a lot of hit songs or original material. These performers would sing two or three numbers with a house band and then run offstage and the next act would perform. Usually, one house band remained on stage the whole time. Bigger stars like Gene Pitney or Bobby Vee would close a show. The local back-up bands we hired had to learn a bevy of songs by listening to the records and, ideally, they'd have rehearsals before live shows. On occasion groups doing long tours of thirty nights or more would bring their own band. Sometimes those backup musicians went on to stardom themselves. I remember the band that backed up a Gene Pitney concert was Bobby Vinton's group. Bobby became a major singing star with hits like *Blue on Blue,* and *Blue Velvet*, written by Bernie Wayne, who had treated me so well during my days at WLEE.

As the concert business exploded, production equipment became easier to find. And it was more powerful and sophisticated, enabling concerts to expand to fairgrounds and stadiums. The biggest acts cashed in, carrying all of the lights and sound equipment they would need, plus their instruments, and charged it to the promoter. They rented or owned eighteen-wheel semis to transport the stuff, and employed technicians to set up and run the equipment. Today, most touring bands have about ten of these giant trucks. You can see them parked out back of the venues where they play. They haul in everything, including special effects and stage sets, and giant TV screens. The performers, of course, travel by private jet, with an entourage of support people and a string of limos and SUV's or luxury coaches for their ground transport.

One of the reasons we eventually got out of the concert business was because the fun stopped. There was no more picking up the act yourself, or going to dinner, or hanging out with them backstage. The entertainers started to live in a bubble with security costing more than we spent on the entire show. Business managers controlled everything to justify their jobs.

• • •

Dick and I had some disagreements with entertainers along the way, but when we started out promoting shows we dealt with problems one on one—not through a wall of managers. A couple of our more famous incidents involved Mick Jagger and Jimi Hendrix. Dick had to break up a fistfight once between Tom Jones and Gordon Waller, of Peter & Gordon. And during one settlement in the box office for Joe Cocker, Dick and Cocker's manager and a representative from the IRS scuffled for the check. There is a story connected with almost every one of the shows we did, some more dramatic and unforgettable than others. I could do a whole chapter on our issues with Chuck Berry.

Back when we first started promoting Chuck locally there were no jet bridges or security going out to the aircraft. Steps were pushed up to the airplane on a runway. As we typically did back then, we stood at the bottom of the steps to greet the artist and help collect their luggage. A flight attendant asked Bill Walker (a salesman and promotion manager at WGH, who we had sent to pick up Chuck), to come aboard. Chuck said he would not get off the plane until we paid him in cash, and up front, his $500 fee for the coming night's performance. Bill did not have $500, so he went to the terminal and found someone at the airline who loaned him the money until the next day. I don't recall if Bill had to leave his watch as security.

Typical IRS letter instructing us to withhold funds from certain foreign entertainers.

• • •

The Rolling Stones' first tour of the US included a date at the
Dome in Virginia Beach, which I booked after their agent kept
sending me telegrams and letters pushing their popularity. It
didn't take much push at all: after the Stones mega-hit (*I Can't
Get No) Satisfaction*, but we had to negotiate a deal that worked
for our very small venue.

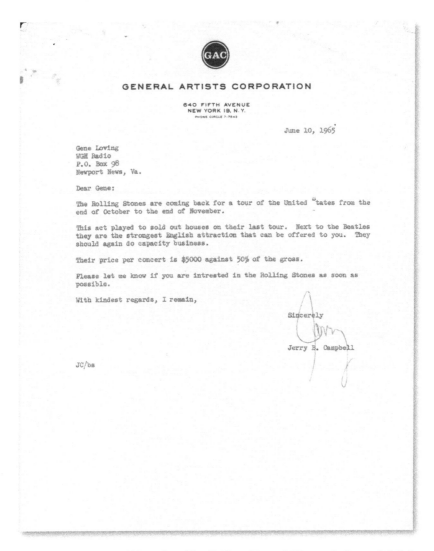

**Note the date, June 1965, when The Rolling Stones' US agent, General Artist
Corporation (GAC), started pitching me on booking the band for a date in Virginia
the following summer. We did promote them at the Dome once I believed (*I Can't
Get No) Satisfaction* had become the breakthrough hit they needed.**

GENERAL ARTISTS CORPORATION

640 FIFTH AVENUE
NEW YORK 19, N. Y.
PHONE CIRCLE 7-7843

August 11, 1965

Gene Loving
WGH Radio
P.O. Box 98
Newport News, Va.

Dear Gene:

Thank you for your letter of August 6th. Get back as soon as possible
to me on the Rolling Stones. Please let me know what date you can use
them on.

Hope to hear from you shortly.

With kindest regards, I remain,

Sincerely,

Jerry B. Campbell

JC/bs

A follow-up letter from the Stones' agent after I let him
know we may book a date during their next tour.

A *Virginian-Pilot* photographer snapped this picture as The Rolling Stones got off their chartered plane in July 1966. I was there to greet them and be sure the limos we hired were set to take the Stones to the Dome. Below you can see me pushing back the curtain on the far side of the stage at the Dome, as the police ring the stage for the first show. Mick Jagger was not a happy guy as I found out between performances.

They said the Stones would not play two shows back-to-back. It took some persuading, but they finally agreed to play two. Even with four thousand available seats to sell, the Stones were expensive. The ticket charges would have to be so high I was afraid the prices would prevent a sellout.

Today, those who control venues like Live Nation, also make money through concession and merchandise sales. Dick and I didn't control any of that at the Dome. We merely rented the building from the city. They sold the drinks. So we had to make our money on ticket sales. At the time we booked the Stones, our top price for down-front seating may have been $7 for The Beach Boys but usually averaging $5. For the Stones we would have to charge $10 for almost every ticket, and we'd have to sell all two thousand seats at both shows. We decided to take the risk. Every ticket was sold within about two days.

We always hired a few local police officers to provide security for our shows. Mostly, they helped with parking and handled any rare rowdy behavior. About four days before the Rolling Stones were to play our date they appeared in Boston and a small riot took place at the show. Kids were throwing chairs and fighting. It made all the papers and TV news. I got a call from the Dome manager who said that the city was thinking of telling us to cancel the date in Virginia Beach. After recovering from the shock of hearing that, I drove out to City Hall to meet with the Dome people, and the city manager and the chief of police. It was agreed that if we hired fifty officers to keep the peace the show could go on.

The Rolling Stones had chartered a plane for the tour. When it arrived and parked at the far end of a seldom-used runway I was there to say hello and talk about the show. I did not mention the Boston riot or that we had extra security. For the Stones we had a limo, and at some point, after hanging around at the airport for a while out in a field near the private terminal, the band followed me to the Beach. By the time we got there the audience for the 7 p.m show was getting seated, and we went backstage. The only special request I recall from the Stones was a TV in their dressing room.

It was showtime. The band went onstage behind the curtain and Dick Lamb introduced them as I helped pull back the curtain to give the side seats a view. As Dick was talking, Virginia Beach police officers ringed the front of the stage and stood guard the entire performance. They had not told us about this plan in advance. Their presence put a chill on the crowd, which gave only polite applause after each song—not what the Stones were accustomed to. At the end of the show, after the curtain closed, Mick Jagger roared every expletive imaginable. He demanded to see me *"Now!"* I heard his rant from the other side of the stage and grabbed Dick. I didn't want to go to their dressing room alone. Jagger was angry and I thought he might get physical.

When we went in, Mick started telling us that in their entire career all over the world the Stones had never had police intimidate an audience like that. If the cops weren't removed they were not going to do the second show.

I explained that we didn't know they were going to ring the stage. We had only expected them to just stand to the sides to be available in case some incident started like the riot at their performance in Boston. All the members of the Stones were standing right there listening to the exchange. Keith Richards said, "No show" unless you get them to become invisible. I left to find the Dome manager and police liaison. I believe they understood that if the Stones walked, the uproar would be worse than if we pulled back the officers to the wings. I went back to tell Mick it had been worked out. The second show's improved atmosphere did make a difference in the interaction between the band and audience. We later produced a Rolling Stones concert at Scope about 10 years later. If Mick Jagger recalled the Dome issues, he never mentioned it.

We would have one more encounter with Mick when the band was doing what was supposed to be its final tour in 1982. It was a two-day event at the Hampton Coliseum, to be broadcast worldwide on HBO. By then, AGL Productions had invested in Whisper Concerts and Bill Douthat handled most of the details. There are lots of scenes from that show that wound up in a documentary film about the Rolling Stones. And there were lots of scenes that didn't get into the film, too, like the goats in the band's bathroom. The Stones insisted on us providing the animals as part of their backstage perks.

Mick, Keith and the boys stayed in Colonial Williamsburg at the 1776, and Mick got lost on an exercise run. He had to knock on the door of a private residence to find out how to get back to the hotel, so they offered to drive him. I found out about it when

Mick asked me to provide his rescuers with tickets to the show. The Hampton shows were great, and they would not be the Stones' last. Mick and Keith Richards, now in their seventies, are still performing—and in my view they're still the best continuing rock band.

• • •

Another big score for Dick and me was promoting Jimi Hendrix—twice at the Dome and once at the Mosque in Richmond. The first Dome show was April 4, 1968, the day Martin Luther King Jr. was assassinated. When I picked up Jimi at the airport there was no news about Dr. King as it had yet to happen. I took him to the Holiday Inn on Military Highway, saying I would pick him up at 5:30 p.m. for the 7 p.m. show. I was driving a white Cadillac convertible with a little bit of history of its own. The British rock band, The Who, which had been doing a concert at the Dome earlier that year, all piled into that Caddy to hear their hit *Magic Bus* for the first time on the radio.

I heard the news about Dr. King while driving to the Dome with Jimi, who sat in the front seat. But I turned down the volume on the radio as I flashed back to when President Kennedy was assassinated and how the radio station cancelled programs and sent everyone home. Then I looked to see Jimi's reaction. He said nothing—*nothing*. In fact we didn't talk about it at all during the ride. We got to the Dome and Jimi went to his dressing room. Not long afterwards a messenger said Jimi wanted to see me right away. Jimi was there with his band members. His first words were, "We're not playing the show . . . unless you fix the marquee right now to comply with the contract." The marquee was supposed to read *The Jimi Hendrix Experience*—not just Jimi Hendrix. His other two band members were known as The Experience. Totally relieved that he wasn't canceling the performance due to Dr. King's death, I immediately found the Dome manager and tried to have the marquee corrected. Hendrix and The Experience seemed to be in a good mood after we explained that the marquee had the band's name on one side but ran out of letters for the second side. The band went onto the stage to prepare for our introduction, and just before I went out to introduce them, Jimi asked me to tie a scarf on his arm. Somebody shot a picture of me doing that, and they sent me a print.

Jimi Hendrix with his two bandmates,
Noel Redding and Mitch Mitchell, who were "The Experience."

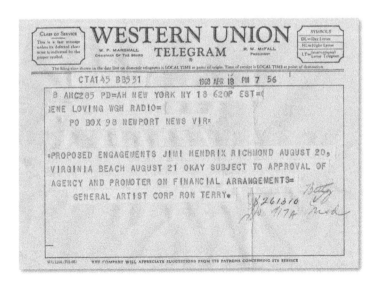

• • •

We promoted two Jackson Five concerts in the mid-70s, one at Scope and one at the Hampton Coliseum the following year.

Michael Jackson was very much the star of the group, the lead singer on all the hits. For the Scope show we booked one floor of the Golden Triangle Hotel next to Scope for security, to give the Jacksons plenty of room to roam. Michael's father, Joe, was the road manager; his mother Katherine handled the settlement in the box office after the show. Janet Jackson was about ten years old at the time and mostly sat in her room watching TV. I spent a few hours with the group at the hotel talking about music and Norfolk. They never had been to our area prior to that day. All the guys kept their doors to the hotel hall propped open so they could exchange visits with each other.

I remember Michael sitting on the floor at the end of a long hall at the Golden Triangle rolling a volleyball back and forth to his brother Marlon.

Hampton Roads Coliseum

P.O. BOX 7309   1000 COLISEUM DRIVE HAMPTON, VIRGINIA 23366

SIDNEY F. MORSE
DIRECTOR

January 20, 1972

Mr. Gene Loving
A. G. L. PRODUCTIONS
c/o WNOR
252 West Brambleton Ave.
Norfolk, Virginia 23510

Dear Gene:

Enclosed is a photo of the latest Jackson 5
marquee to add to your ever growing collection
of "Sold Out" pictures.

Sincerely yours,

Sid Morse
Director

SM/an

Enclosure

CHAPTER 11

DEAL ME IN

Among the local performers I had grown closest to was Bill Deal. He and the Rhondels became a major part of what was known as "Beach Music." As mentioned, they were the house band for a couple of clubs in Virginia Beach, but they also did dates along much of the East Coast all the way from Maryland to Florida. They were well known in Myrtle Beach, South Carolina and Ocean City Maryland. Bill Deal and band co-founder and drummer, Ammon Tharp, loved to play music. In the winter months, when many beach communities closed, the band played lots of college frat parties and in community centers where Richard Levin, Tommy Herman and I promoted them during the off-season.

The Rhondels and other "show bands" were developing their own sound by rearranging popular R&B songs into the more up-tempo "shag dance" beat. These songs and sounds quickly became college favorites, although never radio hits. By the 1980s the East Coast beach sound was its own musical genre. We used Bill's band often to back up Chuck Berry and other performers who traveled alone.

Bill had asked me a couple of times to help him manage bookings with some of the local clubs. Virginia Beach clubs were always competing for popular local bands, and deciding where to play—or not to play—could get political for the musicians. For instance, the Rhondels were the house band at the Peppermint Beach Club before it changed ownership. The owner of the Top Hat had been after Bill for a couple of years to move to his club. As it turned out, WGH had built what we called a "Sky Studio" on the roof of the Top Hat, and it overlooked the Virginia Beach boardwalk and beach. I did my radio show from that studio at least a couple of days a week in the summer. I had gotten to know Top Hat owner, Johnny Vakos, and he loved the promotion on WGH for his club. Bill was happy to move to the Top Hat for summer performances, but he was squeamish about telling the new owners of the Peppermint. So, Bill asked me to be the messenger, and it was as unpleasant as Bill rightly anticipated it would be.

About 1966, I had helped Bill and his band with their first "local" album: I got them access to a recording studio owned by musician Link Wray in Washington, DC. That session produced twelve cuts, and the album sold pretty well at their appearances.

One day I was broadcasting, in the WGH Showmobile, from Norfolk's Southern Shopping Center when Bill came by with a record he had just gotten from the pressing plant, a tune called *May I*. He and the band had decided to record the song in its now-signature Beach Music style because it was constantly requested when the band played clubs. The band pressed about five hundred copies. I liked the song and told Bill I would play it on WGH and that he should put copies out at every area record shop. He did, and within a week they were all sold. The band then ordered one thousand copies, and they all sold. I thought *May I* had national potential.

• • •

Several Tidewater area singers had become nationally recognized. Keely Smith, a Native American from Norfolk, became a major Vegas club star, especially after teaming with her husband, Louis Prima. Gene Vincent & His Blue Caps from Portsmouth made it big with *Bee-Bop A Lula*. And a record producer from Norfolk, Frank Guida, found a few local artists that he recorded on his Legrand Records label—Gary U.S. Bonds among them.

I was friends with one of the record promotion guys, Hal Charm, who for years had worked out of Baltimore on behalf of Mercury Records. Hal had just joined Jerry Ross, owner of Heritage Records, which was distributed by MGM. I sent *May I* to Hal and he played it for Jerry. Hal called to say they wanted to sign Bill Deal and the Rhondels and release *May I*. "Please come to NYC now," he pleaded. The next day Bill, wearing a white suit, flew with me to New York. Bill got a few looks from the passengers on the National jet: they probably thought he was a Southern Baptist preacher. By the end of the afternoon Bill had a record contract and *May I* went on to make the national charts, and even reached No. 1 in some Southern markets.

Bill asked me to start managing the band. The Rhondels were getting offers for dates all over the country, including a week at Disncyland. And Jerry Ross was already calling wanting their next release. Bill started immediately working on it. Not long afterward, I got a call from Bill at 4 a.m. They'd made a recording at Studio Center in Norfolk, and he wanted to play it for me and get my input before they wrapped it up. I listened to the song, *I've Been Hurt,* over the phone. "Bill, it's a hit, don't touch anything" I said, and it was.

I met Bill at the post office in Norfolk a few hours later and we overnighted *I've Been Hurt* to Heritage Records. It shot up in the charts and quickly became another Rhondels hit. A few months later, Bill brought me *What Kind of Fool Do You Think I Am?* It was 1969 and the band was about to have its third national hit. Jerry Ross called to say he wanted to put the band in the studio in New York to make an album. We all went up, spending a couple of days with Jerry, along with professional arrangers, string sections, and other musicians who would come and go to supplement the Rhondels. The song *Nothing Succeeds Like Success* came out of that session. Soon, the Rhondels' name and hits went international due to MGM's worldwide distribution. I was in Germany that year and the album was right there in the record shops. The band also became a favorite in Japan and South America. I was fielding calls from agents seemingly everywhere who wanted dates on Bill and the band. The Rhondels worked all the time, but they wanted to be back home for the summer to play Virginia Beach and be with their families or local girlfriends.

Publicity picture for Bill Deal and The Rhondels during the height of their late
'60s hit record success. Bill is in the center, second up from the bottom,
with Ammon Tharp on his left.

Gene Lowry AGREEMENT v000264

THIS AGREEMENT made this ____ day of November 1969 _____, between WALT DISNEY
PRODUCTIONS, DISNEYLAND DIVISION, a corporation with principal offices at 1313 Harbor Boulevard, Anaheim,

California (hereinafter referred to as "Disneyland"), and BILL DEAL AND THE RHONDELS, c/o

ACTION TALENTS, INC., 300 West 55th Street, Suite 4V, New York City,

New York _____ (hereinafter referred to as "Producer").

It is mutually agreed between the parties as follows:

1. The Producer agrees to furnish, and Disneyland does hereby purchase, for the engagement hereinafter provided,

a complete musical organization consisting of ____ Eight (8) musicians, including leader

_____, which organization shall be hereinafter referred to as "said unit",
upon all of the terms and provisions hereinafter set forth.

2. PLACE OF EMPLOYMENT: Disneyland, Anaheim, California

3. DATES OF EMPLOYMENT: November 27, 28 & 29, 1969

4. HOURS OF EMPLOYMENT: 9:00 pm & 11:00 PM
   Two 45-minute shows nightly

5. PRICE AGREED UPON: $5,000.00 TOTAL

6. The Producer agrees to plan, assemble and furnish said unit as constituted and shall supply and furnish all the
necessary personnel as well as supply all musical arrangements and scripts, if any, subject to the terms and conditions
herein provided. Subject to the terms hereof, the Producer shall have and exercise exclusive authoritative control over said
unit, the details, methods and persons to be employed by it in performing the provisions of this agreement on its part to be
performed. The Producer shall perform and discharge all obligations imposed upon it as employer under the rules of the
American Federation of Musicians of the United States and Canada (herein called "AFM"), Workmen's Compensation,
Unemployment Compensation or Insurance, Federal Insurance Contributions, withholding taxes, and other federal and state
laws and regulations. It shall further file all returns and reports and make all withholdings required by it as an employer
under the provisions of the foregoing, and it shall pay all assessments, taxes, contributions or other sums imposed thereunder
upon or with respect to the salaries or wages paid by the Producer to the persons whose services it engages or furnishes
for this show.

7. Should Disneyland be materially hampered, interrupted or interfered with in the normal conduct of its business
of operating Disney land Park by reason of epidemic, fire, action in the elements, strikes, walkout, labor dispute, governmental order, court order, or order of any other legally constituted authority, act of God or public enemy, war, riot, civil
commotion, or any other cause or causes beyond Disneyland's control, whether of the same or of any other nature, or by
lockout, it is understood and agreed that Disneyland shall be relieved of its obligations hereunder with respect to any performances scheduled for presentation during the period or periods of such hampering, interruption or interference, and the
Producer shall have no claim of any kind or nature against Disneyland relating to such obligations.

8. This agreement shall be interpreted under the laws of the State of California, and this agreement is the entire
agreement between the parties and cannot be changed orally.

9. Disneyland agrees, at its own cost and expense, to furnish a functioning public address system and to assume all
operating costs thereof.

10. SPECIAL PROVISIONS.

See Attached Rider.

WALT DISNEY PRODUCTIONS, Disneyland Division

By _____
                                    Disneyland

Bill Deal _____
                                    Producer

D/254   /ar

**One of the engagements for Bill Deal and The Rhondels during the period I
managed the band. This contract was for Disneyland.**

Coinciding with the "travel less" attitude of the band, I reached an agreement with Jerry Ross and Heritage Records for an annual budget so the Rhondels could record in Virginia, rather than commuting to New York City to spend days in a recording studio. Nick Colleran had approached me about investing in Virginia's first fully equipped multiple track recording studio, so local bands didn't have to go out of state to make a record. Bill Deal, Dick Lamb, Richard Davis, me and a couple of others partnered with Nick to build Alpha Audio in Richmond, which became Virginia's premier venue for music and commercial work for the next twenty years. (Google it)

You never know how your life's straight line will lead to things wonderful—but unforeseen. My work with Bill Deal and the Rhondels would lead to me *owning* radio stations, rather than just working for them. But that journey is not always easy— or pleasant.

Ted Torrock had played football at the University of Virginia, and moved to Virginia Beach after he was cut from the NFL Baltimore Colts. Ted then signed up to play for the Norfolk Neptunes, a team in the upstart Continental Football League. Ted didn't make much money playing for the CFL, but somehow he had managed to develop a club in Virginia Beach called Rogues Gallery. He rented an old Chevy dealership on 17th Street and planned to open in the summer of 1968. There had been some publicity in the paper that I got the record deal for the Rhondels, so Ted called me to book them as his house band at Rogues. That would mean the band would not be available to the other local clubs, and now the Rhondels had hit records. So, if Ted wanted them, he'd have to pay considerably more than the band had been getting, which he agreed to do. Ted's plan worked. His club was packed every night the band performed, and I was hired to emcee a couple of times a week, which meant promoting the band, the club and WGH.

• • •

As the summer of 1968 drew to a close, the Rhondels decided they just could not face another nine months of traveling all over the US to play dates. Instead, Bill asked that I talk to Ted about

thc Rhondels playing every other Friday and Saturday night at
Rogues. The hope was that locals would keep the club open during
the winter. On weekends when the Rhondels weren't performing
other bands managed by my friend Richard Levin would perform.
Meanwhile, the Rhondels would use those off weekends to play
at college campuses in Virginia. Staying at Rogues more of the
time would also eliminate the costs of booking agents and travel.

By mid-November it was cold inside Rogues and the crowds
complained. The club didn't have heat—just air conditioning. Ted
never pointed this out when we discussed the winter schedule,
but now said he couldn't afford to add a heating system. I found
that hard to believe, given the amount of beer the club sold and
the large crowds since it opened. Back in the 1960s only beer
could be sold in clubs—no liquor or wine.

One night in early December Bill called me in a panic. He said
the band had gone to Rogues to play and the doors were padlocked
with some kind of notice posted by the City of Virginia Beach.
It turns out that Ted had failed to pay taxes on admissions and
withholding taxes on his payroll. I had been scheduled to emcee
that night, so I arrived and read the notice in detail and then
called our lawyer to investigate. He found out that Ted Torrok
didn't in fact own Rogues Gallery; the real owner was Richard J.
Davis, a mortgage banker and Portsmouth lawyer. I called Mr.
Davis, explained who I was, and asked about the contract for the
Rhondels. He informed me brusquely that Rogues was closed for
good, and suggested I get in line with the rest of the creditors,
and he hung up.

This was bad. The Rhondels were on salary so Bill Deal and his
band partner, Ammon, had payroll to meet. Plus, they had turned
down opportunities with other clubs so they could play Rogues.
Bill was calling me every thirty minutes expecting his "manager"
to solve this problem. Bill was always a first-class gentleman who
did not curse, raise his voice or drink much beyond a beer. He
remained very professional, but very concerned. Bill had just
bought a dream house for his wife and two children on swanky
Rundee Inlet in Virginia Beach. And he had just bought a Jaguar
XKE from me, so he was not flush with cash.

Here I am putting up the top on the Jaguar XKE in the driveway of the rural Poquoson house. Shortly after this, Bill Deal bought the car.

It didn't take long for my lawyer and me to figure out how and why Ted Torrock was running a club owned by a Portsmouth lawyer. Richard J. Davis was president of Tidewater Professional Sports, which owned Norfolk's AAA professional baseball team, the Tidewater Tides, and had started the Neptune Football team. Apparently, Ted had come to Mr. Davis with his dream of being in the nightclub business, so Davis had backed him and put up the money. (Torrock told a Norfolk newspaper years later that he invested $500 and was part owner.) Davis' wife, Martha, had been going to the club and seeing the crowds and beer sales. It was a shock to both Mr. and Mrs. Davis that Ted hadn't paid his monthly taxes, and Davis closed the club to stop a further cash drain.

Dick Davis was a man of impeccable integrity and perhaps the most distinguished-looking person I had ever met. I don't believe that he had ever listened to WGH, nor had he ever been to Rogues. He had no idea who I was and had never heard of the Rhondels. I explained my background in concerts and promotion, and told him that Bill Deal had hit records and could bring in a crowd whenever the club was open. Dick Davis said the only reason he got involved in the club was to eventually buy the building and land that Rogues now occupied, on the site of a former Chevy dealership.

Looking for a solution, I pitched Dick Davis on Bill Deal and me reopening the club, offering to put in any money necessary to keep it going, and letting Dick's accountant file and pay all taxes while we were involved. Bill and I would own 25 percent of Rogues Gallery each, and Dick Davis would own half. We would run the club, book the acts and promote them. Dick agreed.

• • •

Bill and I completely remodeled what was still basically a cinderblock car shop, adding heat and much improved lighting. Bill found a responsible individual to manage the club, and put his sister-in-law in charge of the door, collecting the cash. The Rhondels started performing there again, fresh with new hits, and attendance was great. Rogues became a big success and the partners were doing well after paying *all* the costs, including taxes. We started booking other name entertainment that were looking for smaller venues to play, including Tommy James & The Shondells, Fats Domino, and The Four Seasons. We went on to develop Mary's Country Kitchen in the front car showroom which was still vacant. Bill Deal and I continued as friends after our business partnership ended in 1977. One morning, Bill went in to take a shower and never came out. I was one of four asked to deliver a eulogy at his funeral. In the spring of 2015, I was walking down Lexington Avenue in New York City and *May I* was playing on a radio at one of Manhattan's many newsstands. The song triggered a lot of memories.

• • •

At the time we took over at Rogues, only beer could be sold in clubs in Virginia. When the state legislature approved selling liquor and wine by the glass, we were the first club in the state to get a license to do so. The next morning Nabil Kassir and

Ed Ruffin, who owned several clubs at the Beach, offered to buy Rogues.

I had known Nabil and Ed since the early 60's when the former lifeguards started into the bar and club business in Virginia Beach. They owned Cheecho's on Atlantic Avenue and Peabody's Warehouse, which, like Rogues, aimed at a younger beer-drinking crowd. On occasion they hired me to emcee an event at Peabody's. At one point they sued the City of Virginia Beach and AGL Productions for using a taxpayer facility, the Dome, to compete against privately owned business, but the suit was thrown out of court. Despite that scrap, I remained friendly with Nabil and Ed, who would buy Rogues from us in 1977. Owning that business—running one—was invigorating and richly rewarding. My eyes grew wider from that experience and as they did, new opportunities crossed before them. In fact, Nabil Kassir and his wife, Debbi, are among our closest friends. A restaurant, Debbi founded, Aldo's, has been a locals' favorite for years.

•   •   •

In 1969, Ambert Dail, the WGH general manager, decided to shuffle the deck at the radio station. He asked if I would give up the music director position to become a WGH department head. I would get a company car, a new title "Promotion Manager", and have an office and secretary. I would still do the 3-to-7 p.m. show, but this was seen as a "promotion." I wasn't wild about giving up the music director job, but this new position meant more money, and it would give me a chance to work with all of the WGH salespeople and management, arranging all of the sales and on-air promotions, and placing all of the station's outside advertising. I accepted, and ended up working more hours because now I really did need to be in the office by 9 a.m.

Among those I had come to know well and admire during my rise at WGH were Hampton Mayor Ann Kilgore and the City Manager Ed Johnson. Ann's husband worked at NASA, and we would often be invited over for Sunday brunch or meet them for dinner. Ann was leading the effort to build a long-needed arena of about ten thousand seats. There was nothing close to that scale in Hampton or neighboring Newport News or Williamsburg to accommodate any kind of large sports event, concert or convention. Ann worked with the Newport News mayor and city council to share the expenses and select a mutually agreeable location, but in the end Newport News backed out. When Hampton decided to go it alone, Ann and Ed asked me to help as an unpaid consultant, since AGL productions was doing 90 percent of the concerts in the Hampton Roads market. Hampton was the first municipality to build a major facility of this type in Virginia, and it was going to cost $6 million. AGL was given the honor of producing the first show and grand opening event.

Another player I befriended was attorney Charles Gordon, known as Flash. He and his wife, Billie, liked going to concerts. They had a stable of race horses based at Pimlico Race Course in Baltimore, home of the Preakness. Plus, he had horses grazing in pastures in Hampton. Flash had the only privately owned limousine in the Hampton-Newport News-Williamsburg region. Once in a while we were invited to go with the Gordons to Baltimore to see one of his horses race.

Charles Gordon owned a local motel and several apartment buildings. But he mostly practiced law every day, alone, in his own office building in downtown Hampton near the courthouse. If you had a traffic problem in Hampton, "Flash" was your guy. His longtime secretary, who was his ace assistant and paralegal all rolled into one, Miss Baker, guarded the door and kept order in the always-filled waiting room. And if I came in, no matter what was going on, I was escorted into a conference room where Flash would soon appear. It was a real experience to go to lunch with him as he always had the best table and would always draw a crowd, greeted by other lawyers and even judges.

Flash wanted to invest in AGL's concerts. At some point after the Hampton Coliseum opened, and all the cost and risk went up, Dick and I invited him into a few shows that did well for all of us. To all of our deep dismay, Flash dropped dead one day at his desk. I was honored to be a pallbearer at the funeral, along with Virginia Lieutenant Governor Henry Howell.

Liza Minnelli and Charles "Flash" Gordon with me, just before
Liza's sellout performance at the Hampton Coliseum.
Note the corduroy suit and long hair, my '70s look.

• • •

As I mentioned earlier, WGH was owned by the Newport
News *Daily Press.* As WGH promotion manager, I now interacted
much more with other executives and key corporate types
within the company, and was occasionally invited to national
conventions, as WGH was a member of the BPA (Broadcast
Promotion Association).

Ray Bottom, who then was in his late thirties and a member
of the family that owned 50 percent of the *Daily Press*, remained

in an office at WGH rather than the newspaper. The Bottom family was very influential, and one of Ray's best friends was state Senator Hunter Andrews from Hampton.

Ray began regularly inviting me and the WGH sales manager, Howard Jernigan, to social gatherings. Ray was not married, was very active in the Air Force reserve, and focused his time at the WGH offices on the FM station, which played classical music. His hobby was flying his own airplane. His Austin Healy with plastic windows and a top that was tough to raise was a car he brought from Europe where he was stationed while on active duty. I thought, *Here is a guy who can buy anything he wants, and he is wrestling with this old automobile.* One year, I went on vacation for two weeks and Ray asked me if he could take care of and drive my Corvette, and I agreed. I figured maybe he was trying out the Corvette and was going to buy one, and when I returned from my trip I was told Ray had bought a new car. But when I looked in his designated parking spot, expecting to see a new Vette, I saw he had replaced his Austin with a VW bug, one of the first in the US.

Often Ray rented a cottage on the ocean in Virginia Beach, and he invited me and Howard Jernigan to visit many times. It was my first exposure to really high-end first-class party time, hanging out with one of the WGH owners, a state senator, their buddies, with a bartender in the house, and catered food. I was beginning to understand that there was a big difference between my place on the beach in Poquoson and the north end of Virginia Beach. I had a new goal, and it wasn't to own a VW.

• • •

The City of Hampton scheduled a college basketball game at its new Coliseum as sort of a test run for the first event, not really promoting it too energetically, but giving the parking people a chance to see how traffic flowed, and making sure the tickets matched the seats. We were surprised by the resulting full house. It showed the potential for this big new venue.

AGL Productions was asked to do an opening concert and then find something special for the official Grand Opening the same week. We selected a band that had never appeared in Tidewater, The Association, known for its hit single, *Cherish*. The show did not sell out, but the eight thousand in attendance was twice the audience of two packed Dome shows in Virginia Beach. The Coliseum was now the biggest stage in eastern Virginia.

I tried to get Bob Hope for the opening, but he was already committed elsewhere. Bob's agent suggested Jack Benny. I called Jack's manager, who responded enthusiastically, but the price for Jack was $25,000, plus we had to hire Jack's specified opening act, a singing actress named Shaini Wallis who had just won an Academy Award for the movie *Oliver*. Plus, Jack wanted a full orchestra.

About half the seats were going to be guests of the city, so Dick Lamb and I had to sell the other five thousand to cover the cost of everything. WGH was going to "present" this Grand Opening so they allowed me to go all-out with full page newspaper ads in the *Daily Press*, on TV and constant radio promotion.

I was more excited than I had been about anything in a long time—even more than when I was invited to Washington to the meet the Beatles. Jack Benny was an entertainer I had grown up with; my parents never missed his radio show in the 1940s or his TV show when he went on NBC starting in the early 1950s. Even in 1970, his twice-a-year, one-hour specials for NBC were always among the highest ratings. Jack had created an image as being the stingiest, cheapest guy around and his show had a cast of characters who had become almost as well-known. Benny started his career in the days of vaudeville and had rubbed shoulders with every big star for the past fifty years. He was a regular on Johnny Carson's *Tonight Show*; Carson said Benny was his all-time favorite comedian and influenced him more than any other. As it turned out, when the contract came I was expecting a long list of demands including limos and security. Nothing more was required. Jack, his manager, Irving Fein, Mrs. Fein, and one of Jack's writers, Hilliard Marks, were coming in two days early. I would pick them up at the airport. Irving had also been involved in Frank Sinatra's comeback in the early '50s, and he was a well-known Hollywood character.

The local press was going crazy to interview Jack, so we set up a full press conference at the Holiday Inn in Hampton where Jack would be staying. I thought maybe Jack would want to take a nap after arriving, but he didn't. Jack was surprisingly energetic, and he liked press conferences.

• • •

Every local newspaper, TV station and some radio stations sent reporters. We held the press conference in one of the Holiday Inn meeting rooms and the place was packed. The interaction was lively and lasted an hour.

Afterward, Jack asked me to walk him to his room and then invited me in. I knew Jack had to be tired after his long flight and the press conference, and I figured he was just being polite, so I respectfully declined when he asked me to come in and sit down. He was, after all, seventy-six at the time. He insisted I stay, saying he was not going to nap. Instead, he was curious about the plan for dinner and wanted to chat about the show. I told him that the restaurant in the hotel might be sufficient for tonight, but also reminded him they had room service "No, no," he said. He wanted to take our local entourage out to dinner. He asked me to invite my wife and Hampton's "lady mayor," Ann Kilgore, whom he was going to joke about in his monologue. When I phoned Susan, and then Ann, they were both excited by the invitation and agreed to come right over.

I stayed with Jack and arranged a private dining room for the six of us. That evening with Jack Benny remains one of the highlights of my life. He was funny and gracious, telling us about his various Hollywood experiences, including some road-trip antics with his best friend, George Burns. Irving, by the way, was George Burns' manager, too. Jack answered every question we asked about the old days in radio and the start of TV. Jack was engaging and, most notably, the most humble marquee star I had ever met.

Over the prior dozen years I had spoken with many of the biggest names in music, promoted many of their shows, and spent time with actors in town to promote a movie. All of the music stars wanted to stay in their hotel prior to an event, napping, watching TV, or meeting for a meal *after* a show. Jack Benny was the first big star to ask us to show him the local sights. Jack said he'd always wanted to see Colonial Williamsburg. Through contacts at the radio station I arranged a private tour. A car picked up Jack at the hotel the next morning. Jack, Irving and his wife left for Williamsburg while I met with Hilliard Marks to work on Jack's monologue for the next day's Grand Opening of the Hampton Coliseum. Hilliard asked me questions about local politicians whose names he would insert into jokes, and the same with city names and controversial issues. Our same group had dinner together again that evening.

I spent most of the next day at the Coliseum, making sure everything was ready for the show. Local orchestra players had been hired and rehearsed the numbers Jack wanted to play on his violin. For those who do not know, Jack was actually one of the best violinists around. He started in show business as an orchestra member in the pit of big shows. He could play anything by memory. A lot of his act these days was to start a number with the orchestra and then about halfway through yell "stop, stop, stop," tease some member of the orchestra for being off key and then segue into a series of jokes, never finishing the song.

Before the show, I was with him in the dressing room. Several of the top dignitaries were ushered back to meet Jack and have a photo taken, including Virginia Governor Linwood Holton. Many entertainers want to be alone before going on stage. Not Jack. I had expected him to be reading, and rereading, his script for the monologue, especially so he could remember all the local names of people and cities and events. Instead, Jack showed me how to hold the violin and play a couple of notes. Then be blew me away— Jack gave me the violin as a token of appreciation for having him here to open the Coliseum. I asked him to autograph it. The violin remains one of the most prized possessions in my office.

There was one condition attached to the extraordinary gift. Jack wanted me to toss him the violin and then, after about fifteen seconds, the bow—on cue, across stage during his monologue. Both needed to land near his feet. He kept his personal violin on a stand near the orchestra. The stunt brought a huge laugh. He picked up the violin, stared at it for a few seconds, then gave it to the conductor who handed him his own violin.

Here I interview Hampton, Virginia Mayor Ann Kilgore
regarding the opening of the Hampton Coliseum. 1970

Me with my favorite entertainer of all time, Jack Benny, just prior to the grand opening show at the Hampton Coliseum. Jack gave me the violin and was showing me how to hold it.

Opening weekend, Mayor Kilgore and I watch
the first musicians to play the Coliseum, The Association.

Backstage with Jack Benny, just before the
grand opening show at the Hampton Coliseum.

Jack's act was hilarious. At that time, Hampton was the largest processor of crabs in the US, and most days you knew it from the smell. Jack teased about cutting a ribbon on a building in a town known for crabs and said he had been able to remain "crab free" all his life. Next he teased about Hampton's female mayor. Dick Lamb and I had a small part as presenters of the program, wearing tuxedos instead of our red WGH jackets.

The next day I drove Jack and his entourage to the airport. Irving Fein invited me to visit him in California to have dinner with Jack and George Burns. Unfortunately, Jack died at age 80 about four years after we met and before I was able to make the trip. That's always been one of my big regrets. No star has impressed me more. If you want to know more about Jack, I recommend *Jack Benny, An Initimate Biography*, which was written by Irving Fein.

One of Jack's famous lines is "Age is strictly a case of mind over matter. If you don't mind, it doesn't matter." How true.

CHAPTER 12

FM RADIO

The decade of the 1970s offered lots of promise and watershed change for both my radio and our concert promotion careers as the music scene continued to evolve. Dick and I were now staging shows in the ten-thousand-seat Coliseum and, soon, in other new mega-venues. Our company did the grand opening of Norfolk's Scope arena with Dionne Warwick, and The College of William & Mary Hall with Sly & the Family Stone. Best of all would be the birth of my daughter, Lynne. Susan and I remodeled the house, bought a larger boat and began being accepted in our adopted hometown, Poquoson, which was famous for shunning outsiders.

There were some fundamental shifts in the radio world, too. For about a year, I had been noticing that teens at the hops were requesting songs we didn't play on WGH. In fact, very few Top 40 stations played Jimi Hendrix's songs as it was considered too "hard." Yet Jimi was selling lots of albums and had been getting some of his cuts played on FM radio, which was slowly creeping up as FM became more available. One reason: US automakers started installing AM/FM radios without extra charge.

Until the very late 60s, FM radio wasn't available in cars unless you bought a very expensive receiver and installed it under the dash. Some broadcasters in the 1950s and early 60s actually gave their FM frequencies back to the FCC not seeing any future. New technology changed that. FM developed stereo capability giving it a better sound for music, and transmitted with less interference than AM.

Owners of FM signals started getting inventive, using it to play alternative music or genres with limited audience, at the start. WGH-FM's classical music was in that category. At some point around the start of 1969 WNOR-FM started what was termed an "underground show" on Saturdays from midnight until six in the morning. The format was almost entirely album cuts that did not qualify to be on Top 40. I could tell from requests at record hops that a lot of teens were listening to that show. Asked where they had heard the song, invariably they said WNOR-FM. The station expanded its underground midnight-to-dawn show to seven days a week.

I started stopping by Ray Bottom's office to talk about the changes in FM radio. WGH-FM was Ray's baby. The FM station did not have anywhere near as many advertisers as WGH-AM. WGH-AM covered what was lost at the FM, which had better studios and a staff of classical music buffs. Sensing the surging popularity of underground rock music, I tried to persuade Ray to flip the formats with WGH Top 40 going on the FM and classical music on AM. The idea of playing Bach on AM while the Beatles aired in stereo FM made no sense to the owners of WGH. Next I tried to rent the midnight-to-6-a.m. time block on WGH FM, taking responsibility to sell enough advertising to cover the cost and hopefully make a few dollars for myself. "Not a chance," I was told. My instincts were screaming that "underground" would soon surface around-the-clock on an FM station—somewhere.

WGH's general sales manager, the second-highest executive in radio after the general manager, was a very nice man named Howard Jernigan. Howard, like Gene Creasey and me, had started his career at WLLY in Richmond. I had always been friendly with Howard, stopping by his office to chat and doing some social things with him. Out of nowhere in March 1970, Howard resigned become general manager at WGH's biggest format competitor, WNOR, which had been purchased for $1 million by husband-and-wife lawyers from Texas. As part of his deal, Howard could earn a small equity interest in WNOR-AM *and* FM.

I called Howard to express my surprise, and congratulations.

"Gene! I'm so happy you called . . . " Howard asked me to become general manager of WNOR-FM and to do with that station what I had proposed for WGH-FM. And the pay—a 50 percent increase. The deal included me doing a radio show from 3 until 6 p.m. on WNOR-AM, but with weekends off. And, I could do concert promotions through WNOR, just as I had been doing through WGH. I was just twenty-eight years old and thinking I wouldn't make general manager until I was in my 40s.

I went home and talked to Susan, who at the time was pregnant and was due in the fall. Changing jobs would mean a long commute from Poquoson to Norfolk, at least a forty-five-minute trek each way. On the plus side of being Norfolk-based was that it was closer to Rogues and other events I was hosting south of the James River. We decided that I should take the job. My heart was with WGH, but I doubted they would make the inevitable FM transition any time soon.

I handed in a letter of resignation and was immediately summoned to the office of WGH General Manager Ambert Dail. He had just lost his sales manager, so this was a double blow to Ambert. I had the top-rated radio show in the market. Ambert tried, but failed, to talk me into staying. He wanted me to work out my two weeks. My sign-off at WGH was a Saturday in April, and the very next Monday I was on the air at WNOR.

I remembered that Bob Calvert had failed to take his audience with him when he switched from WGH to WNOR. So I figured the same would be true for me. I thought my loyal audience would even feel betrayed. But thankfully, that was not the case. The first Pulse rating for WNOR-AM showed a big increase in the 3-to-6 p.m. show; within a year we beat WGH-AM.

Thanks to an improved line-up across the board during mornings and afternoons, WNOR-AM started matching or beat WGH-AM during daylight hours. WGH had a superior signal once the sun went down and continued to do better at night. WNOR became so popular that even Bob Calvert rejoined the WNOR team for a while, before moving on to WFOG-FM, where he finished out his career.

• • •

My GM office at WNOR-FM was plush compared to my space at WGH. In fact, the WNOR facility was a showcase for modern radio. Technically, I served two masters at WNOR: I reported to Howard Jernigan as CEO of everything, and to Paul Lucci, program director for the AM. I liked Paul and respected his ear as he guided WNOR-AM, and our business paths would cross significantly in the future.

In 1961, I took this picture of the just completed WNOR offices and Carousel Studio. Also shown is the yet to be finished Brambleton Avenue. The white curb is a reflection pool.

My main goal and focus was to transform WNOR-FM into a stand-alone profitable station. That meant building its audience and a solid advertising base. I needed to have independent leadership in the sales department and quickly sought out Jim Lowe, whom I first met when I went to work at WGH. While I was at WGH, he and I had promoted a few dances together. He eventually signed on with WNOR-AM as a DJ and started selling advertising. Jim had lived in an apartment at Hague Towers in Norfolk, next door to the radio station, before getting married and moving to Bay Colony in Virginia Beach. At the time, the Hague Towers building was owned by the father of Donald Trump, and often, young Donald was sent there to collect overdue rents.

I offered Jim the sales manager job at WNOR-FM. Jim accepted and would supervise two others on the FM sales team. Another longtime WNOR salesperson, Joe Burton, had just resigned to take over management at another local AM/FM station. Little did I know that Joe would become another player in my future career. Up until then most AM and FM sales departments were intermingled with the same people selling both. But I wanted a 100-percent focus on FM.

The demands of building an FM station, hosting a radio show, promoting concerts, managing the Rhondels, and a co-owning of Rogues Gallery, along with the commute to Poquoson, made for some very long days for me. When our daughter was born I wanted to be home more, and backed off some night work. However, the money from the combination of my various opportunities was important to us. Howard, my boss, saved the day: he offered to let us rent an apartment over his garage on 54th Street at the Oceanfront in Virginia Beach during the week. Susan and I jumped at it, so she and I and our baby daughter, Lynne, would occupy the apartment at the Beach during the week, and we all went back to Poquoson on Fridays for the weekend. Suddenly, we had two places and two different lifestyles, and we had more time together.

My AGL concert partner Dick Lamb was working about a block from WNOR, at Channel 3 doing his morning TV show, and then served as program director at WTAR-AM. Dick had become the best known broadcast face in Hampton Roads. He was a local star, but one without a designated parking spot. It was first-come, first-served at WTAR, and he was not well served.

I suggested to Howard that we give Dick a reserved spot in the WNOR lot because he and I were promoting concerts for WNOR. It wasn't a hard sell; Howard liked Dick. Besides, WNOR had plenty of parking spaces. Now I could see both my car and Dick's from my office. We each had recently bought a new Cadillac Eldorado. My blue car was much better looking than the strange yellow with a brown top Dick had ordered.

Occasionally Dick would invite me to walk over to the WTAR-TV studios to appear as a guest on his show. One year Joe

Perkins, the station's program manager, asked me to host the annual WTAR-TV high school spelling competition broadcast live on Channel 3. Another big local WTAR star, Jeff Dane, was the regular host of a weekly fishing show. Jeff was later to become involved with us in the launch of a new TV station. When I first met Jeff, he snubbed Top 40 DJs, including me. Big TV stars never acknowledge lowly radio rats. Fate works in funny ways. In the not-too-distant future I was to be his boss.

· · ·

One of the best things about working in downtown Norfolk every day was lunch. As one of America's original chow hounds, I love a good meal out. Back then there wasn't much of a selection in Hampton, maybe three places that were good, otherwise you drove to Williamsburg. In Norfolk, we had at least four and they were all close to WNOR. Most of the time we went to lunch at the Golden Triangle. In those days I could not qualify or afford to join the Harbor Club, a swanky private restaurant and lounge with meeting rooms on the top floor of one of Norfolk's signature office buildings. The Golden Key Club at the Golden Triangle was also out of my reach. It was a lunchroom frequented by most of the big wheels in the region.

One person I did get to know was Walter Chrysler who had just moved to town after Norfolk agreed to accept his art collection and rename a public museum for him. Additionally, a twenty-two-hundred-seat performing arts center downtown next to the Scope arena was named after Walter. WNOR was about two blocks from the Chrysler Museum and the home where Walter and his wife lived, so we often walked over to the Golden T together. Dick Lamb would join us for lunch, along with others from WTAR.

For me, another perk of working at WNOR was a company car. I had one at WGH as promotion manager, but it was a well-worn station wagon painted with the WGH logo. Radio stations trade advertising for rolling stock in most cases, exchanging commercials for the dealer for a car or van. In this case, the only car my sales manager Jim Lowe could barter for was a brown two-door Buick. The car drove beautifully, but it was ugly—worse than Dick Lamb's Eldorado colors. I can see why the dealership traded it for radio time—nobody would buy it. I labeled it the brown turd, mostly leaving it at home and driving my Cadillac instead. I did get some satisfaction when it came time to get a new car, which ended up being a red Buick Riviera. We sold Dick Lamb the brown Buick for his wife, and he often drove it to work. There is no accounting for taste.

• • •

By 1974, FM radio was starting to gain on AM radio as more FM stations went into the business of playing what we also called "alternative," or "progressive" music, replacing the "elevator" music that many FM owners aired throughout most of the '50s and '60s. Some stations stuck with the stodgy format into the '70s, while others, like WOWI, evolved with the times with a 24/7 progressive rock album format. Soon the same owner I worked for in Richmond at WEZL in 1959, the Benns family, started WMYK-FM at the Virginia-North Carolina line, calling it K94. That station had a major signal and was licensed to Moyock, North Carolina, which is just south of the core Hampton Roads market. The station was initially envisioned by the FCC to service the expansive rural county of Currituck, but instead of putting the tower in a spot to serve just that area, the Bennses moved it right up next to the Virginia-North Carolina border to better reach the cities of Hampton Roads. This was perfectly legal, and was known in the business as a "move-in."

K94 broadcast from a trailer in the woods and soon cut deeply into WOWI's progressive-music audience. WOWI's owners retreated, selling the station to a preacher from Portsmouth, Bishop Levi Willis. So we took WNOR-FM on a more commercial route by playing soft rock with an all-female DJ staff because even then, few advertisers would buy time on alternative rock stations.

My boss, Howard, was starting to have some major health issues and faced several months of recovery. So he named me station manager of both WNOR AM and FM. Howard was still my boss, but now I was in charge of the entire outfit.

In 1970, an article in *The Virginian-Pilot* when I left WGH for WNOR-FM.

Gene Loving: Stereo boss at WNOR-FM.

he's a mover

Gene Loving, afternoon disc jockey for WGH the past nine years, has moved to Norfolk's WNOR as station manager for FM radio and as afternoon disc jockey, Monday through Friday, on AM.

"Lean Gene," as he's known to thousands of young fans in Tidewater, has been rated No. 1 deejay in Tidewater for the past nine years by Pulse and since its beginning in 1965 by American Research Bureau. He will be heard on AM from 3-6 p.m.

He has been a music director, promotion director and has developed a syndicated radio interview program featuring worldwide personalities, now heard throughout the world.

He switched from WGH to become FM station manager because "Quite honestly, I feel in the next two years FM will be as listened to, if not more, as AM. The public today wants to hear music just as it's performed in the studio. It's really exciting to think a radio station can duplicate this and bring it to its listeners. FM offers clarity of signal and music in stereo. Stereo adds realism not matched in anything else."

He says, "I feel the future of the radio business is in FM stereo. It has a young staff and it thinks young."

In late 1974, Paul Lucci urged that we move the WNOR-FM format to what is today called "classic rock," which meant it would include top commercial artists like the Rolling Stones, but leave out traditional Top 40 songs termed "teen" or "bubble gum" music. I thought this was a very positive idea from Paul whose job was tied to WNOR-AM. Paul knew the classic rock format on FM would cannibalize the AM ratings. I discussed this with Howard one evening. I was still renting the apartment behind his house and saw him almost daily during his recovery.

Howard agreed with me: it was time to give up the soft music on the FM and change with the evolving taste of the audience. Paul Lucci was then promoted to program director of both WNOR-AM and FM. We decided the FM needed a new logo and on-air identity. So Paul and I went to see a local advertising agency. Ron Primm designed several new logos for us to review, and the one we selected, FM99, is still being used.

• • •

Another of my responsibilities at WNOR was overseeing construction of a new tower for the FM station. The prior owners had just been using a shorter old tower near the Elizabeth River, never going to the five hundred feet allowed by the FCC license. Height in FM radio equated to reach. You either built what was allowed or you lost that right in the future. Going though that process proved to be a very valuable lesson for me in the years ahead.

By late 1974, FM99 was positioned to be a major competitor, and we were busy. And promoting and presenting concerts through AGL Productions bolstered WNOR's image. Dick and I brought Sonny and Cher to Scope in 1973 and Hampton in 1974, both major sell-outs at the height of their CBS TV show. We had our biggest financial success via a deal with Three Dog Night to play at the new Hampton Coliseum, a contract I had signed months before they became superstars. The band had previously played for us at the Virginia Beach Dome to a sellout crowd.

I remember that show at the Coliseum well. Just before the start, Cory Wells, lead vocalist, sent word he wanted to see me in the dressing room. I anticipated a complaint. Instead, Cory floored me with an apology. "Gene, I just want to apologize for my condition when we last played for you at the Dome. Danny (Hutton) reminded me I was spaced out when we played at the Dome and not in very good voice . . . I promise, tonight we are going to put on the best show ever." I thanked him, accepted his apology and left the dressing room. I had no idea he wasn't up to his best at the Dome show.

Another big promotional success was Led Zeppelin in 1971. It was the first hard-rock band to play the Coliseum. City Manager Ed Johnson was very nervous that Zeppelin fans, who had caused damage elsewhere, would tear up the new upholstered floor seats. The band left the stage, the crowd went nuts and the city manager was relieved because no damage was done. Then, I asked the band to play an encore. The city manager went crazy, believing the show was over and his plush seats had survived. The seats did survive, and I spent an hour at city hall the next day explaining that encores are a standard part of rock concerts. If the band had not done an encore there very well could have been a riot.

Often we would be a "co-promoter" with others who had "contractual rights" but no "local knowledge." That was the case with the Jackson Five and Osmonds. Dick Clark owned the rights to the tours of both groups for the entire country. Dick Clark stayed loyal to Dick Lamb and me. He had not forgotten the times we risked significant money to book some of his earlier "caravan of stars" tours. All of our productions in association with Dick Clark were winners.

WNOR opened offices and studios on the Peninsula for the first time in Newport News in 1971. I originated my daily 3-to-6 p.m. show from that location two days a week as the Norfolk station established a footing beyond the Southside of Hampton Roads.

Me with The Osmonds shortly before they took stage at the Hampton Coliseum, 1972. Marie, 13 years old, was back stage with her mother, Olive, and father, George, who managed the tour and settled the box office.

Me with The Jackson Five. The girl in the center was a contest winner who got to go backstage to meet the group. Seems she was focused on Michael, maybe she had a sense he would become the biggest star in "pop" about twenty years later.

• • •

My fulfilling, happy days at WNOR were disrupted in 1975 when I came in to work and learned that the station owners had fired Howard Jernigan over the phone, in part because of absenteeism due to his health issues. While sad, this was not an unreasonable position for owners Arnold and Audrey Malkin to take. A week or so later, they arrived with consultants they had hired to revamp their Fort Worth station. That evening, three of us from WNOR had dinner with the consultants and the Malkins, who asked a lot of questions. The next day, while I was on the air, Paul Lucci was fired. When my show ended the owners summoned me to Howard's office. They said they were going to make a change in management and operate the stations through the consultants from Fort Worth. They were firing me. I tried to make the argument that the stations were doing well financially and FM99's new format was already ahead of its prior year's ratings. They were adamant, and essentially said I was Howard's guy and they wanted someone else, someone who would take directions from Fort Worth. They described a decent severance package. I didn't understand it at the time, but they had just created an opportunity that would have never happened had I stayed comfortably employed at WNOR.

I packed up my office and drove to Rogues Gallery for my regular gig with the Rhondels. It was now 1975, and I was out of a salaried job for the first time since 1958. If not for my various other income sources, I would have panicked. As I drove home that night I imagined that once the word got out that I had been canned, the phone would ring and I would be back playing hits on the air, somewhere.

That evening, after giving the news to my wife and telling Howard in person, I called Paul Lucci to let him know I was out. We eventually found out that the consultants thought they could save a bundle by running both Fort Worth and Norfolk without upper management or program directors. Then they promoted WNOR-AM sales manager Fred Gage to take the place of three people. The owners didn't understand the long-range implication of their decision. They were lawyers and investors, not radio station operators: they had not personally experienced that the strength of radio is "live and local" with the most important element being local. Radio stations become part of a community's fabric, a personality that dispenses local information, and a staff that is involved in the community. Some stations play the same music; it's what's in between the music that makes a difference. Once the leader of a local station disappears from civic events, or is not available to meet with those who want the radio station to promote a local charity or become a sponsor of something like the Neptune Festival and Hampton Bay Day, the station misses talking about things important to the community. And you can bet the competition will be talking about those things. It took about a year before the owners realized their mistake. WNOR fell in the ratings and the owners fired the consultants. Eventually FM99 went on to become a stable and highly rated station, but only after the Malkins sold it.

Jim Lowe, the sales manager of WNOR-FM, had survived the purge. He had become my friend over the years and we would have dinner at each other's homes a couple of times a year. When he heard I was out, he had called me right away to express his concern, not only about me, but about WNOR. Jim asked me to keep in touch, hoping that perhaps we would team up again at another station.

DJs and radio people in general move around a lot to improve their job positions. I never had that ambition. I did not want to give up a good job on the Virginia coast to fight a ratings game in a big market with thirteen-week contract renewals, so I was not thinking about looking outside of Hampton Roads for a job. Once, when I was at WGH I was offered a DJ slot on WDCA in Washington, DC. Susan and I went up, looked at the impressive facilities of the radio station, and house-shopped, but in the end I just didn't want to move away from the ocean, or give up the concert business.

The next day I did something bizarre for a guy out of work. The WNOR company car was not part of my severance pay, and while Susan and I each had relatively new Cadillacs, I decided they both should be traded in for something brand new to inspire me to find a job to make those new car payments. I bought my wife a new Corvette and myself a new Cadillac Eldorado convertible. Dick Lamb threatened to resign from our promotions company because I had acted so irrationally, but he calmed down after a few days. I kept assuring him I would not ask him for a loan if

I ran out of money.

Fortunately, AGL Productions had several concerts on the books so I had something to keep me busy. I remember one of them was Average White Band at Chrysler Hall, which sold out two shows. My Rogues Gallery partnership with Dick Davis and Bill Deal was also going well: we were dividing up money almost weekly and paying down the mortgage.

We had only one problem at Rogues. In the early '70s not only did we have Bill Deal and the Rhondels, and a couple of other local regular bands, but we featured major national acts to play one or two nights a week, for so called "pick up" dates, when they were between bigger jobs. The problem was we were selling too much beer compared to food sales. Virginia ABC laws at that time required sales to be at least 50 percent food in order for a club to maintain a license to sell beer. And there were no mixed drinks in those days. We offered hamburgers, pizza, and other typical bar food, but we were not selling enough food. We were giving away popcorn to each table and reducing the price of a beer so we could allocate part of the check to food. The balancing act was a constant struggle, and the ABC inspector had urged us to improve our food sales. We all agreed we needed to establish a restaurant at Rogues, maybe serving breakfast as people left the club during early morning hours. What was created still remains one of the top restaurants in Virginia Beach, even forty years later.

Bill Deal often ate lunch at a restaurant on Virginia Beach Boulevard, which was primarily known for breakfast. He got to know Mary Craft, who ran the business and cooked most orders herself. She mentioned to Bill that her lease was coming up for renewal and the owners were hiking her rent, which she couldn't afford. Bill thought about the empty space at Rogues, the front all-glass auto showroom from old Clark Chevrolet.

Rogues Gallery was located in what had been the shop-service area in back of the building. We used the space in the front mostly as a dressing room or a place for bands to take a break. Bill called me and proposed building out the car showroom as a restaurant and turning it over to Mary Craft to run. We were entitled to include all the food sales in our revenue report to the ABC agency as it was our restaurant. Mary would then keep whatever profit she made with breakfast and lunch, and consider it her salary. I loved the idea, but then asked Bill where we would get the thousands of dollars necessary to build out the kitchen, put up real walls to replace the glass, and equip the space with all the booths and tables. Bill said that our club manager, Al Mailes, had mentioned "Big George" Lineberry of Southern Amusement Corp. might advance us the money. George was a good source for financing in exchange for the rights to the jukeboxes and pinball machines.

We were already sharing 50 percent of the profits with George from the foosball tables inside of Rogues, which was nice additional income. George agreed to fund the build-out for what became Mary's Country Kitchen, with him getting all of the money from the amusement machines until he was repaid; after that, we would split fifty-fifty. Dick Davis signed off on the plan and we moved ahead. People still line up for breakfast at Mary's, even though she has long passed to that big kitchen in the sky.

• • •

After a week or two of being out of radio, I was actually enjoying not having to be in a studio somewhere at an exact time each day. I loved spending some weekdays out on the boat. Dick Lamb, who was the program director at WTAR radio, felt sorry for me and asked that I fill in a few nights when one of his DJs was off. And WAVY asked me to host a couple of TV specials. I liked filling in; no long-term commitments; no being shackled to an office or studio.

I stayed in touch with old colleagues, including Jim Lowe, who was not liking the WNOR atmosphere. Jim had expected me to find a new job right away and see if they had a spot for him. He was getting concerned that I had yet to even look for a job. I did have a meeting with my old boss at WGH, Ambert Dail, who called out of courtesy, and reported that Ray Bottom remained recalcitrant; Ray was never going to switch WGH-FM away from classical. So WGH was in my rearview mirror.

CHAPTER 13

JOY AND HEARTBREAK

My hiatus from being a full-time DJ gave me time to think—and explore. The radio business could be exhilarating, but as with any business, it had a cruel side. I had seen revolving doors sweep people in and then out just as quickly. While I loved the celebrity of being on-air, I now understood the fickleness of being a radio jock, having seen so many of my colleagues come and go. But many of them were climbing the ladder to bigger markets. Now, with FM there was a load of competition. You needed that rare blend of talent and foresight to stay ahead of the game. And, you needed to seize opportunity and take some risks. Having lots of allies also helped—a lot. That much I knew for sure.

Jim Lowe from WNOR kept an eye out on my behalf, and his. Jim mentioned to me that the salesman he had once worked with at WNOR, Joe Burton, was now running stations WTID-AM, a country format, and WQRK-FM, a Top 40 format station that branded itself as Q104.5. Jim was thinking that Joe may want me on the FM station to help build its credibility and audience. I had met Joe a few times at trade association meetings, so I called him and we met for lunch. It was clear Joe wasn't in need of a manager—and certainly couldn't meet my salary expectations for DJ-only work. He said his stations were just breaking even, which I interpreted to mean they were losing money. I also didn't expect Joe to release someone to make room for me. I got the impression things at WTID-WQRK were shaky and the properties might be sold, but I needed to find out more about it. *Who owned those stations and what would they cost?* The Malkins paid $1 million for WNOR a few years back. But where would I get that kind of money? At the time I had a net worth of about $100,000—on paper. The first step was to find out as much as I could about the station and its owners, so I hired a Washington lawyer familiar with FCC ownership and filings, which were public records.

We quickly discovered that WTID and WQRK's principal owner was a Maryland physician named Norman Berger. I called and left a message that I wanted to talk to him about his radio stations in Hampton Roads. About five minutes later Norman called me back. When I asked if he would consider selling the stations he almost jumped through the phone to shake my hand. Apparently, Dr. Berger had been trying to find a buyer for some time. He also told me not to discuss this with Joe Burton because Joe had wanted to buy the stations but couldn't raise the money. So that's why Joe had been so evasive when we met.

The price? One million dollars—same as WNOR—must be the magic number for sellers.

Dr. Berger asked me a lot of questions about my background and ideas. He also gave me the name of his brother-in-law, a Washington lawyer who handled Norman's business affairs. When I hung up, I had a new focus—radio station ownership. I was just thirty-three years old and had figured ownership was still at least two decades away.

So, how was I going to raise $1 million?

The only true millionaire I knew was Dick Davis, my partner in Rogues. Dick and I had developed a decent working relationship and our venture at Rogues had been successful. I knew his family, and he knew mine. And by now I knew that Dick Davis had invested in several businesses as a silent partner, just as he had with Rogues. He had also been one of the original local owners of WAVY-TV, so he knew a bit about broadcasting.

We met and I explained all that had happened at WNOR and

my talk with the owner of the radio stations I now wanted to buy. Dick asked to see the stations' financial statements for the past few years, which I had yet to obtain. I was encouraged; at least Dick Davis hadn't said "no."

I called Dr. Berger's business manager and obtained the financial statements which showed that the doctor had been shelling out $50,000 a year to cover losses. I could see why general manager Joe Burton did not have backers rushing to help him buy WTID and WQRK since he was already running them and could not make money. Dick Davis and his accountant reviewed the financials and quickly concluded the stations were not worth the asking price. He told me to offer $500,000, which I did. Dr. Berger's advisor had a few choice words and hung up on me. I figured it was game over. That night the doctor called and also expressed disappointment with the offer. He said he knew I was the right buyer and that he really wanted me to have the stations; he offered to sell them for seven hundred and fifty thousand.

The next day Dick Davis told me to counter offer $750,000. "Tell Dr. Berger we will pay $200,000 at closing if the doctor will take a note for the $550,000 balance." We would pay off the loan in seven years plus 6 percent interest. Dr. Berger called back the next day and accepted. I was stunned. We had just agreed to buy an AM-FM radio combination in a market I knew. The deal was confidential until the contracts were signed and Dr. Berger had a $50,000 deposit. I agreed to keep my mouth shut but was busting at the seams to call Jim Lowe and Paul Lucci to say we soon might be working together again.

The next day, a ten-page contract was drafted. While that was going on, I called my FCC lawyer in Washington, Bill Barnard, about transferring the stations to our new company, which we called Bay Cities Communications. Getting FCC approval could be cumbersome and time consuming: it's a process that must be advertised to seek community input. Airwaves are considered public property, so regulators need to be convinced that the invisible space would serve the community's best interest under our stewardship. Transferring ownership of an FCC license involved canvassing groups of community leaders about their concerns, and potentially addressing them by covering the issues on the radio. That survey process can take months.

Broadcasters formed associations to expedite the tedious

process. Instead of meeting with seventy-five or so different individuals in the community and then cataloging the results, the FCC allowed stations to get through the canvassing process by doing it all together with various leaders throughout one day. Broadcast managers would gather as a group in a hotel meeting room and, one-by-one, listen to input from people like the mayor or chief of police. This system cut a couple of months off of the approval process. I had been attending those meetings while working at WNOR and could already document the answers.

My deal with Dick Davis had to be disclosed in our FCC application. The Davis family and I would be equal partners in Bay Cities. As such, I needed to ante half of the $50,000 deposit, which meant I had to scrounge around for $25,000 in cash. I wound up borrowing the money from my old friend in Hampton, attorney Charles "Flash" Gordon. I don't think Dick Davis knew I had to borrow to cover my end of the deposit.

Next came an even bigger bombshell. Dick Davis wanted to borrow the remaining $150,000 we needed from a bank. He essentially wanted me to secure my half of the bank loan with my salary and personal assets, and he would secure the rest. We couldn't use the radio stations as bank collateral because they were already being used to secure the note Dr. Berger was holding until we paid him off.

Seventy-five thousand was a lot of money back then, about three times the value of my Poquoson house. I would have to pledge close to my entire net worth to secure the loan. Plus, Dick Davis told me I had to find a bank to agree to our plan. I wanted this deal badly, so I started making appointments with bankers. After several different meetings, the Bank of Chesapeake came through with the money, and the loan was made on the strength of Dick's financial statement—not mine. One condition of the loan was that Bay Cities would have to bank with our lender. Dick's lesson to me was that you never want to use your own cash unless absolutely necessary. Paying interest on a loan is a business expense. It took three different bank visits before we got the financing, but the only money we each contributed to buying WTID and WQRK was $25,000 each.

• • •

Having to go to a personal friend for money and a bank for a loan after earning so much for such a long time caused me to rethink my spending habits. The vacations to Europe first class, weekends at the Homestead resort, horses, maintaining two residences, private school for Lynne, fancy new cars, had all soaked up much of the money I could have saved. So first, I cancelled the apartment lease in Virginia Beach. Fortunately, Dick Davis offered to let us use his oceanfront apartment at Oceans II if we wanted to stay overnight at the Beach. Dick also decided to let his wife, Martha, be the 50 percent shareholder for the Davis family. That was great news to me, as I really enjoyed Martha's personality and she loved music.

Once the deposit was posted and the application to FCC filed, Dr. Berger and Bay Cities issued a joint press release announcing the sale of WTID and WQRK. I had asked to meet with Joe Burton in his office for the same morning before the press release was issued, wanting to deliver the news personally. I figured Joe would be disappointed that he wasn't able to buy the stations and worried that he might be sacked. I was right. Joe was angry and asked if I wanted him to pack up his desk. We didn't own the station yet, I told him, and besides, I wanted him to stay and focus on sales at WTID while I managed WQRK. Joe said he would think about it. A week later he called to apologize and accepted my offer to run sales at WTID.

WTID already had a long history in the market as a country station when AM radio was the only band in the car. WTID's shortcoming was that it was daytime only, signing off at dark. Even so, the station had decent ratings. It was the station where Wolfman Jack started in radio. In the early '70s at the height of his NBC-TV *Midnight Special,* I brought the Wolfman to town for an WNOR promotion. At dinner he told me his WTID story about after he left the Army having been stationed at Fort Eustis, hitch hiking to Newport News to find a job. He was hired to sell advertising on WTID, not do DJ work.

Joe had been working from a sales office in Norfolk. I wanted him and the sales team to instead set up shop in Hampton where WTID's transmitter and studios were located, so the AM and FM staff would see themselves as involved and dependent on only the station where they worked.

Next on my list to notify, Paul Lucci, who I wanted as the new program manager for WQRK, and Jim Lowe as sales manager. Jim had a job and could wait until the deal closed. But Paul was out of work and couldn't wait around to see if our deal went through. So, I called Joe Burton and asked if he would hire Paul Lucci early, which he agreed to do since Paul would be good for the station even if our deal failed to close for some reason.

We bought WTID and WQRK in late September of 1975, five months after I lost my job at WNOR, and there was plenty of eleventh-hour drama. My lawyer, Bob Curren, and I drove to Washington to meet with Dr. Berger and his financial adviser. They were accompanied by their FCC lawyer, Jason Shrinskey, which seemed odd. My FCC guy wasn't with us as we saw no need to bring him. Dr. Berger's FCC lawyer started saying frightening things: They wanted a yearly consulting fee of $50,000 for Dr. Berger until the note was paid off. They had essentially added $350,000 to the purchase price, and unless we agreed Dr. Berger would not sell, the lawyer insisted. That unforeseen demand took the deal back up to the original asking price of $1 million plus another $100,000.

I had negotiated plenty as a concert promoter and partner in the Rogues deal. Never had I been so angry or surprised. We had a contract and, if necessary, I knew we could sue them, but that wouldn't get us the stations anytime soon. I picked up my papers, told my lawyer to gather his things and we headed for the elevator. As we waited in the hall, Dr. Berger came running out, asking us to stay. We did, closed the deal and drove home. We had planned to go out to dinner and celebrate, but I was still too upset and headed straight for home. Thirty years later I would deal with Dr. Berger's FCC lawyer again.

• • •

During the summer as I waited for the deal to close, Dick Davis told me to start taking a salary for time spent planning the stations' future. We would write a check for what was owed me once we took control. I thought this was very generous of him and completely unexpected. It enabled me to repay Charles Gordon my deposit money loan as soon as we took over the stations.

Dick Davis was chairman of the board of Bay Cities; I was president and general manager. Our wives were also on the board. My first decision was a big surprise to everyone: I decided not to go back on the radio. People had expected me to leverage whatever on-air name recognition I had developed in the market over the years. But I knew that if I did go back on the air and the ratings went up, I'd be trapped in a DJ slot. I was starting to think that my time would be better spent working with the entire staff and meeting clients.

I had been off the air for months and simply didn't miss it, much to my own surprise. Being a DJ had been my life and passion; it's why I got into the business. My decision was clinical; I had accomplished my goals and it was time to move on. It proved to be the right decision.

• • •

Rogues Gallery and the concert promotion business continued clicking along. In April 1976, Dick Lamb and I scored one of our biggest talents ever—Elvis—for the Hampton Coliseum. We figured this would be a huge feather in our caps and a lot of cash in our wallets. Boy, did we get it wrong!

Landing Elvis for the Coliseum was a huge deal. Elvis was making a comeback and still had a massive following. He also had a very controlling manager, Col. Thomas Andrew Parker, who severely restricted access to Elvis. He was as possessive with Elvis as Brian Epstein had been with the Beatles. About the only time the Colonel hadn't been glued to Elvis' hip was when the rock star served in the Army and was stationed overseas. Col. Parker was of Dutch extraction and had entered the US illegally. He therefore never tried to obtain a passport to accompany Elvis in Germany or anywhere outside the US. It's why Elvis had never performed overseas.

I had hoped that Elvis would want to meet me to shake my hand for bringing him to Hampton, and for all of the support playing his records over the past fifteen or so years. In eastern Virginia, my old station WGH led the way into the new era of playing popular rock 'n roll, especially Elvis's music. A "thank you" and a picture with "the King" would have been nice, and appropriate. But Col. Parker had other notions.

We had landed the show because of connections we had with the main promoter of Elvis' tour, Jerry Weintraub. Jerry told us

Elvis would play either Baltimore or Hampton, and the catch was that Elvis does not pay rent for a venue. We were told Hampton should consider it an honor to host the King. *Rent-free?* At first I thought it was a joke.

I called the Coliseum manager who said we needed a higher approval than his. So I had a meeting with Hampton's mayor and city manager. Bringing Elvis to their city would be coup, so they bit. I told them they would make more money on parking than the rent anyway, as it would be the first time for two shows in one day. I called Concerts West, who was working for Weintraub, with the good news. I had expected AGL, our company, to handle selling tickets and split the profits as usual. Wrong again! I was told all ticket proceeds went to Elvis and the companies behind his tour, and that they totally controlled all the tickets. The only bone we were thrown came from Col. Parker; he would let me "buy" the front row to both shows. Which I did.

On the night of the performances Col. Parker allowed no one back stage. After all of that, I didn't even get to meet Elvis—but my friends and I did have excellent seats.

• • •

While Dick Lamb may have given me a hard time about working for nothing on the Elvis deal, the other Dick, Mr. Davis, couldn't have been happier with the financial results from the radio stations. The financials were better than projected so Dick Davis suggested we refinance our debt, take some money out and pay Dr. Berger the balance we owed him. As it turned out, Dr. Berger and I became friendly. He blamed his lawyer for almost scuttling the deal. Dr. Berger liked the steady checks from us and was disappointed when I said we were thinking of paying off his loan early.

In early 1976, Bill Archer of the National Bank of North America in New York called me on the phone one day to tell me that his bank was getting into the business of doing broadcast loans. I assume he was just going down a list of radio stations, calling owners. If we wanted to buy more stations, or had other needs, please call him. A couple of years later when we wanted to do the refinancing, I did call and said we wanted to borrow $1.5 million to pay off existing debt, buy some new equipment and pay some money to ourselves. The stations now appraised for $2.5 million, more than twice what we paid. After about a month we got the loan. I remember going to New York with my lawyer, Bob Curren, to sign the documents and pick up the check. We rode the subway back to Midtown for a meeting thinking that I could now afford a cab; Bob had the check for $1.5 million in his pocket. In future years Bob Curran was appointed as judge of the Circuit Court in Newport News.

The Davis family and I split $1 million. Uncle Sam took about half, and I used the rest to pay off every bill I had. Now in my early thirties, I was debt-free and with the cash I had left over, plus my share of Rogues Gallery and the radio stations, I had a net worth of more than $1 million. Life was great and I felt incredibly blessed. Then, in late 1978, the earth shifted under my feet.

· · ·

Lynne, at 18 months old.

Our seven-year-old daughter, Lynne, was a very active child with lots of neighborhood friends. She did sleepovers, enjoyed school, and, from the earliest age, entertained herself with crayons and picture books. Because we were in a rural setting we bought her a pony and a cart. It was often used to give the neighborhood kids rides. She and her friends also swam in a pool we had put in our back yard. She got to meet the stars we brought to town. Her biggest thrill was meeting Donny and Marie Osmond at the height of their TV show, when they performed at the Hampton Coliseum.

I knew Donny from prior Osmond performances, but the *Donny & Marie* show made a big TV splash and vaulted their popularity. I recall how very friendly Marie was when I took Lynne back to meet her. Marie came toward us extending her hand saying, "Hi, I'm Marie Osmond. It's such a pleasure to meet you." Marie asked if Lynne would be so kind as to have a picture taken with her. I am so glad I was able to arrange that meeting and see the joy in my daughter's eyes.

One day I noticed a bump on the side of Lynne's nose. I took her to a doctor in Poquoson who said it must be an inflamed sinus. A few days later, no improvement, and the lump was bigger. We found a specialist at Riverside Hospital who operated to remove the growth. He called to ask that Susan and I come to his office and told us Lynne had cancer. The next day we were in Charlottesville at the University of Virginia Hospital to see a specialist, Dr. Robert Cantrell, who focused on the type of childhood cancer afflicting Lynne. The doctor gave our daughter a 20 percent survival rate. He wanted to operate immediately to remove all the tissue around where the tumor had been, and then start chemotherapy and radiation. I called Jim Lowe at WQRK and told him it looked like we were going to have to stay in Charlottesville for a few weeks. I drove home, picked up clothes and Lynne's things, and Susan and I moved into a hotel room near the hospital.

• • •

We ended up staying in Charlottesville for two months. Our daughter was very sick, her energy depleted from chemotherapy and radiation treatments. Some days we would take her in the car to Skyline Drive or out to dinner, although she ate very little. I would drive back to the office for a few hours once a week. Lynne appeared to go into remission for a few months, but the tumor started to grow back next to her nose. She had lost her hair, was wearing a wig, and was embarrassed to go out, but once her friends started to come around she had a few days of near normalcy.

We decided to seek treatment at Memorial Sloan Kettering in New York, among the world's premier cancer hospitals. We made that trip, stayed a few days, and the experts there said their treatment would have been no different than what we received at UVA. No other treatment was available for this kind of cancer.

I was very fortunate that WQRK was doing fine by the time Lynne got sick. I could do most things by phone and had a great team in Jim Lowe and Paul Lucci. We hit our business goals in 1977 and were on track to do the same in 1978. I received a lot of emotional support from my colleagues and friends during this very troubling time in my life.

Lynne died in October the next year, shortly after she turned age nine. She spent the last three months at home in bed with a nurse during the day, and Susan and I took care of her at night. I was having lunch at the Crow's Nest restaurant on Newtown Road when one of our WQRK staffers came in and told me Lynne had been rushed to Riverside Hospital. By the time I got there she was gone. My wife never got over Lynne's death. Susan always believed our daughter would recover.

Watching a loved one suffer with a fatal disease is emotionally draining and frustrating. You do all you can, think of every option, call everyone and anyone who might help, read books, do research. Pray. What you can't do is personally heal someone who is fatally ill.

Lynne's death took a heavy toll on my marriage. Susan didn't think we had done enough; she was upset that we hadn't found a doctor who could cure our daughter's disease. Over the next year we saw three different marriage counselors, but made little progress. The third one advised me to leave the marriage—for Susan's sake and mine. Susan was unable to deal with a divorce in any rational way, so my attorney advised that I sign over to Susan everything we owned together—except for the businesses. I did, and also agreed to pay a substantial alimony so she could be cared for, until she remarried, which she never did.

Susan bounced back some, attending travel agent school and becoming an airline ticket agent. Sadly, the job didn't last long. Susan died in a mental institution in Roanoke after moving to several different cities trying to escape her demons.

CHAPTER 14

ULTRA HIGH FREQUENCY

About a year before Lynne got sick, I was told by my FCC lawyer, Bill Barnard, that a license was available in Norfolk for CH 33. At that time there weren't many UHF TV stations, so the FCC was anxious to see these frequency allocations activated. In those days, about the only UHF TV stations were public broadcasting affiliates. All of the main network channels were VHF. Early TV sets didn't even have tuners that included UHF. In the 1970s you could receive UHF, but you had to use a separate knob on the television and have a special UHF antenna.

Bill Barnard believed Dick Davis and I could get the license for Channel 33. But I'd have to jump through the FCC hoops and solicit community input, just as we had done when buying the radio stations. UHF seemed to me at the time to be the TV equivalent of what FM radio had been just a few years earlier. Grabbing a license now, when it was available, could be a great opportunity.

We filed for the permit in late 1977 but quickly met with resistance from local competitors. The owner of WVEC-TV and its two sister radio stations objected, arguing Bay Cities Communications would have too much "control" in the marketplace. That argument seemed hypocritical since WVEC's fiefdom was comprised of one TV and two radio stations in the same market—exactly what we had hoped to achieve.

We filed a response and while our application was pending, the FCC changed ownership rules. UHF licenses would not be issued to "controlling" shareholders of other broadcasting companies in the same market because the FCC wanted to ensure ownership diversity. FCC's evolving stance on media ownership was creating lots of whiplash, even forcing some companies to divest TV or radio stations. Among those was Norfolk-based Landmark Communications, which owned the two dominant daily newspapers, a couple of radio stations and one of the big-three TV network affiliates, WTAR. That fight, led by a local lawyer trying to use the new rules against WTAR, lasted ten years before Landmark agreed to sell the TV station.

The FCC's idea of "diversity of ownership" was understandable. So, my group took a different approach and amended our FCC filing. My two associates at WQRK-FM, Jim Lowe and Paul Lucci, were brought in as investors and would each hold 5 percent ownership of the TV station. Dick Davis and I also lowered our ownership interest to 10 percent each. We would sell the remaining 70 percent and create a Virginia-based ownership group. We had little problem lining up investors and eventually we included a couple of sharp Norfolk lawyers, Joel and Charles Cooper. Joel, who liked media companies and owned a local magazine, Metro, said he had considered applying for the Channel 33 license himself. We decided to call our company the Television Corporation of Virginia. Joel would serve as president and I would be secretary.

With the Cooper and Davis names behind Channel 33, we easily found others to ante in, including some of Dick's affluent friends like attorney Herbert Bangel, plus a retired congressman and a Portsmouth insurance executive. I drove to Richmond and met with my original inspiration in broadcasting, Harvey Hudson.

The Television Corporation of Virginia
The brains and bucks behind Channel 33

Sitting: Herman Valentine, Richard J. Davis, Brad Bangel, Stockton Fleming. Standing: William Allaun, Thomas Downing, Harvey Hudson, Gene Loving, Joel Cooper, Jim Lowe, Paul Todd, Hugh Hoff. Not pictured: Tim McDonald, John Trinder and Martha Davis.

WILLIAM ALLAUN: *Secretary* and *Member, Executive Committee;* Newport News attorney, former owner of WBCI and WMBG, Williamsburg; currently Chairman of the Board of the Middle Peninsula Savings and Loan.

BRAD BANGEL: Vice-President of Bruce Farms, Inc., a development firm based in Chesapeake.

JOEL COOPER: *Member, Executive Committee;* Norfolk businessman; Cooper, a former director of WAVY-TV, and his family own Seaside Park in Virginia Beach and various media interests.

MARTHA W. DAVIS: Director of Bay Cities Communications Corp.; member of the Executive Committee and Board of Directors of Television Corp.; director of Virginia Investment and Mortgage Corp.; director of the Tidewater Children's Museum.

RICHARD J. DAVIS: *Advisor to the Executive Committee;* Mayor of Portsmouth and Chairman of the Democratic Party of Virginia; President of Virginia Investment and Mortgage Company and former Chairman of the Board of Fidelity American Bank.

TOM DOWNING: *Chairman of the Board and Advisor to the Executive Committee;* former U.S. congressman for 28 years and now a Newport News attorney.

HUGH HOFF: *Treasurer;* President of Hoff Cadillac and a director of the Bank of Virginia Beach.

HARVEY HUDSON: Vice-President and General Manager of Neighborhood Communications Corp., owners of WKGN, Knoxville, and applicants for WJJS and WLGM, Lynchburg; he is also one of Richmond's best known broadcasters.

GENE LOVING: *Member, Executive Committee;* President of Bay Cities Communication Corp., owner of WQRK and WTJZ; a past president of the Tidewater Association of Radio Broadcasters and a member of the Board of Directors of the Virginia Association of Broadcasters.

JIM LOWE: General Sales Manager of WQRK, a former sales manager of WNOR-FM and WGH-FM and past president of the Advertising Club of Tidewater.

TIM McDONALD: *President and General Manager;* formerly of WTTG, Channel 5, Metromedia in Washington.

PAUL TODD: Account Executive with WQRK; President and co-owner of WKEX in Blacksburg.

JOHN TRINDER: *Vice-President and General Sales Manager;* formerly local and regional sales manager of WTAR-TV, Norfolk.

The founding investors of WTVZ-TV, CH 33, the anchor station of TVX Broadcast Group. (Top row, L-R:) Bill Allaun, Tom Downing, Harvey Hudson, me, Joel Cooper, Jim Lowe, Paul Lucci, Hugh Hoff (Bottom row, L-R:), Herman Valentine, Richard Davis, Brad Bangel, and Stockton Fleming.

Harvey had been in the industry for forty years but had no equity in any station where he had been employed. I offered Harvey 10 percent of Channel 33 and he accepted. I also offered Dick Lamb 10 percent, but Dick's bosses at WTAR-TV frowned and said that would be a conflict of interest. If Dick bought in to Channel 33 he would have to resign from WTAR. Dick stayed at WTAR and declined my offer, which was a big disappointment to me.

We spent a lot of money on legal fees to defend our FCC application, which was still being challenged by competitors. That battle added a year to the process. By the end of 1978 we knew the FCC would approve our application. We had to pick call letters for the station, so I had Bill Barnard do a search of four letter combinations. All new stations on the east side of the Mississippi started with a *W*, and on the west side of the river a *K*. When I saw WTVZ on the possible combination list, I called Bill and told him to file for those letters. The station is still using that name today.

The WTVZ name also fit nicely with the new call letters for our AM radio station. As I had expected, FM radio had chewed deeply into the radio listening market, forcing lots of rejiggering. One way we responded was by turning our AM station, WTID, into an all jazz format and renaming it WTJZ, the *JZ* being for jazz. By then Joe Burton had left and my former boss at WGH, Roger Clark, came to work for me handling sales at WTJZ and doing a weekend jazz show. I was fortunate during this period to have a great chief engineer, too. Jim Seaman had joined the radio stations after a stint in the Navy. He was smart and well organized, a can-do guy. I asked Jim to investigate costs of equipment for our TV startup, the main components of which would be a UHF transmitter and antenna installed at the top of a tall tower. Jim brought us three proposals. Prior to Jim, engineer Andy Booth handled a few challenges for us at WTJZ. We obtained a license to also broadcast at night on WTJZ, and Andy built those nighttime facilities.

The FCC wanted to know how we would pay the expense of building a TV station from scratch. So, costs and financing were huge factors. Obtaining a license to broadcast is one thing, but spending millions to make it happen can be a staggering hill to climb, and so you had to prove in advance you had the money before the government issued a construction permit. I'm guessing the other two commercial TV stations, besides WVEC, in the market didn't fight us too hard because they assumed we would never get the money to actually build the station.

We were serious, and considered proposals for transmission equipment from RCA, Harris, and a company in Europe called PYE, which was owned by the Dutch company, Philips. Philips was viewed as the GE of Europe and already sold lots of products in the US under different names. Magnavox was their TV set brand. Philips had a finance company in the US which would lend money against their products, but RCA and Harris did not. So, we went with Philips.

A major consideration was where to locate a transmission tower, a huge expense. It meant getting permits, buying or leasing land and then erecting a massive thousand-foot tower. And without the proper tower location you were sunk. Back in the pre-cable days, TV reception came via rabbit ears or roof antennae. So you needed a strong, unobstructed signal beaming into households.

In the late 1970s, all of the area TV stations had thousand-foot towers at an antenna farm in Driver, Virginia, an outpost on the western edge of Norfolk-Virginia Beach region. I was looking for an alternative to building a tower, so I went to see John Morrison, the general manager of Norfolk's PBS station WHRO-TV. I knew he had a tower in Driver and that his station was always trying to raise money for their operations. PBS is non-profit and didn't sell advertising, and John agreed to rent us space on his tower.

Making a deal with WHRO-TV was good for them and for us. It gave the public TV station a steady monthly income, and it saved us a ton of money and time. Another plus was that there was another UHF station already in the market. Channel 27 belonged to the Christian Broadcasting Network, which was operated by its founder, Pat Robertson. Pat used the station to broadcast his 700 Club program. He went on to create other Christian-based content, and launch The Family Channel on cable, which he eventually sold for over $1 billion. Pat's son Tim Robertson deserves a lot of the credit for creating the value of the Family Channel and taking it public before its eventual sale. And Tim Robertson would one day play a role in the future of our company.

Channel 27 broadcast a few older family-oriented sitcoms in the evening, which was helping attract some viewers to the UHF band. So, now there would be two stations trying to convince people to add an Ultra High Frequency (UHF) antenna to their TV set.

• • •

By the time we were ready to start making Channel 33 a reality, our Television Corporation of Virginia ownership group had fourteen members. Each of us signed a personal guarantee to pay back any money we borrowed, based on the percentage of ownership. We already had $1 million in equipment financing lined up from Philips without personal endorsements. So, we borrowed another million to handle the rest.

We received a construction permit from the FCC in early 1979. We were ready to get the transmitter site construction underway but still needed a place in Norfolk for our studios and offices. We wanted the person we hired to run Channel 33 to have a say in the office location. Television Corporation President Joel Cooper's magazine editor, Paul Katabian, suggested John Trinder, local sales manager at WTAR-TV, Channel 3, for the job. The CBS affiliate was the highest-rated and most prestigious station in the market at that time. I knew John from business and professional meetings, and had seen him when I visited Dick Lamb at WTAR.

John Trinder had a terrific job and local sales staff. Advertising poured in to WTAR. To entice John we would have to offer him comparable pay, a company car and, mostly importantly, an equity stake in Channel 33. John thought it over for a few days and accepted our offer. He agreed to resign from Channel 3 about six months before the WTVZ launch. John's bosses at WTAR thought he was nuts and wrongfully predicted he would come begging for his old job back.

Our ownership group had expected me to be involved in the operation of Channel 33, taking care of the programming and doing the same kinds of things I did in radio. One problem; I didn't know anything about buying movies and syndicated old network TV shows, which we needed 24/7. John had not done this at WTAR either. Unlike radio, television eats content. You can only broadcast a program so many times before the public has seen it enough, or the rights to air it expire. No one in Norfolk had ever bought programming for a purely independent station. So I wasn't sure who to turn to for help and advice.

As soon as news got out that a new station was going on the air, film companies started calling us. I asked a few of their salespeople to name someone they thought was the best programmer in independent TV. We got a couple of names, contacted them and arranged for them to fly in to be interviewed by John Trinder, Joel Cooper and me.

We liked Tim McDonald best: he was at MetroMedia at Channel 5 in Washington. He had worked for MetroMedia off and on for a few years, including in New York City at WNEW as promotion manager before going into programming. Tim agreed to join us, but only if he was president of our new enterprise, had a 2 percent ownership position, and other CEO-style benefits. John Trinder and the rest of us agreed to his terms.

With key players in place we started shopping for locations, settling on the old Rice's department store on Granby Street, downtown Norfolk's main street. Construction started immediately, and Tim and John began interviewing prospective employees and crafting a promotion campaign. Tim also scouted up content, buying movies and thirty-minute sitcoms. Their office during those start-up months was a glass conference table in our radio station's conference room on Newtown Road. My job morphed into protecting our investors' interests mostly by making sure we stayed within our planned budget.

Two big WTAR-TV on-air personalities ended up becoming part of our first year launch. Dick Lamb agreed to do a weekly interview show as part of our public service FCC requirements, allowing us to run promos throughout the week saying "watch Dick Lamb's show on Channel 33." By then Dick had left Channel 3 to join Larry Saunders in a new radio company, buying WVEC-AM and FM, and renaming it 2WD. The other most unlikely local TV star who had been on WTAR-TV for decades, Jeff Dane, did a weekly fishing show and had other duties. He had a falling-out with Channel 3 managers and had decided to retire. Jeff had bought a house on the Albemarle Sound in Currituck County, N.C. and wanted to just hang out there rather than keep up the daily grind in Norfolk. Tim, John and I drove down there and pitched Jeff on signing with us to continue the fishing show. He agreed, so we were able to promote Jeff, too, giving the impression everyone was coming over to WTVZ-TV.

. . .

During the summer of 1979, while Tim and John were getting everything ready for the big WTVZ-TV sign-on, I took a call from our FCC lawyer Bill Barnard who pointed out to me he was starting to see activity in the UHF band in a lot of medium-sized markets. If we wanted other UHF stations, we had better hurry up and apply, he advised. I acted quickly, calling a meeting of the Television Corporation of Virginia owners. I lobbied hard for us to look beyond Virginia for opportunities to either obtain a UHF license or buy a struggling independent station at a deep discount. Everyone agreed, and each partner anted $500 to cover legal costs. That was the first cash any of us had ever put into our TV business.

Tim, John and I studied a book on TV stations for every US market. We selected Nashville, Tennesse., Little Rock, Arkansas., Jackson, Mississippi, Austin, Texas, and Buffalo, New York. Next, we looked for existing UHF stations struggling financially or owned by people not in the commercial TV business. We found one in Winston-Salem, N.C.

Around the time we were shopping for other UHF station opportunities, WTVZ-TV went live. It was September 1979. Norman Lear came in for our client sign-on party at the Omni Hotel. We had secured the rights to a couple of Norman's sitcoms, so he flew in to help us kick off the station. The night after the party was his birthday, so he stayed in town to join us for a dinner at Ship's Cabin where I made a birthday toast. The entire sign-on week felt as big as any music event we had promoted.

One of the shows we bought from Norman Lear was his hit program *Sanford and Son* starring Redd Foxx. The sitcom had never aired in the Norfolk market, off Network. Response was so strong we aired back-to-back episodes during the 7-8PM period. Building audience took time because most viewers did not know how to receive UHF TV stations. They had never hooked up the additional receiving antenna they needed because there just wasn't anything on the UHF dial they wanted to watch. We started giving away small hoop-shaped antennas at 7-Eleven stores, with instructions about how to activate UHF. We basically needed to teach viewers how to find us.

One huge break that jumpstarted UHF viewing was an FCC ruling implemented just months before we started broadcasting. The FCC decided that all television sets manufactured from that point on had to have a single tuning knob for both VHF channels 2 through 13 and UHF channels 14 through 60. Suddenly, one turn of the TV knob landed viewers on UHF stations. That put UHF on the map.

• • •

Dudley Simms and his twin brother, John, had built a substantial business called Piece Goods Shops that sold knitting and sewing supplies all over the US. The company was headquartered in Winston-Salem, N.C. The brothers decided to give back to the community by activating a UHF television station that broadcast religious programming, similar to what Pat Robertson had done in Portsmouth, Virginia. But they didn't have a quality show like Pat's *700 Club* to anchor the channel, and an even bigger problem was that they went on the air themselves, doing commentaries about how they saw life and local issues, alienating a lot of viewers with their strident style.

The Simms brothers had lost about $1 million operating their station, and had invested another million dollars in their UHF facilities, and could not see profits anytime in the near future. They invited us to Winston-Salem to see the station and talk further. The first thing we learned was they had a very poor location for their antenna on top of a downtown bank building and the signal fell short of much of their market. We would have to get clearance to move the transmission facility if we were to buy Channel 45.

The Simms gave us a tour of their Piece Goods facility and TV studio. There was one very attractive young woman with a personality-plus attitude who served as the station's sales assistant and public relations director. I could see why she handled public relations. Her name was Angela Jordan. As I flew back to Virginia I thought, *If Angela comes with the station, let's buy it tonight.*

One big problem was that we had big eyes and small wallets. Our co-owners had put up some money for legal research to apply for UHF stations in a few markets, but we had not secured funds to buy a station. First things first. Before taking the proposal to the investors, I needed to find out about the cost of moving the transmission antenna. Jim Seaman, our chief engineer, found a spot on a mountain near a state park. There was no road access, and it took us an hour and a half out of Winston to get to the location. The landowners agreed to give us an option to buy if we secured the deal with the Simms brothers. The next question— how much would we have to pay the Simms for their broadcast license? Five million, they said.

I spoke to my longtime partner Dick Davis about raising a few million dollars. His response, "Good luck." He wanted to see a much lower number before we went any further. I met with the brothers again and they asked for $3 million; I offered two and returned to Norfolk without a deal. The next day they called and accepted our offer. I figured it would take about six months or so to clear FCC hurdles, which would give me time to raise the cash. After adding in the cost of building a transmission tower and other operational expenses, our initial investment would be about $3.5 million.

I called our owners together for a meeting to discuss the plan and expense. Two of the owners were having financial stresses so they offered to withdraw from the company if they were released from all TV debt obligations. This left a new 20 percent ownership position available. Others in the group seemed intrigued, so I met with a bank president to discuss a $2 million loan to be secured by the assets of Channel 45. The bank agreed if personal guarantees would stand behind the debt. Five in our ownership group agreed to a personal endorsement. In exchange, those five members received larger ownership interest in both the Virginia Television Corp. and the new North Carolina company. Philips Credit loaned $1.5 million against the new tower and transmitter. Bottom line: we would be able to borrow the full amount.

CHAPTER 15

RERUNS

B y the end of 1980, word was out via the national trade papers that we were acquiring a second TV station to serve the North Carolina Tri-Ad market of Greensboro, Winston-Salem and High Point. Companies selling shows to TV stations flocked to make us a client. Until now, 90 percent of the old network TV shows and popular old movies had not been available in smaller TV markets like Norfolk and Greensboro because there were no independent TV stations to air them, or limited time on stations focused on a Christian message. Local stations affiliated with ABC, CBS and NBC didn't have room for many reruns because most of their programing was new material from the national network; plus, they needed to use key time slots for local news and the popular game shows like *Wheel of Fortune*.

To make buying network reruns and old movies affordable, we traded advertising. Here's how it worked: In an hour, eight minutes were available to sell commercially. So, the syndication company providing us with content used four minutes for their national client and we sold the other four minutes to local advertisers. This arrangement meant we did not have to pay cash for the show itself. But some of the very best shows were not available via barter.

Top thirty-minute sitcoms (situation comedies) like *Good Times* would air between 6 and 8 p.m., so-called prime access. The asking price for a show of that caliber was $2,000 per half-hour. We kept the price reasonable by negotiating deals that spanned two or three years, allowing us to run each episode multiple times. One of the amazing testaments to the popularity of these shows was their staying power. Common sense suggested—at the time—that viewers would grow tired of watching the same reruns after a couple seasons. Instead, we found that the ratings for these shows held steady. Viewers would watch each episode four or five times—sometimes more. *I Love Lucy* is still playing today, as are many of the most popular sitcoms from the 1950s and 1960s: *The Andy Griffith Show, Bonanza, Gunsmoke, Leave it to Beaver, The Beverly Hillbillies.* Additionally, by the time the 1980s rolled in there was an eruption of made-for-independent-TV programming for new stations like ours.

One way we preserved ratings for these old shows was to change the time of the day they aired. We might initially offer a rerun at 7 p.m., but then show it next year at 11 p.m. when there would be a different audience tuning in.

It truly was a build-it-and-they-will-come scenario. Viewers were nostalgic and hungry for these old shows, and for alternatives to what the three major networks were offering.

We also discovered a niche with early morning and mid-afternoon kids' cartoons. Toy advertisers loved this programming and quickly became big supporters of independent TV stations. Kids' programming was a springboard for an entire industry of toymakers and toy stores who could now reach tiny tots directly by advertising on daily cartoons. Before independent TV, most kids' programming was limited to Saturday mornings. The biggest kid show, *Sesame Street,* aired on the nonprofit PBS network, which did not sell advertising.

Our market analytics all pointed in the same direction. We had affordable content that was in high demand by an underserved audience. We couldn't wait to launch in North Carolina.

• • •

The deal with the Simms brothers hit a few more snags, requiring me to make a few more trips to Winston-Salem. The Simmses had created a lot of issues because of their political screeds. As part of our purchase agreement, they pledged to stop airing their editorials during the FCC review period. We didn't want the Simmses to provoke viewer protests or boycotts, which could scare away advertisers and increase scrutiny from regulators.

The Simms twins ignored our agreement. Not only did they go back on the air with their extremely conservative and strident political views, but they also put up billboards to draw attention to their commentaries. The local newspaper went crazy with editorials and letters to the editor. The brothers were also supposed to maintain existing staff and programming, which was costing them about $100,000 a month in losses.

I met with the Simmses in Dudley's office. I had decided to be direct. I told them that they had violated our agreement, that the station remained too controversial, and that we wanted our deposit back. They were stunned. The brothers were not used to being challenged. We knew from interviewing station personnel that the Simmses were unpredictable, and they believed some of their employees were trying to undermine them.

I remained resolute, telling the brothers that we were withdrawing our FCC application, ending our contract with them and that our lawyer would be in touch. As I stood to leave, they looked panicked and asked me to wait while they spoke in private. While waiting, Angela Jordan, the woman who attracted my attention on our first visit, saw me sitting alone. She came in to shake my hand and say how much she was looking forward to working for us. About that time the Simmses came back and Angela left.

The Simmses were contrite, asking me what I needed to preserve the deal. I said I had not come to negotiate, and before any new agreement could be reached I would have to discuss terms with my partners in Norfolk. I excused myself and called John and Tim to tell them what was happening and ask their advice. We decided that if the Simmses reduced the price by $100,000 to cover the cost of additional advertising for our launch, then we would go forward. We also wanted all editorials to stop and all billboards supporting their views taken down. The brothers agreed, I left. The lawyers adjusted the contract.

As soon as I was gone the Simmses brought Angela back into their office and questioned her about her conversation with me. She told the truth; she merely stopped in to say hello. The brothers didn't believe Angela, suspecting she was a spy. John Simms called Channel 45's sales manager Leo Derek and told him to fire Angela. The sales manager talked Simms out of being punitive on the basis that the purchase agreement said there could be no staff changes until the closing.

Despite the drama, the sale went through in mid-1981. Several of us from Norfolk drove to Winston to move the TV station's equipment and furnishings to another building. Angela wasted no time getting the word out that Channel 45 had new owners. She arranged a newspaper interview for John, Tim and me at the Omni Hotel in downtown Winston, and she met us there to introduce us to the reporter. All three of us liked Angela and invited her to stay for dinner after the interview, but she had to go to a church meeting. I was extremely disappointed. The good news: now that the station was ours I knew I would see Angela again—soon.

• • •

After taking over WJTM-TV Channel 45 in North Carolina, we started regular monthly visits to the station, especially during the reconstruction and relocation of the transmitter and antenna facility from downtown Winston to a mountain overlooking the Tri-Ad market. Around March 1981 the station's public relations person, Angela, invited me to lunch. I had done a little research on her and was going to ask her out, but hesitated when I heard she was leaving the next weekend on a cruise with her boyfriend. *Ouch!*

I was impressed that she selected "Bob's" for lunch as it showed she was a real down-home girl. She ordered a peanut butter sandwich and I had a hot dog. I found myself opening up to her, discussing my failed marriage and the death of my daughter, which I hadn't talked about for a year. I normally didn't like to talk about personal issues. I was so comfortable with her from the start. The discussion seemed so natural because she was such a good listener. I said that if she ever came to Virginia

Beach I would love to take her to dinner. A few weeks later she called to say she and her brother and his wife were coming to Norfolk for a convention and asked for a hotel recommendation. I took her to dinner, breakfast and another dinner. Actually, our first "date" was a milkshake at Wendy's right after they had checked in around 11 p.m. I learned that she was not serious about the guy who was her cruise companion. He was in the used car business, and I dubbed him "Hub Caps" for future reference.

The next time I was in Winston for a Channel 45 visit we went to dinner and then held hands walking the campus of Wake Forest College. I couldn't stop thinking about Angie, so a couple of weeks later I sent her an airplane ticket to come visit me in Virginia Beach. Later we went to New York for a very memorable weekend. I asked her to resign at Channel 45 and move to the Beach. She took an apartment in Birdneck Village and became what most know as a "Kelly Girl," working for various businesses while key employees are on vacation. One of those jobs was for Dr. Bill Magee at his surgery center just as Bill and his wife, Kathy, were founding Operation Smile. Later, Angie and I were to become very involved in that international mission. She also continued her modeling career, signing with Barbara Lewis at Charm Associates.

Angie
Loving

Pictures from
Angie's modeling
portfolio. 1982

My first impression of Angie turned out to be well founded. She had accomplished a lot at an early age, qualifying her for the PR job in TV. She modeled for several national magazines while still in high school, had competed in the Miss North Carolina pageant after winning Miss Thomasville, and to pay her living expenses held three jobs at once, including legal secretary for the most prominent attorneys in Greensboro, Cahoon and Swisher, a cashier at a local cafeteria style restaurant, and a make up artist at a department store.

By June I asked Angie to marry me. She said she would think about it. It was going to be, and was, a wild summer. On November 18, she organized a surprise 40th birthday party for me. After everyone left, including her parents, Ernestine and William Jordan who had driven up from North Carolina, Angie said yes, let's get married, which we did at city hall the next weekend—without telling anyone. But we told her family and our friends we were engaged, with a North Carolina wedding set for April 1982. Several of my associates chartered a bus to bring my friends to Thomasville, North Carolina, Angie's hometown, for the wedding. My partner, Dick Davis, who was by then the Lieutenant Governor of Virginia, and his wife, Martha, filled in for my parents who were not up to that kind of trip. Once the Virginia group found out we were not serving alcohol at the church community center at the reception, they decided to party on the bus heading back home, while our other guests enjoyed our full-service every-flavor ice cream bar from Mayberry's.

We left for a two-week honeymoon in California and Hawaii, returning to live at Cove Point in Virginia Beach where our condo had a boat slip for my twenty-seven-foot Chris Craft speedboat. It took about year or so to convince Angie that my boating skills were sufficient for outings on the Chesapeake Bay. She went with me every time but hung on like a leech to Humphrey Bogart in the *The African Queen.*

• • •

Buying Channel 45 had proven fortuitous for me, both personally and financially. Word quickly spread of our efforts to convert a UHF station from religious programming to a viable commercial independent. Among those taking notice was

Chuck McFadden, who sold TV programming and movies for Paramount Pictures on the East Coast. Chuck had been in every kind of job in TV since the 1950s, and he saw the potential for UHF and independent TV.

In those days, our radio station WQRK-FM had an advertising trade deal with the Sheraton Hotel on Atlantic Avenue in Virginia Beach. We used the Sheraton for client parties, taking advertisers or agency reps to dinner, and for impressing job candidates. We invited Chuck McFadden to interview for general manager of our renamed WJTM-TV, Channel 45 in Greensboro, and made sure Chuck had a nice room at the Sheraton. WTJM's new call letters stood for John Trinder and Tim McDonald. John, Tim and I agreed Chuck was a great fit for our North Carolina venture. And we were right. Chuck became part of our company and in 1999 formed his own, bringing us in as partners. That relationship lasted thirty years until Chuck died. An oil painting of Chuck with his golden retriever hangs in our company headquarters conference room. Chuck's daughter Kimberly Guadagno was elected to a second term as Lieutenant Governor of New Jersey in November of 2013.

• • •

Not long after we closed the North Carolina deal, my phone rang. It was Harvey Hudson. "Gene, we got the license for Channel 35 in Richmond, and Morton Thalhimer is having second thoughts about investing the money to build the station. There may be a chance for our Norfolk group to do a partnership with Morton; please come to Richmond to talk to him."

I wasted no time taking up Harvey on his invitation. I went to Richmond to meet with Morton, Harvey, and the longtime radio engineer I knew from my days at WLEE, Tom Kita. Morton was aware that we were losing money at WTVZ-TV in Norfolk, more than what we had originally projected, and he was afraid that Richmond, a smaller TV market than Norfolk, would be a real financial challenge for a startup UHF station. Also, no one in his organization, which included a real estate company, movie theaters and radio stations, had enough experience to start a TV station, so he would have to hire everyone. I let him know we would like to be his partner. He agreed we could come back with more information. A couple of weeks later, John Trinder, Tim McDonald, Jim Seaman and I met with Morton, who was accompanied by a TV consultant. We were astounded when the advisor said UHF just didn't work well and would never be competitive with the network stations. The guy also said that the coverage area projected for Channel 35 in Richmond was overstated. Harvey and his radio engineer sat silent; they didn't want to argue with their boss. My group spoke up, however. "Come to Norfolk, take the original FCC predicted coverage map, drive to the edge of the signal and turn on a TV set and you will see it works just like it's supposed to. We have been on the air for over a year and can prove the audience is growing by simply looking at the ratings."

Shockingly, Morton declined our invitation. Instead, he offered to sell us the license for Channel 35 for what he had invested to date—about $90,000. We agreed, suggesting we pay him 90 percent of the money and he keep 10 percent of the ownership. But Morton didn't even want to do that. He seemed convinced UHF TV was a loser. So Harvey pounced on the opportunity, offering to buy the 10 percent stake we had offered Morton.

We called our contacts at Philips Credit Corp. to say we wanted to buy another complete package of equipment, but this time we needed about $2 million in credit; half would be to build a one-thousand-foot broadcasting tower in Midlothian, just outside of Richmond. Philips agreed. We borrowed another million from the Bank of Virginia in Richmond to cover start-up losses. Again, several of us from the original Norfolk group received a slightly larger slice of equity in the Television Corporation of Richmond for our personal guarantees on the bank loan. We were on the way to our third independent TV station.

Less than three years later we sold our Richmond TV station to the owners of *The Baltimore Sun* newspaper for $14 million. I called Morton Thalhimer to tell him so he wouldn't have a heart attack when reading about the sale in the newspaper. The station was named WRLH, for *R*ichmond, *L*oving, *H*udson, and it still has the same call letters today.

• • •

I was starting to spend most of my time on the TV company. So, around 1982, I appointed Paul Lucci as general manager of our two radio stations. One of Paul's key hires was a new salesperson, Linda Cochran. Within a year she transferred to sales at WTVZ-TV. Linda went on to manage our Raleigh, N.C. TV station, our Syracuse, N.Y. TV station, got married, and later managed all four of our Montana TV stations. Thirty-five years later, Linda Cochran Gray is running our NBC and CBS stations in Bowling Green, KY, and she looks exactly the same.

I was on the road two or three days a week related to TV, so it was time for a transition. I needed to spend more time on doing deals and building a TV company, which meant dialing back on my other efforts.

Dick Lamb and I were still promoting concerts through AGL productions, but we didn't have the same deep connections with up-and-comers. By the 1980s, progressive and hard rock had taken hold and we didn't have much experience with those newer genres.

Some local promoters started booking bands into clubs, hoping they would eventually build enough of a fan base to merit concerts at Norfolk's Scope or the Hampton Coliseum. Among them was Bill Douthat who formed Whisper Concerts. Bill, and Cathy Moore who focused on local bands, had a good eye for talent. But they didn't have enough money to back the big shows. Bill learned what I had learned many years earlier—you can easily lose money producing concerts, and some promoters lost major money. Fortunately, AGL Productions had more winners than losers every year.

Recognizing what we knew—and what we didn't—Dick and I shifted into silent partnerships for some of the top album acts Whisper wanted to promote. Douthat decided to book the album acts not only for Norfolk, but Richmond and Roanoke as well. He opened offices in the Golden Triangle Hotel. Bill asked to meet with me to talk about a partnership. AGL agreed to invest in Whisper, and my Television Corporation partner Joel Cooper wanted in, too. Joel and his family had been associated with entertainment for decades with ownership of the Ocean View Amusement Park, and Joel's dad, Dudley, was one of the wealthiest men in the area.

Over the next few years, more and more of the shows were

promoted under the Whisper logo as Bill focused full time on securing talent. AGL continued to do events separately, but mostly with the traditional stars. Many of the biggest name acts were signing contracts with a single promotion company for all their dates, thus squeezing out local promoters such as AGL. So without the best shows to offset the ones that did not make money, we concluded that it was almost time to exit the concert hamster wheel.

AGL began to add other forms of entertainment and sports to our production business during the 1980s. Professional tennis was especially popular as the game's elite players had real celebrity status. We even landed the biggest name in sports, perhaps of all time.

We brought Muhammad Ali to the Hampton Coliseum for an exhibition match shortly after he ended his professional career. He showed up unceremoniously wearing a business suit. I was in the star's dressing room when Ali arrived. When we met he asked me to sit; he seemed serious and said he needed to talk about something. We sat on sofas at a coffee table. I was expecting him to ask about something related to the match, or interview requests from the dozens of reporters waiting outside.

"I'm having problems with my Rolls Royce," Ali said. He had driven his car to the Coliseum. Somewhat surprised at the subject, I told him the closest Rolls dealer was Moors Motor Cars in Richmond. Then amazingly, he started to describe to me what the car was doing and asked what I thought it was. I gave some vague answer. He wanted to know how long it would take him to drive to Richmond. No chauffeur. The Champ had come to Hampton—alone. He apparently liked traveling by himself.

We chatted about cars for a good hour, past the time I thought he would be getting ready for the fight. About fifteen minutes before he was due in the ring, a guy came in saying, "Come on Champ, let's get you ready." Ali excused himself and shortly afterward came out of a dressing area wearing trunks and gloves. I assume his associate had wrapped his hands. After the match, which lasted all twelve rounds, Ali came back to the star's dressing room, showered and came out wearing the same suit and tie like he was going to a board meeting. He had me draw a map to the Rolls dealer in Richmond, shook my hand, and left.

CHAPTER 16

TVX BROADCAST GROUP

B etween radio and TV our senior people and sales managers were traveling to New York City weekly. Many of our national advertising clients had offices there, and in the early '80s taking an advertising-time buyer to lunch and pitching a specific promotion on a local broadcast station could get you some business. Jim Lowe, our head radio salesman, was also doing some TV sales and had arranged a deal with a hotel that is now a Marriott at the corner of Lexington at 49th Street. Biff Halloran, whose giant oil portrait hung in the lobby, owned the hotel. Whenever we were there we got the best available room, which most times meant a suite. One of my regular stops was Philips Credit Corp. on 42nd Street across from Grand Central Station where I visited with Gene Shaw, our contact for the TV equipment financing. During one of my early visits I was introduced to Walter Corcoran, president of Philips Credit. Walter was an attorney and had served as Philips' in-house counsel for several years before being promoted to head the company. I also met the very tough Philips lawyer

Beth Walman who negotiated with our lawyers for our station equipment loans. Walter and Beth became people I spoke to almost weekly as we built our TV company.

In addition to visits to the Philips offices, Gene Shaw and Walter Corcoran often invited me for a drink at about 6 p.m. at Trumpetts, which was the restaurant in the Hyatt Hotel next to Grand Central. The restaurant was named for the hotel owner, Donald Trump. Sometimes we had dinner before they both took the train to their homes in Greenwich, Connecticut. My relationship with Walter has spanned thirty-five years. Angie and I often joined Walter and his family at Big Moose Lake in the Adirondacks during their annual vacation to hike the mountains and build some great memories. We attended his daughter's wedding there in 2016. In later years, after his retirement from Philips, Walter was a US business representative in Ireland. Philips Credit had financed most of the cable systems built in Ireland and Walter was on the board of several, traveling there all the time prior to leaving Philips. I spent a week with Walter in 2003 driving all over Ireland meeting with his many local friends, staying at those places you see in the travel magazines.

Each fall a major music event and dinner was held at the Caramoor Estate in Greenwich, Connecticut. For years, Philips bought tables and invited clients to attend, which included hotel accommodations at the Ritz Carlton and limos for the weekend. One of Walter Corcoran's favorite stories, which he told at his daughter's 2016 wedding, was about the night six of us were being driven back to the hotel around midnight. The driver, in the pre-GPS days, got so lost we rambled on country roads for over an hour. Finally, when the driver tried to enter an expressway via the exit ramp, I made him turn the limo over to me. I did not put on the driver's hat.

There were enough of our broadcast executives going to New York weekly that we decided to rent a limo to take us into the city each time and remain with us as we made our rounds. We liked one particular driver, Michael Smith, so we always requested him. I was taking a lot of personal trips to NYC too, so my limo bill was getting pretty outlandish. After a couple of years I decided to buy a Lincoln limo and let Michael rent it out to clients when we weren't using it. That covered Michael's salary and all basic operating costs, an arrangement that lasted five years. During that time Jim Lowe did a trade deal with the Waldorf Astoria for their best available rooms. We were going up so often the gate staff at Piedmont airline got to know us, making sure we received preferred seating. We had it pretty good in the early '80s—a top shelf hotel, limo service around town and dinner at swanky restaurants and bars entertaining ad agency clients.

• • •

Success came quickly for our UHF stations, and we had brokers calling every week with new opportunities. But we knew we could no longer borrow from banks based on our personal guarantees, as we had reached our personal financial capacity.

One of our original investors was William A. Allaun, an attorney and businessman from Newport News. Bill had been in business for a long time and knew a lot of people all over the country. He connected us with a Baltimore firm that helped companies raise capital. That company was Legg Mason, and they got Tim McDonnell, John Trinder and me to develop some projections based on our experience in Norfolk and Greensboro. We created a "road show" presentation which we took to help us persuade venture capital firms to invest in us. A few expressed interest, and two seemed very interested at about the same time—Citicorp and First Chicago.

Looking back, the dollar figure seems small, but then it was pretty big: we were trying to raise $6 million. Before they would invest in us, the capital firms expected us to refinance all of our bank loans, thus eliminating any personal risks we had assumed. Our new bank loan would also have additional money available for each new station we added in the future. Philips Credit would continue to have their equipment loans, plus make more loans for future stations. Consolidating and restructuring our debt, and having a source to finance new acquisitions, would make us a much stronger company with the resources to grow, even though the new venture capital investors would dilute our collective ownership by 49 percent. We arrived at a basic deal with both venture companies, and then Tim and I, along with our lawyer, Tom Frantz, spent several days in Chicago negotiating final terms of the deal. John Canning, who headed First Chicago Venture Capital, took us to dinner a couple of times, and he attended a few of our company board meetings at Joe Hoggard's Ships Cabin restaurant in Ocean View. John Canning later became the principal owner of the Tidewater Tides minor league baseball team in Norfolk.

Meeting with bankers and potential investors, and ferreting out new acquisitions, took all of my time. This was precisely why I had delegated day-to-day operations at the radio stations to others, and it felt like a long way from my days playing dedications on WLLY in Richmond.

Although my heart had been in radio for two decades, I realized it was time to sell WQRK and WTID-AM so I could focus entirely on building a TV company. Once the stations were sold, I would become chairman of a combined TV board. The Davis family and I wound up selling the radio stations to the same group in Baltimore that would later buy our TV station in Richmond for $14 million—the A. S. Abell Co., owners of the *Baltimore Sun*. The sale enabled Angie and me to build a house in the Alanton section of Virginia Beach on Linkhorn Bay. Our designer, Gene Roebuck, won the top award for our house design, beating out a home built by Barbara Streisand. We moved in the winter of 1985. We had a beach and a pier with water deep enough to park my thirty-two foot Searay Pachanga.

• • •

By the mid-1980s, John, Tim and I used to joke about buying a company jet because we were flying around so much. We argued about who would pick the interior colors. At the time, the appropriate color would have been red, as in "red ink."

The reality was that we couldn't afford to buy a plane, or afford any extravagance because cash was tight. Just as we had projected, our new TV stations were eating the profits of our established properties. But we were optimistic that our newly acquired investments would quickly move from red to black on the ledger sheet. In fact, in the future, we finally were able to buy a corporate jet and I picked the colors.

Despite our cash flow crunch, we remained on the hunt to expand our UHF holdings.

On the tarmac in St. Kitts, in the Caribbean, (L-R:) Bill Barnard, Steve Burke, Al Rider, Dick Foreman, and John Trinder in front of the MAX jet (I took the picture) celebrating the sale of the original MAX Media to Sinclair Broadcast Group.

• • •

I could easily write a chapter or two about each of the additional nine television stations that we developed and added to the company that ultimately became TVX Broadcast Group. If I did that, the book would be 500 pages so I'll pick a couple of markets to highlight.

By the end of 1983, Citicorp Venture Capital and First Chicago Venture Capital had each invested $3 million in our existing TV stations—Norfolk, Greensboro and Richmond. We used those funds to continue buying or building new markets. We obtained licenses for independent stations in Little Rock, Buffalo, and Nashville. We bought troubled Channel 49, WNOL-TV in New Orleans, and a station in Raleigh. We partnered with someone to build a new TV station in San Antonio. We also partnered with locals in Memphis who had just obtained the license for Channel 30.

To build our portfolio, we had to involve local leaders in the start-from-scratch stations, and we had some interesting partners owning up to 20 percent combined in each market where an original license was issued. We applied for a license to build a TV station in Austin, Texas and Jackson, Mississippi, where I spent considerable time evaluating community needs by visiting with dozens of public and private institutions and governmental authorities. Among our investors in Austin was former Congressman Joe Kilgore, and the wife of the head of the Texas Rangers. Two other groups also applied for the license. We backed out after one of the competing groups offered us a ten-year consultancy to let them get the permit for Austin. We also stepped away from Jackson, Mississippi once we determined we were unlikely to win the final round.

Among our partners in Nashville were Ammon Carter Evans, publisher of *The Tennessean* newspaper, and Nashville Mayor Richard Fulton, who had served several terms in Congress. We rented a building from entertainer Charlie Pride to use for our studios and offices.

I recall sitting in Mayor Fulton's office when the phone rang and he told me he had to take the call. I overheard a very personal conversation. Fulton was speaking to Mae Axton, best known for writing *Heartbreak Hotel* for Elvis. Mae was a force in the city's country music scene. I did not have the nerve to tell Mayor Fulton, who obviously thought highly of Mae, that I had once threatened her son Hoyt when he showed up in the late '60s as an opening act for *Three Dog Night* at the Virginia Beach Dome. I had never heard of Hoyt Axton, and by the end of the first show I knew why. Mae's son was one of the most foul-mouthed people I had ever met. Even the lyrics of the songs were offensive. I went straight to the Dogs and told them if Hoyt said one four-letter word on stage or didn't change his song content in the next show, I would have the Virginia Beach police physically remove him from the stage. Hoyt acquiesced and cleaned up his performance for the second show, as he saw me and the cops standing in the wings.

We had reserved the call letters WCAY-TV for a station we were trying to buy in Miami. (Cay and Key are island names.) When the Miami deal fell through, we used the letters for the Nashville station.

Our next opportunity to grow also came in Tennessee. We read that a local investment group in Memphis had just gotten a permit to build Channel 35. That cadre included Ed Taylor who was an early pioneer in satellite TV. Ed had suggested that Ted Turner put WTBS on Ed's satellite. Doing so made Ted's local

Atlanta station into one of the first superstations with nationwide distribution.

Ed Taylor was a partner in the Memphis license group along with Dr. George "Sonny" Flinn, who had played a major role in developing ultrasound scans for expecting mothers. He received a royalty from every ultrasound machine sold. Radio and TV investing were a hobby for him. Another partner in the Memphis group was Kemmons Wilson, founder of the Holiday Inn chain and the guy credited with inventing the franchise business.

One of our Virginia partners, Bill Allaun, had met Kemmons years earlier when he visited Newport News looking at property for a Holiday Inn. Kemmons Wilson and his sons built and owned four hundred Holiday Inns before they took the company public. Bill called Kemmons and asked if he would meet with us about Channel 35.

John Trinder, Tim McDonald, Bill Allaun and I flew to Memphis expecting to take a cab to Kemmons' office, but when we got off the plane he was standing right there. We crowded into Kemmons' Cadillac and he drove us to his office, which was not too far from the airport. Kemmons was one of the nicest, classiest guys I had ever met. He was beyond humble, considering the company he had built and his financial position. Most guys like him had assistants doing everything.

Kemmons admitted that he knew nothing about TV and was considering what to do with the Memphis broadcasting permit he had obtained. We proposed being equal partners, each putting up half the money to build the station with our group having the operating contract. He agreed. Next, with our flight not due out until that night, he had sandwiches brought in as we asked him a lot about the formative years of Holiday Inn and his history in Memphis. He was surprisingly candid about family details, the design of the Holiday Inn sign—everything.

After lunch, Kemmons asked if we would like a quick tour of Memphis, which we accepted, and he drove us around. He asked if there was anything we would especially like to see, and I said St. Jude's Children's Hospital and Graceland, home of "the King." He agreed, and on the way over he told us his Elvis story.

Kemmons was a friend of Sam Phillips, who owned Sun Records, and had loaned Sam money from time to time. He says one night Sam called. "Kemmons, I just had an offer from RCA to buy my new artist Elvis's contract for $25,000. What should I do?" Kemmons told Sam to take it. After that, Sam stopped calling Kemmons for advice; Elvis became a sensation worth millions.

Over the years, anytime I met someone for business in Memphis. they wanted me to show them Graceland. I visited so often I think I could recite what the tour guide says.

We grew to like and respect Kemmons, who agreed to be a director on our board after we took the TV company public. It was a big honor for us to have him, as he turned down dozens of similar invitations since leaving Holiday Inns. He left after having a fight with his board about putting a casino in a Holiday Inn in Vegas. He came to Norfolk several times for our meetings, and I would go to Memphis to see him. Once he walked me down Beale Street in Memphis, stopping at an old theater to explain how he started out there as kid selling popcorn.

Eventually we held one of our board meetings at Kemmons' time-share property at Orange Lake next to Disney World. At the same meeting, Angie and I had dinner with Christie Whitman, together with our board member and her husband, John, who worked for CitiCorp. I had been to the Whitman farm in New Jersey a couple of times and supported her when she first ran for county commissioner. She went on to become governor of New Jersey and then head of the EPA in the Bush administration.

• • •

By early 1985, we had built or acquired more new independent TV stations than any other broadcaster. We had invested aggressively, had spent the $6 million we received from Citicorp and First Chicago, and still needed to raise additional equity to keep expanding. So, we turned to the public market.

Virginia Investment Corporation in Norfolk partnered with Salomon Brothers in New York to take us public. By then we had changed our name to TVX Broadcast Group and we hit the road telling our story. John, Tim and I toured dozens of the principal money-center cities across the country on what is called a "road show" arranged and managed by Salomon Brothers. It was an exciting and educational experience, involving big-name financial institutions and insurance companies that buy stock when it is first issued for sale to the public. It's called an Initial Public Offering, or IPO.

We were doing breakfast meetings in San Francisco, lunch meetings in LA and dinner meetings in San Diego. We repeated that routine throughout the country. Limos met us at each airport, taking us to the finest private clubs for first-class events where we seldom got to eat the excellent food being served to our audience.

Prior to all of this, we had spent a solid couple of months helping the lawyers gather information on our stations, their markets, and the TV industry in general. These were the lawyers who were experienced in taking companies public and dealing with SEC requirements. Many of these legal sessions were all-nighters in New York and Washington. Fred Stant, of the Virginia Beach firm Clark and Stant, wrote much of the prospectus about TVX and our future. Three lawyers from the firm, now known as Williams Mullen, also worked very hard on the documents—Tom Frantz, Steve Burke and Tom Snyder. We were on the Salomon Brothers' trading floor standing with the firm's CEO, John Gutfreund, when the bell rang and trading started. Our IPO sold out and we had the capital we needed to continue building TVX.

The TVX Broadcast Group Board of Directors
(L-R:) Richard Davis, John Trinder, John Whitman, me,
Bill Allaun, Tim McDonald, Paul Finnigan, Kemmons Wilson. 1987

John Trinder, president, and me, chairman of TVX Broadcast Group in the
Presidential Suite, Excelsior Hotel, Rome, Italy, client trip. 1989

Angie and I chat with the wife of the ambassador
to the Vatican during a TVX client trip to Italy.

Me with comedian, TV and film star Martin Lawrence, and local Norfolk boy who made good in Hollywood, Dick Robertson, president of Warner Brothers Television.

Richard J. Davis (center), my business mentor, mayor of Portsmouth, chairman of the state Democratic Party and lieutenant govenor of Virginia with his best friend and one of our early investors, Herbert Bangel.

As chairman of TVX, it was my job to interact with the new shareholders, Salomon Brothers and our expanded board, which now included Kemmons Wilson, who I believe added a lot of street credibility when we were shopping for IPO investors. I also remained very involved in the construction of any new TV stations by traveling to each of the markets, meeting with our local partners and taking the officers of the lending banks to see what was going on.

Tim and John were running the business, especially the stations that were staffed, programmed, and selling advertising every day. Once in a while I would join John and Tim in New York to help pitch one of the big national sales companies that sold advertising for TV stations like ours.

National firms handled about half of all advertising that went to a local station. It took us a lot of meetings before we secured the right firm, one that would take an upstart independent company like ours. We started off with national rep Adam Young. Two years later we were offered a 20 percent interest in one of the country's best TV-rep firms, Seltel Inc., with John Trinder on their board. We agreed to move all twelve of our stations to their representation.

Things went along as projected financially for about a year, which was important to our credibility in the public stock market and with our lender. At one point, Citibank's venture capital unit held a lot of TVX stock in addition to loaning us over $100 million. That relationship boosted Wall Street's confidence in us. I would speak weekly with some of our key investors and supporters.

It was not unusual for Tim, John and me to be out of town on separate trips three to four days a week. We were all personally known by all the agents of the airlines in Norfolk. We competed with each other to see who could walk on the plane at the last minute, cutting it the closest. Tim won for a lot of reasons, week after week, month after month. My nature drove me to be first on the plane most of the time.

If we were going to New York, the limo I had personally acquired would be waiting when we landed. Our hotel had improved due to Jim Lowe arranging the trade-for-advertising deal for us at the Waldorf Astoria. They always upgraded us to the best available room, which often was a several-room suite. The deal at the Waldorf allowed me to extend a business trip into a personal weekend. A few years later, the Waldorf manager took over at Caesar's Palace in Vegas, which enabled us to enjoy many benefits at yearly broadcast and network meetings held there.

For several years, Dick Lamb, his wife, his daughter, and Angie and I spent the week after Christmas at the Waldorf, staying over for New Year's Eve for the big CBS Guy Lombardo broadcast. We were among the tuxedo and gowned dancers bringing in the New Year.

• • •

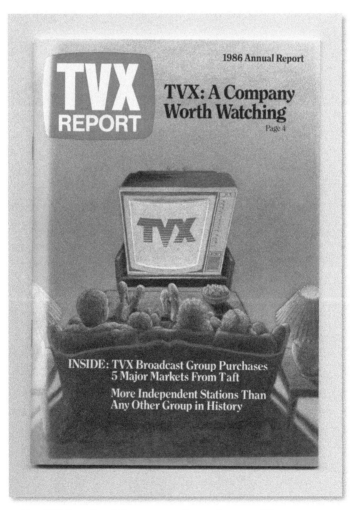

Our TVX Broadcast Group annual report as a public company, designed to look like *TV Guide*.

Another year passed and business remained very good. TVX was now the second largest group of non-network TV stations in the country that was not Spanish-language. The largest was an upstart called FOX. We received a call from Barry Diller who had accepted the job as the new FOX Network president. At that point, the "network" was comprised of a group of TV stations owned by mogul Rupert Murdoch, which he bought from Metromedia. Barry pitched us on being first to sign with the new FOX network, which we did. This immediately doubled their coverage footprint in the US. Believe it or not, this was a risk on our part for a lot of reasons. The FOX network's first show, featuring Joan Rivers, failed. Eventually FOX developed a show called *Married with Children,* which became the anchor one night a week. We became heroes to Rupert Murdoch by being first to bring such a big group of stations into FOX, and we enjoyed a lot of interaction with him personally at FOX affiliates meetings during the first formative years.

FOX would eventually add NFL Football to a strong nightly primetime schedule. The result was that our independent stations had become more valuable than many of the traditional ABC, NBC, or CBS affiliates.

• • •

In late 1986 an opportunity presented itself when Taft Broadcasting decided to sell their group of independent TV stations. Taft Broadcasting was one of America's original premier TV and radio companies. The founding family was that of 27th US President William Howard Taft. At the time, the FCC allowed one company to own no more than twelve TV stations, so we would have to sell a couple of our stations to stay within the FCC limit, if we won the bid for Taft. With the Taft acquisition, we would become the largest independent TV group in the US by number of stations. Taft had quickly bought UHF stations from various owners without fully accepting what could happen when major balloon payments for programming agreements came due a the end of the contracts. It was an acquisition strategy based on starting with low monthly payments and the assumption that station values would aggressively appreciate before the principal balance had to be paid. They believed they could borrow money against the stations' increased value and thereby satisfy all the creditors. It was precisely the same kind of thinking that led to the housing collapse in 2008-09.

Tim McDonnell, John Trinder and our lawyers, along with analysts at Salomon Brothers, went over all of Taft's programming contracts in detail. They then developed more realistic projections based on our company applying medium-market expense controls at the big-market independent TV stations Taft was selling.

Industry gurus were predicting the Taft group would go for half a billion dollars. But our financial model proved that the stations were worth 20 percent of that. Salomon Brothers agreed and offered us a bridge loan to buy the Taft Group for $110 million, plus a refinance of the debt on the TV stations we already owned. That meant a loan of $350 million that we would have to pay back within a year by refinancing all of it in the public market. We were confident we could quickly do so by attracting investors. Our financials were as solid as our track record in the smaller markets.

No one else was willing to bet what they were led to believe would be a several hundred million dollar bid, so they never floated an offer. We won, acquiring Channel 6 in Miami, Channel 29 in Philadelphia, Channel 20 in Washington, plus stations in Dallas and Houston. All of the stations were in the Top 10 markets, as defined in 1986. The industry was astounded that little ol' TVX just swallowed the famous Taft independent group, akin to a minnow swallowing a whale.

Prior to our bid for Taft, we gained big-finance acquisitions experience when trying to buy the Spanish-language stations now making up UNIVISION. We bid $500 million, but came in second behind Hallmark Cards. I had been talking with Raul Topia, who had been special counsel to President Jimmy Carter for Hispanic Affairs, and who brought us the San Antonio opportunity and was a partner in that station. We knew Hallmark Cards was also going to bid for the stations. Raul and I met with Irvine Hockaday, Jr., who ran Hallmark. We proposed that we form a merger to jointly buy the TV stations, but Hallmark wanted to go it alone. I lived at the Beverly Hilton for two weeks doing due diligence on the deal along with our financial advisors. It was a real education on going after the big prize. Oddly, our bid was supported by Citicorp Venture Capital; Hallmark was backed by First Chicago Venture

Capital. Both institutions were investors in TVX at that time. I
remember a meeting, actually a walk though Beverly Hills, with
one of the First Chicago guys: I was trying to convince Hallmark
to merge the bid. It didn't happen, but it did set us up to go after
Taft when they decided to sell.

Everything was going great after buying the Taft stations,
and we started working on refinancing the Salomon bridge
loan of $350 million. We hit the lawyers' offices in New York to
rewrite a prospectus to raise new investor money. We expected
public financing to pay off Salomon's bridge loan, plus additional
capital for improvements at all the stations.

On October 17, 1987, John and Tim were in California
getting ready to make a pitch about TVX and its future to a LA
insurance company. I was in New York discussing a potential
TVX investment with the Chairman and CEO of Prudential
Securities Interfunding John Whiteman, who had left Citicorp
and our board to run a division of one of the best known names
in financing and insurance.

The Prudential building overlooked the East River about
two blocks from Wall Street. I was sitting in John's office when
word came that something was wrong with the stock market. We
went downstairs to the trading floor and watched as the market
dropped 500 points, which was so bad that some finance guys
later committed suicide. It was the worst plunge in value on a
single day since the Great Depression. I joined John and some
of his team for a too-shocked-to-respond session for hours at
a local bar. I got a call from Tim and John telling me Salomon
Brothers cancelled the TVX presentation and they would meet
me back in Virginia. The next day we realized we had a $350
million loan due in a few months and nowhere to go for the
money: the finance markets were dead. To say I was worried is
an understatement. We would soon be bankrupt without new
financing to pay back Salomon.

We went from feeling great with twelve TV stations, five in
the Top 10 markets, into a frightening financial free-fall. As luck
would have it, we were the smallest bridge loan at the time for
Salomon Brothers. They had an oil company and drugstore chain
owing them billions. They told us to sit tight and do nothing;
they would call at some point.

For the next eight months, Salomon kept pushing our loan

out month-to-month beyond the due date as they dealt with much bigger problems. Fortunately for us, the TV advertising business remained strong, thus enabling our management team to implement the plans to run the TV stations we bought from Taft on a much tighter budget.

Instead of pulling the plug and sinking us, Salomon helped us by updating our prospectus to find investors. We were thankful for the help and patience, but we were anxious to attract investors to pay off that bridge loan. It was a stressful period, but our board held steady.

Tim McDonald had been a colorful character since he first came to work at the Norfolk TV station. He was a bachelor, saying he would never marry again, living near the oceanfront, often working until midnight picking movies to play on the TV stations, based on his personal knowledge. Normally this kind of thing is left up to the local station's program director—not the president of a company that owned twelve stations. But picking movies for ratings periods was Tim's hobby.

Tim had a lot of fun, often at parties at his house on weekends hosting advertisers and friends he had made in Norfolk. But one morning we all woke up to a newspaper story about a witness in a drug trial saying that they had seen "cocaine used at a party at Tim McDonald's house." Tim was not accused of anything, and that is all that was said. But because Tim was the CEO at a big TV company, this story found itself in the industry trades almost immediately, and it was a killer for a business trying to raise money from new investors.

Salomon summoned John, Tim, and me to New York to discuss the situation. It was agreed Tim should keep a low profile and that Salomon would hire someone to investigate the allegations. Meanwhile, John and I worked on how we would change our presentation.

The investigation turned up nothing, so it was decided that we would all go back out on the road together to pitch TVX to investors. We raised about 80 percent of what we had hoped, with Salomon Brothers buying the difference to get the deal closed. However, it was evident that the bad publicity linking Tim's name to cocaine had damaged his reputation and, by extension, that of TVX. Salomon used its ownership weight to push for Tim's release and a healthy severance package. The Salomon officer responsible for our account would come to Norfolk to explain their position. The next day, John Trinder took over as CEO of TVX, while I continued as chairman of the board.

• • •

In late 1989, Salomon Brothers called to ask John Trinder and me to meet with the President of Paramount Pictures Television, Mel Harris. Paramount had an interest in buying the TVX stocks owned by Salomon Brothers. We met Mel at the New York headquarters of Gulf and Western, the company that owned Paramount. We had a candid and far ranging conversation about TVX and how we saw TV in the future.

Paramount went on to buy Salomon's position, provided they could have two seats on our board, to which we agreed. Mel Harris would take one seat and Lucy Sulhaney the other. She was recognized as the most powerful woman in TV at that time, going on to become president of the FOX network after leaving Paramount. Harris and Sulhaney invited us to hold some future board meetings on the Paramount Pictures lot in Hollywood, which we were more than happy to do. We also became the first to sign the new *Arsenio Hall Show* developed by Paramount and taped daily on the Paramount lot in the old Desilu Productions studio, home to *I Love Lucy*. We and our clients attended many of these shows. I also often enjoyed sitting on the set of *Entertainment Tonight* while they were taping at Paramount, even though we did not air *ET* on the TVX stations.

Angie had one of her many "this is so exciting and thrilling" moments during this phase. We were around lots of Hollywood types and high profile CEOs. One day we had lunch in the Paramount commissary with Sherry Lansing, and on another occasion we dined with Frank Mancuso, chairman of Paramount Pictures. He gave us access to some of the movie soundstages where the big stars were filming. We had our own dedicated golf cart and driver. For several of our TVX board meetings the Paramount officers flew to Norfolk on their big Paramount jet with the famous Paramount logo on the tail.

**John Trinder and me with a paralegal in New York City
signing the documents to sell TVX to Paramount Pictures.**

• • •

For me and our board, one big moment came in early 1989 when CBS offered us $65 million for WCIX, Channel 6 in Miami. That was more than half of what we had paid Taft for all five of its major-market TV stations. The offer from CBS was too good to turn down. I spent a month Mondays through Fridays staying at the New York Hilton while working on contracts for the CBS deal at Black Rock, the CBS offices that were across the street. Steve Burke of Clark & Stant from Hampton Roads was with me most of the time. Representatives from Salomon Brothers would drift in and out with advice. I have a video shot in the WCIX news studio in Miami of me and Eric Ober, later to become head of CBS news, announcing the sale to the WCIX staff.

Every year a meeting of the TVX Broadcast Group general managers and sales managers was held at a resort to play golf, give awards to individuals for meeting goals and make plans for the next year. Palm Springs, CA. 1990

Our radio and TV general and sales mangers during
mid-1990s Max Media days. John Trinder is front and center.

CHAPTER 17

DÉJÀ VU

In late 1990, John and I were on a client trip to Vienna, Austria, when I received a call from Salomon Brothers telling me that Paramount wanted to buy all of the TVX public stock and take the company private. They asked me to come to New York right away. The next day—after we had listened to the Vienna Boys' Choir sing to 600 of our best advertisers from across the US—Angie and I took a 6 a.m. flight to London to connect with the Concorde, to arrive in New York for an 11 a.m. meeting the same morning. Our Vienna flight was late and they held the Concorde for us, which was unbelievable. Afterward, Angie flew on to Norfolk and I checked into a hotel to try to freshen up prior to going over to Paramount.

Steve Burke, our lawyer from Norfolk, would join me. We had also asked Fred Smith and Michael Connelly to meet us. Fred and Michael headed the media division at First Boston, another investment bank we had engaged for advice, knowing this day may come. We needed an impartial third party to help us negotiate the deal.

When we arrived at the Gulf & Western building, Martin Davis, CEO of Paramount's parent company, introduced us to Steve Ratner who would negotiate for Paramount. Later in his career, Steve was President Obama's "Auto Czar," handling General Motors and Chrysler bankruptcies. Paramount made a per-share offer, a premium to where our stock was trading. But the offer was about half of what we wanted, and after some negotiating we declined Paramount's offer and left. However, the upshot was that our company was now in play with Paramount. We were hoping the entertainment behemoth would sweeten the deal, which it did.

A few days later the call came. In early 1991 we sold TVX to Paramount Pictures for about $500 million. Paramount offered John Trinder a chance to remain as CEO if he moved to California. He turned down that opportunity. Instead, John and I would start over, launching a company that would come to own TV and radio stations in seventeen markets. I celebrated the Paramount sale by purchasing an even bigger boat and taking trips with Angie.

• • •

Leading up to the sale to Paramount, we started selling some of our smaller markets so we could improve our balance sheet and focus on the big market stations we'd bought from Taft, plus Raleigh and San Antonio. We sold Buffalo to the Knox family who owned the NHL Buffalo Sabers; we had one buyer for both Nashville and Memphis, and another broadcaster bought Little Rock. We had earlier sold our Greensboro station to Norman Lear who started a new TV company called Act III. Our New Orleans station, WNOL, Channel 49, went to Quincy Jones. I met with Quincy but did most of the negotiating with Bob Pittman who later became CEO of Warner Brothers and now runs iHeartRadio network.

During these selldowns of the original markets, the man who had been our third main employee, Chuck McFadden, had left Greensboro to manage our Raleigh TV station for a short time. He then moved to Norfolk to run WTVZ and manage all of our smaller stations. Now Chuck decided he wanted to buy WTVZ. Most all managers want to own their stations but few have enough cash to make a down payment. Such was the case with Chuck; he had major school expenses for five children.

John Tinder and I offered to loan Chuck some money with

the right to convert to stock if he had not paid us by a certain date. Chuck accepted, and bought WTVZ for around $10 million. I also introduced him to our financing source at Philips Credit, which provided a lot of the purchase price. Over about ten years we had become Philips' largest borrower, surpassing their biggest client, Walt Disney.

Me with Chuck McFadden at the 10th Anniversary Party of WTVZ-TV, at the Chrysler Museum, Norfolk. I'm holding a bronze reprint of the station's program log from its sign-on in 1979, presented to me as the station's founding partner.

• • •

By the time the sale to Paramount closed I was exhausted. All the traveling had put a lot of stress on my marriage to Angie. I was just gone much too much. We did not have children, and Angie was alone much of the 1980's. I knew I needed to take a break before thinking about what was next. It was a very happy day when I went to New York to get my check from Paramount.

(Top) The guy on the left is Frank Mancuso, chairman of Paramount Pictures. I'm center, and on the right is Martin Davis, the CEO of Gulf and Western. (Below L-R:) A picture of me with the CFO of Gulf and Western, Ron Nelson. Our closing dinner at Pasta e Pani and most importantly, the check.

In January 1991, Angie and I left on a ninety-day world cruise through the South Pacific, New Zealand, Australia, Africa, India, Thailand, China, and Japan plus many other remote ports. About three weeks of the trip were spent on overland excursions off the ship, some of which became very dangerous. Angie refused to do the overland in India after being in the middle of an uprising in Kenya. We also got caught in a storm at sea with fifty-foot waves. The captain said it was the worst he had seen in his thirty-year career. The trip was a terrific diversion from the norm and very educational, but it wasn't always relaxing.

We were caught in two typhoons coming at the ship from different directions as we traveled from Australia toward Africa. We had no advanced warning, because that part of the world's oceans had not yet been covered by weather satellites, as there was almost no commercial shipping between those two continents. Trying not to show Angie my concern I insisted we go up for breakfast. We and the waiters were the only ones there. The captain ordered everyone to stay in their stateroom. Grand pianos chained to the floors in three sections of the ship broke loose, careening into walls, one of which was glass. All the cabinets along the corridor leading into the dining room fell over, destroying hundreds of bottles of wine. Three cooks were scaled and had to be airlifted to a hospital once we could get near an unscheduled island. For someone who entered our relationship as prone to sea sickness, I was pleasantly surprised how well Angie did under such scary circumstances.

• • •

Over the years of our marriage, both of us have enjoyed one—to two-week cruises as total getaway vacations because you can unpack once and see something different every day. We have been fortunate enough to experience ships of all sizes traveling to some of the great historic destinations of the world. Our favorite trips have been on Windstar ships, mostly in the Caribbean on vessels carrying no more than eighty couples.

Although I planned to take at least a year off, I was back to work shortly after our trip. John Trinder and I started meeting with Chuck McFadden to discuss a new broadcast company. Chuck had discovered another opportunity, to buy a station in Syracuse, New York, but still lacked financing. We included discussions with the person who had served as CFO at TVX since about 1984 about being part of a new company. We ended up launching MAX Media, located in the same office building where we had been for several years, at 5501 Greenwich Road.

We immediately started looking for other TV properties and focused on a troubled NBC affiliate in Dayton, Ohio. Citibank agreed to hire us to oversee the operation before we bought it.

While I had been working almost exclusively since about 1982 on TV, my friend and concert partner Dick Lamb and his partner Larry Saunders had been deep in the radio trenches. They bought a couple of stations in Kansas City, adding to their 2WD base in Norfolk. Around 1986 they decided to sell out. 2WD was sold to Gary Edens, who signed long-term contracts for Dick to continue the morning show and Larry to continue as general manager.

During the real estate recession of the early '90s, Edens had fallen on hard times, and Dick and Larry approached us, knowing we had some cash from the TVX sale. They wanted to buy back 2WD, plus WRVA and WRVQ in Richmond, also owned by Edens.

John and I had a few dollars, but not the kind of money needed to buy the two best stations in Richmond plus 2WD. We had heard that Wheat First Securities in Richmond had a venture capital division, so we went to see them. Wheat said they were co-investing in deals with a company in Charlottesville and they would both perform due diligence on a potential radio transaction, having never been in radio before. Wheat and the Charlottesville company, Quad-C, came through with financing but unfortunately for us, someone outbid us for the Richmond stations, so I spent a great deal of time on the phone with Gary Edens talking about his Norfolk property. He had paid $7 million for 2WD and we offered him $4 million. He came to Norfolk where we exchanged harsh words about values in the parking lot on Greenwich Road: Gary had been insulted by my offer. The next day he called and we agreed on $5 million. So we were now back in radio and TV at MAX Media, and Dick and Larry became our partners, too. We were also now in business with deep-pocketed investors—Wheat First and Quad-C. Al Rider and Jimmy Wheat joined our board, along with Tony Ignaczak and Terry Daniels from Quad-C. It was already starting to feel like a repeat of TVX.

• • •

In April 1995 we hired David Wilhelm as our new chief financial officer— we replaced the former TVX financial guy because he was not big on adding more radio stations to the new company. He remained a shareholder until we bought him out a couple of years later. David has been part of the team ever since. David eventually hired Laura Poole as controller, who has been with us 16 years. I enjoy following Laura and her four rescue dogs on Facebook. In 1996 the secretary-assistant John and I had shared for seventeen years, Betty Albertson, tragically died in an auto accident on Interstate 64 on the way home from our office. Debbi Haddaway (now Debbi Babashanian) filled that tremendous void and, amazingly, she is still here twenty years later.

• • •

MAX Media launched at the time the FCC was changing ownership rules. It would now allow one broadcast company to own multiple FM stations in certain markets. In Norfolk, you could now own four. Prior to that, it had been no more than two FM stations and before that just one FM station and one AM.

We moved quickly, acquiring two more FMs in Norfolk. We also bought four FMs in Greensboro. Next, we turned to Las Vegas, buying a station there for $4 million. The station was located behind the old Dunes Hotel, which is now the Bellagio property. Eventually, after some very fun times in Vegas, we sold that station to Walt Disney's brother Roy, who was acquiring assets for estate planning for his children. He paid us $15 million.

On the TV side of MAX Media in the 1990s, we ended up buying the NBC station in Dayton that we had managed as trustees, plus FOX stations in the Tri Cities of Tennessee and Cape Girardeau, Mo. We also bought the NBC station in Tyler, Texas and the UPN station in Charleston, South Carolina.

Just like back in the 1980s during our UHF days, we started building new stations. One was in Paducah, Kentucky and the other in Syracuse. We affiliated both with the new (UPN) United Paramount Network.

Radio and TV had become very good investment vehicles by the time we really got MAX rolling. We were receiving calls almost every week from someone who wanted to buy one or more of our stations; a couple wanted to buy everything. We sold the Vegas FM first because it was a chance to more than triple our investment. Next, a public company in Baltimore, Sinclair Broadcast Group, wanted to buy WTVZ-TV, the Norfolk FOX affiliate. We really didn't want to sell our hometown station: it had a tremendous sentimental meaning for me as the anchor upon which we built TVX. But at some point the offer was too high to refuse.

During the early 90s, as we considered the growth of cable and satellite TV, we decided to apply for wireless microwave licenses in order to construct the first "over the air" programming service that would duplicate much of what was traditionally aired on cable, like CNN and The Weather Channel. By 1997 we had constructed Hampton Roads first wireless cable TV system, transmitting from the Channel 3 WTKR site in Driver, Virginia with offices on Newtown Road. Eventually we sold the business to a public company, which had systems in several communities.

• • •

Our business success seemed to be a repeat of TVX, and my personal life seemed like a flashback, too. Again, traveling demands of building the business took a toll on my marriage. I was away two or three days just about every week. By 1993, Angie had had enough. She left for her hometown of Thomasville, North Carolina. We had tried counseling, which had not really helped because I just could not turn off the business side of my brain. So, in 1994 we divorced.

MAX Media was making money, but we owed a lot as well. We needed to keep buying and selling to sustain the business and keep investors happy. My close associates were also spending too many nights away from home, so our board agreed that it was time for a company jet, something I wish had happened two years earlier. It would have meant a lot less time away from home for me. Getting to small markets took lots of time and expense. Now, with our own jet, we could be in and out within hours instead of two days.

One day, after a year or so of not talking or seeing each other, Angie called to ask if I would come to Greensboro to help her make a decision on a condo she wanted to buy. I went. A few months later she called to say she had found a local counselor who did not know me and was someone she respected. I was delighted to be back in Angie's life and agreed to fly to North Carolina once a week for therapy sessions.

Often a third party can point out things a couple misses on their own. The experience was gut wrenching, but we both came to understand how we could each make changes, which made our relationship stronger than before. After about a year of counseling, we remarried in 1998.

We had a simple early-morning beach ceremony performed by Pastor Larry Shoaf. We sent the following announcement to our friends and family.

WE ARE RISING TO THE OCCASION
TO BRING YOU UPLIFTING NEWS

ANGIE AND GENE ARE SEEING EYE TO EYE!

We happily announce our marriage and
we appreciate the love, encouragement and support
of all our friends.
You'll be pleased to know that we
saved all the gifts from April 1982,
so your prayers for our future will be enough to send us
on our voyage into an exciting new life together.

. . . all things are become new
II Corinthians 5:17

Angie and Gene Loving were married at 6:42 a.m.
Tuesday, September 9, 1997
in a private ceremony on the beach
at the North Carolina and Virginia border.
Their main residence will be Virginia Beach, Virginia.

**The announcement sent
to our friends after our
remarriage. 1998**

Having a corporate airplane definitely alleviated much of the tension of my absences. But the real credit for our ongoing happiness belongs to our original Shih Tzu dog, Star, who distracted Angie on those much less frequent occasions when I still had to go out of town. The little creature peed on all our rugs, which of course upset Angie but took the focus off me. After twelve great years, Star went paws up. It took two rescue Shih Tzus, Bella and Cuddles, to replace Star. We continued in the same house we built on the Linkhorn Bay when we first married. We also kept Angie's Greensboro condo, and purchased a condo in Fort Lauderdale in 1999.

We visit her home area a couple of times a year, mostly during Thanksgiving and Christmas. I have no living relatives, so Christmas in Richmond stopped twenty years ago after my parents died. For the first two decades of our marriage, we would spend Christmas morning with Angie's family in North Carolina, drive to Richmond, have dinner with my parents, and then check into the Williamsburg Inn on Christmas night to stay for a couple of days. There's nothing like Christmas in Williamsburg. Angie's family continues. The Jordan name is alive and well. Most holidays we now see her father's sister, Aunt JoAnne, her aunt Vivian and her husband Bob Ruden who is from Suffolk, plus Lary & Sharon Jordan and our nephews Rocky, Nick, and Jay. Nick and his wife Taylor already have two little Jordans, so about 12 of us gather to celebrate Christmas.

• • •

In 1998 the Baltimore Sinclair Group came to us with an offer to buy all the MAX Media Radio and TV stations for $380 million; we took it. We sold everything but the MAX name. The new MAX, where I continue to serve as chairman and CEO, is an equal partnership of me, John Trinder, The Chuck McFadden family, Tim Robertson who sold the Family Channel to Rupert Murdoch, and an entity owned jointly by Dick Lamb, Larry Saunders, and a couple of their associates. Quad-C in Charlottesville and Colonnade Capital in Richmond (former Wheat First Venture division) are both back as investors, along with new-to-us Golden Gate Capital out of San Francisco. After the sale of the first MAX Media in 1998, I was fifty-five years old and my only real hobby was still boating. So, I decided to look for the kind of vessel I really wanted.

· · ·

Our first new MAX investment in 1999 was 50 percent of three FMs and one AM radio station in eastern North Carolina, mostly serving the Outer Banks. We later acquired the other half, and added two more to give us five FM stations. We also became 50 percent partners of an online digital newspaper, the *Outer Banks Voice*.

In 2000, our next investment was in Studio One in New York, an online creator of content for big advertisers like P&G who wanted a national website to showcase a particular product. Next, we bought a group of TV stations located in every town in Montana. There are not a lot of people in Montana. It's beautiful and remote—but watch out for rattlesnakes in the toilets at highway rest stops.

After the transition in TV from analogue to digital, we could put two signals on the same antenna. So we doubled our holdings by signing on Montana FOX stations in Helena, Great Falls, Missoula, Butte and Bozeman. We already had ABC stations in all those places, plus the NBC station in Billings. We bought the NBC station in Bowling Green, KY and rebuilt all of the technical facilities, plus new studios and offices. And we hired Radar, the weather dog, and added the CBS Network via the new digital antenna capacity.

The new MAX grew as rapidly as its predecessor; in fact, we wound up with twice as many media properties as the old MAX had before we sold it. Our cache included the FOX station in Portland, Maine, and four TV stations in Puerto Rico; radio stations in Arkansas and along the Susquehanna River Valley in Pennsylvania; and stations in three other radio markets in Missouri and Illinois. In 2005, we built a new start-from-scratch CBS Station in Tyler, Texas, which we sold in 2008 for $25 million.

In 2006 the owners of four local FMs and WGH-AM in Norfolk decided to sell. We never anticipated being back in our home market. We paid $80 million for EAGLE, WAVE, HOT100 and ESPN, and WGH-AM. Dick Lamb moved over from our old station 2WD to do mornings on the new WAVE.

History repeats itself, and I am so grateful it has. However, the 2009 recession had a big negative impact on many businesses including broadcasting. If it were not for the goodwill of our investors and lenders, we could have ended up reorganizing under bankruptcy laws like so many other media companies. Newspapers were hit particularly hard. The *San Francisco Examiner* and the *Rocky Mountain News* in Denver closed. *The Washington Post* was sold to the owner of Amazon, and the *New York Times* had to sell a major portion of its corporation to Carlos Slim from Mexico. Fortunately for MAX, buyers wanted a few of our stations for special reasons and paid us well above market prices. We believe we will still be in broadcasting for the foreseeable future, along with our "new media" investments. As mentioned, we invested in a small electronic newspaper published on the Outer Banks and have been scouting the Internet landscape for other digital media opportunities.

CHAPTER 18

BOATS, BOATS, BOATS

My love of boats became even more infectious than my passion for cars. I like being on the open water with friends aboard, and I like it even better when we're going fast.

During the '60s and '70s I graduated to longer, more powerful boats with more seating. By the mid-'80s I was all in with a 32-foot Pachanga cigarette-style boat built by Sea Ray—top speed of 75 knots, which is about 86 mph. My Pachanga had an outside exhaust that bypassed a muffler, which made it roar. Angie was thankful that it could also be switched to a much quieter underwater exhaust, provided the speed was no more than 35 knots. She liked the slower ride, and that the boat had a head and place to sleep. But due to a lack of air conditioning, we only slept overnight on the boat once. That gave me the excuse to buy an even bigger toy.

When we sold TVX to Paramount, it was time to trade in the Pachanga for something we could start to use together, built more for comfort than speed. First came a 39-foot Express Cruiser named *Sea Eagle*. In 1992, I did my first Intracoastal Waterway trip south, along with three friends. I learned that if you could follow a chart you could easily get from Virginia to Florida safely. After several Intracoastal trips, I started leaving the boat in Fort Lauderdale for the winter, flying down on weekends.

Predictably, commuting between Virginia and Florida by boat gave me the itch to buy something even bigger, which I did—a 40-foot Sea Ray we named *Frequenseas*. Next up, a 45-foot Sea Ray we called *Airwaves*.

With Dick Lamb on the Intracoastal Waterway, Myrtle Beach, South Carolina taking the 45 ft. SeaRay, *Airwaves*, to Fort Lauderdale.

Cabin-styled express cruisers were reasonably fast, comfortable and seaworthy. As we cruised, we explored coastal towns along the way, and in the summer focused on marinas in small towns on the Chesapeake Bay. The trips became my vacations, and we often brought friends along. About every other year Angie would do one Intracoastal trip. But we eventually decided that we loved Florida, so we purchased a condo next to the Marriott Marina Hotel, now the Hilton, across from Pier 66 on 17th Street near Port Everglades. Yes, the condo had a boat slip.

After selling Max Media in 1998, I had more time to spend in Florida, staying connected to the office by phone and email. We decided it now made more sense to stop moving the boat between Virginia and Florida. It was time to keep one boat in Florida and another in Virginia. Having two boats may sound exorbitant, but it actually made economic sense. Fuel, overnight dockage fees and meals for cruising up and down the Intracoastal Waterway twice a year was about as much as buying and maintaining a second boat. Plus, we saved wear and tear and associated maintenance costs.

My dream boat was a 63-foot Sunseeker built in England. I had seen a few around and was smitten. It was the very first unique European design, with a gorgeous all-wood interior and every nautical gadget you can imagine. The 1995 model won every award as the best new thing on the market. We went down to Florida to look at a used 63-footer, which the salesman was going to bring to our condo to be sure it would fit in our slip. After the test, we went to the dealership to look at the boat's service records.

Sunseeker had just advertised in several boating magazines introducing its newest bigger boat, an 80-foot version of the used boat we had looked at. The new 80-ft. Predator was the sharpest, fastest boat of its category ever introduced. People like me drooled over this thing. Sunseeker was using new Arneson Surface Drives, which gave it tremendous speed for a boat its size and weight. The company claimed the 80-footer would do 45 knots, or about 50 mph, which was unheard of. The interior felt like a five-star hotel suite, plush with exotic woods and leather. The boat even had a boat—a hidden dinghy bigger than my first boat.

When we pulled up to the dealer in Pompano Beach, a brand new 80-foot Sunseeker Predator was sitting out back, the first in the US and just delivered the day before. The salesman asked if I wanted to take a look. I said there was no way I could afford it, so why torture myself? After several pushes from Herb Bopp, their top sales guy, Angie and I decided to board the boat for a sniff. I knew the cost from the ads I had read. Despite the sticker price, it was love at first sight, and Angie could see it in my eyes. Apparently Herb could, too, because he pressed me to make an offer. I kept telling him I could not afford it, and that I didn't want to insult them with a lowball number. Undeterred, Herb brought out the owner of the dealership. I told him the most I could even consider was 25 percent below their sticker. He took it. We were floored; and I was now in an embarrassing spot of having to make good on an amount I never believed we would pay for a boat.

The owner and Herb asked that I come back the next morning with a deposit check and to sign the contracts. We would have lots of paperwork to process things like offshore registration due to tax laws, and we had to start thinking about a name, required like a license plate. My head was spinning. Our friends the Stantons had accompanied us on the trip, so we all went out to dinner and discussed what we were really going to do. It was not too late to back out, they assured me. I appreciated the advice, but I was hooked. With Angie's full support we committed to buy the boat. That night, I decided to name my dream boat after my dream girl, *Angela Dawn*.

A few days later we met for breakfast with the man who had been the designated captain for this luxury yacht and had been at the factory in Poole, England during its construction. The dealer had suggested we hire him, so this was really an interview. I found out from the captain that I probably could have paid even less for the boat. A Japanese businessman had ordered it, specified a lot of upgrades, and when it was finished he backed out because he'd lost a lot of money in Japan's stock market crash. Sunseeker sent the boat to Florida, usually the best market, hoping to recoup the balance, and then some. The 25 percent discount that looked so good to me probably looked even better to them. We ended up hiring Mike Fridley, a former submariner with twenty years in the Navy, to be our captain, rather than the individual who we first interviewed.

Angela Dawn, Atlantis Bahamas, 1999

Buying the 80-foot Sunseeker was one of our best decisions ever; it allowed us relaxed vacations without lugging suitcases through airports. Having made the investment we decided to use it as much as possible: weekend trips with family and guests, parties, fundraisers for politicians and charities, or just taking it to a waterfront restaurant for a great meal. Since the boat is crewed fulltime we loaned it to others for special occasions. A couple of times the board members of the Virginia Association of Broadcasters, and their spouses, have been aboard. We hosted media mogul and Christian broadcaster Pat Robertson and his family for a dinner cruise in Florida for Pat's 70th birthday.

We welcomed Bob McDonnell for a fundraiser when he ran for Virginia Attorney General. Former Virginia Governor George Allen was on board, along with several of Virginia's top CEOs, including the president of Northrop Grumman's Newport News Shipbuilding and Dry Dock Company, the Navy's principal warship builder. He was sitting at the helm of our boat commenting on how much he liked it, asking all kinds of questions. I returned the compliment, saying that I really liked the kind of ships he built, especially submarines. He asked for my business card and said he would arrange for me to go out on a sub. Our boat event had been organized by our friend Jeff McWaters who at that time was CEO of AmeriGroup, a company he founded. A few years later Jeff sold his interest in AmeriGroup, and went on to become our state senator from Virginia Beach. Jeff and his wife Cindy have taken some memorable trips with us on the *Angela Dawn*. We have also enjoyed going to Saint Michaels, Maryland by water to join the McWaters at their beautiful estate. In 2015 they purchased a "luxury coach" which has enabled us to be part of their "land cruises". The coach is as much fun as the destination.

On November 17, 2000, I received a phone call inviting me to take a ride—the next day—on a nuclear sub out of Port Canaveral, Florida. So that evening I flew down on our corporate jet and the next morning was taken aboard the USS Montpelier. Spending the day on the Montpelier at sea, deep diving, riding in the conning tower with the Captain, eating with the crew, looking through the periscope, has been one of my best experiences, and it was my birthday.

One of my biggest thrills, 500 feet under the ocean aboard *USS Montpelier*, checking the surface via periscope, assisting the navigator. Riding the conning tower with Captain William Frake, and crew members at the ready to defend the submarine. On my birthday November 2003.

Aboard the submarine *Montpelier*.
Standing on the conning tower at sea.

Great boats need great captains, and over the past eighteen years we have had five wonderful skippers of the *Angela Dawn*. Boat captains change jobs about every two years on average. In 1999, after only eight months on the *Angela Dawn*, our captain Mike Fridley was seriously injured in a flight over the Everglades in which the pilot died. Rupert Lean was then with us two years, and is still a friend who we see in Florida often. Our next captain, Rob Mase, stayed ten years and only left because his young family needed dad at home; we often see him and his wife, Kate, who he met in Virginia Beach. Rob had lived a Jimmy Buffet life, with stories to match. Next came Andrew Reid and his dog, Sassy. Actually, I hired the dog and Andrew came to take care of her. One nice bonus was that Andrew is an excellent chef.

In 2008, we sold the original *Angela Dawn*, after signing a contract to build a new boat, a 77-footer with more interior room and four state-of-the-art Volvo IPS drive engines. The boat uses half the fuel of the original big boat, and although it is not as fast, I appreciate comfort more than speed as I age. I realized that it is more pleasant to sit outside on deck when the snacks and drinks aren't blowing away, which happens above about 25 knots.

Travelling by boat has enabled us to see a lot of the country we would have never likely visited by car, especially the small towns and villages all up and down the East Coast including the Hamptons, Martha's Vineyard and Nantucket. Every winter we go to some section of the Bahamas and focus on islands in that region. Most don't realize the Bahamas, Bimini, is only 50 miles from Fort Lauderdale, which is about a two-hour run from our condo.

Some of our most memorable trips have been in the North cruising the Hudson River into Lake Champlain, stopping in Burlington, Vermont and other small New England towns around the lake. Gail and Michael Simone, who lead Spring Branch Community Church, made that trip with us. It was our second time with them doing the Hudson. Newport, RI, Boston, Maine and New York City are all regular summer destinations.

Other notables on board in recent years include Bill Hybels, founder of Willow Creek Church in Chicago, and forty pastors from around the country. They were in Fort Lauderdale in 2015 for an annual conference. Dr. Henry Cloud, who has written several amazing self-help books, was also there as the conference speaker. Jan Brewer, the well-known governor of Arizona, has cruised with us. She claims Arizona has more registered boats than any other state.

And, of course, there have been a bevy of old friends and longtime associates, whom I embrace like family, some bringing me back to my past. Among them is John Wilson, my friend going back to the WEZL days in Richmond in 1959. In November of 2015, John made the Virginia-to-Florida Intracoastal trip with me. As we sat on the deck of the *Angela Dawn,* passing the serene little towns and watching sunsets, I couldn't help but feel blessed to have had such a wonderful life and so many great companions like John.

CHAPTER 19

BEYOND BROADCASTING

Maybe it was the inspiration of my original backer, Richard J. Davis, who enabled me to begin owning businesses of substance, but by the mid-'90s I started to listen to presentations from people who wanted to start a business, needing private investors to make it happen. One of those was Tom Naughton, and later his partner Nicolas Valcour. They were trying to raise capital to expand New Dominion Pictures (NDP), based in nearby Suffolk, Virginia. I became a partner and went on their board. They created a lot of solid entertainment, mostly documentaries and drama series, for cable TV. Their shows included *Tainted Love, FBI Files, Special Forces, The New Detectives*, and *Ghost Stories*.

Nicolas eventually bought out his partner, and I became more involved with NDP, remaining on the board while helping to raise money to create new shows, some of which went on to be hits—*A Haunting* and *FantomWorks*. Our dog, Cuddles, appeared in one of the *A Haunting* shows. Cuddles is female but played a male dog. Our now-deceased dog, Star, also had a cameo in a NDP film, *The Deadly Dentist*.

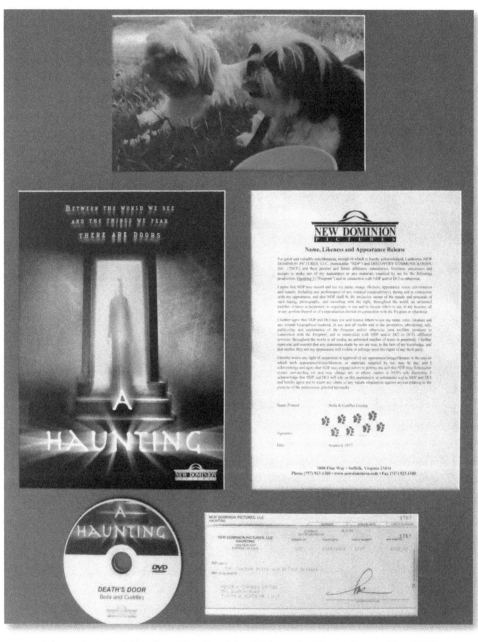

A framed presentation from New Dominion Pictures that hangs in my office. NDP recognized the excellent acting ability of our dogs, Bella and Cuddles, when they appeared in an episode of *A Haunting*. Their check is bottom right.

Another opportunity outside of broadcasting came in 1997 when I was invited by founder John Fain to serve on the board of his public company, Metro Information Services. The company had offices throughout the United States, advising and servicing many of the nation's top businesses on their computer and software needs. It was a great opportunity to learn firsthand how important the new technology-based companies had become to the country's economy. Metro's biggest competitor, Keane, acquired Metro in 2001, following the big new millennium issues in 2000 that challenged so many who relied on computers in their business.

In chapter 6, I wrote about my partnership with Richard Levin regarding our development of commercial properties in Ghent. In 2016, we sold The Colony Coffee House buildings to investors who plan to turn those historic landmarks into upscale residences.

• • •

Around 2003, one of our MAX private capital investors from Richmond came to me with an opportunity in another startup movie company. The principal owner would be Dave Matthews of the Dave Matthews Band based in Charlottesville, Virginia. The CEO, Temple Fennell, was excellent at finding or producing movies. We called the company 12th Floor Films because the office building where it was based, owned by Dave Matthews and his manager, Coran Capshaw, had twelve floors.

Back in the early 2000s, Blockbuster and other DVD rental stores were prospering, which gave us a source of pre-release income as the retailers bid to have a movie first. Our releases returned a nice profit to the investors at 12th Floor. Dave and Temple decided to continue in motion pictures with a new movie company called ATO (Art Takes Over) Pictures, the same name as his record company, which was based on Wall Street in New York. Dave asked me to continue as one of five board members for ATO Pictures. Titles released by ATO were *The Oranges, The Monk, Thin Ice, Last Call at the Oasis, The Woman in the Fifth, Mao's Last Dancer,* and *Casino Jack* starring Kevin Spacey.

By 2012 the DVD market was drying up and soon would be replaced by streaming on Netflix, and the box office for non-action independent movies had diminished. By 2014, ATO

Pictures folded. Despite the outcome, it was a very interesting ten years in the movie business with one of the biggest names in entertainment.

· · ·

Although radio and TV were my staples, the itch to try other entrepreneurial ventures really started in the early 1970s when Bill Deal and I developed Mary's Country Kitchen. I spent a lot of time and money in restaurants. A great waitstaff, excellent food service in comfortable surroundings is, in essence, another form of entertainment. One of my favorite haunts in Richmond was Ruth's Chris Steak House, and I became friendly with the owner who recalled listening to me on WLEE. We talked about trying to do a Ruth's in Virginia Beach, but by then Ruth's Chris parent company was not approving new franchises, and just opening locations it owned directly. Years earlier I had dinner a couple of times with company founder Ruth Fertel at the original Ruth's in a New Orleans neighborhood when we owned WNOL-TV in that market. So, I had long admired the success of her company.

Since we couldn't open a Ruth's, my MAX associate John Trinder and I decided to join with the Richmond Ruth's principal as equal partners to create a new Italian restaurant called Bottega's, which we built next to Ruth's in the Midlothian area of Richmond. It became very successful. Next, John and I invested in a start-up steakhouse developed on the main town mall in Charlottesville. It is the Downtown Grill, and ten years later the Grill is still going strong. Please try it.

Next, Tom Beers invited me to become a 50 percent non-operating partner for a new breakfast and lunch establishment on Great Neck Road in Virginia Beach. Angie picked the name Sunrise Café, in honor of a place she frequented for eggs in her hometown of Thomasville, North Carolina. Fortunately for both Tom and me, after three years of building the business he got an offer he couldn't refuse. The new owners today have great food and we go there mostly after church.

In 2005, Ruth's Chris started to do local franchising again so we raised the money from six local partners and established the business that is now in Virginia Beach's Town Center. Three years later, right before the Great Recession crushed the economy, our operating partner of Ruth's Chris bought out our ownership of the Town Center restaurant and Bottega's in Richmond. Timing is everything; a year later, sadly, Bottega's closed.

Over the years I never lost my fondness for my hometown. Richmond is where I started in radio, developed the FOX-TV station, and enjoyed spaghetti at Bottega's. I have kept ties to the town and even joined a venture that seems far removed from my core competencies,—boarding and washing dogs. How is that for reinventing yourself? My friend Al Rider found this opportunity. Angie and I both wanted our own interest in a business that benefited dogs, so we became partners with Al and Jimmy Wheat. It has been so successful as a doggie daycare center and kennel that we now have three locations. The best part is, the customers just wag their tails and are always happy to see you.

CHAPTER 20

FAITH AND PHILANTHROPY

Most of what I have shared in this book dwells on my professional life and the numerous business associates accompanying me along this incredible journey. Throughout these pages, I've shared stories about becoming successful in business, and meeting rock stars, Hollywood moguls, major TV and radio personalities, and Wall Street wizards. I've disclosed intricacies of business dealings and the many partnerships formed to make them happen. Over the years I have often pondered, *Why me?* The answer, to a large degree, is my Christian faith.

Through my decades of wheeling and dealing and building relationships, I have always been guided by my conscience, and by trying to do right by others, respecting their opinions. I'd like to think that many of the great opportunities presented to me over my many decades in business came because I was trustworthy and honest. That moral guidepost is firmly grounded in my deep and abiding faith in God and the teaching of the Bible. For my deep-seated faith I credit my mother who kept me involved, as a boy, in our Presbyterian Church. Many times during the course of my career, and during vexing personal trials, I turned to prayer. Without prayer, I doubt I would have achieved anything. I have story after story of how things turned out well for me when there was no logical reason they should have.

During my formative years, when my interest in radio evolved, I was a leader in our church's Youth Ministry, and once I was on the air I think that slight amount of "fame" I had as a teenager gave me stature among the kids in the group I tried to help. After leaving Richmond, I always attended a church in the community where I was living, including taking my daughter to Sunday School and driving her to any event where she could be part of a group of Christian kids her age. When my daughter died, my faith was sorely tested but remained firm.

My wife, Angie, and I are active in the faith-based world, and we are close with those leading the churches we have attended over the years. We have been fortunate to count as our friends fantastic people like Larry and Brenda Shoaf, whom we met when he was senior pastor at Virginia Beach Community Chapel. More recently, we've spend a lot of time with Gail and Michael Simone after they started Spring Branch. Over the years we took several vacations with both the Shoafs and Simones. Angie is godmother to the five Shoaf grandchildren. And Michael Simone and I have mutual interests in good food. We continue a many-year quest to find the best hamburger around New York, where Michael grew up in nearby New Jersey. The Simones, like Angie and me, have two Shih Tzus.

Our commitment to the Church and its mission to help others has led Angie and me deeper into philanthropy. We were early supporters of Operation Smile, and served on its board. The nonprofit medical service organization is based in Virginia Beach and was founded in 1982. It provides cleft lip and palate repair surgeries to children worldwide. I served as temporary CEO for eight months while the organization searched for a permanent replacement. I took my lunch to their offices almost daily to sit with Kathy Magee, discussing missions and fund raising, and to hear her husband, Dr. Bill Magee, talk about helping disfigured children lead more normal lives. Bill has been one of the country's preeminent surgeons. He could have retired early, financially comfortable after practicing cosmetic surgery in Norfolk. Instead, he and his wife dedicated their life to helping kids in the US and overseas.

Just as in business, whom you know leads to others with whom you get to know. One of the most inspiring contributors to the community I met was Tom Frantz, an attorney who is still chairman of the powerful law firm, Williams Mullen. Tom recruited me to join the board of the Virginia Aquarium, which turned into a serious commitment of time. I accepted various roles that placed me on the executive committee, which met every couple of weeks. I was eventually appointed treasurer during one of their significant fund drives to remodel and upgrade the exhibits and facilities. Seeing the crowds that visit the aquarium and its state-of-the-art theater warms my heart. The institution's mission includes a stranding center where rescued animals are rehabilitated. I had a small part in helping bring together Virginia Wesleyan University in Virginia Beach with the Aquarium, to share the cost of the new marine science boat, which is now one of the principal tools of both institutions.

Since Angie and I were not paying college tuition for Bella and Cuddles, we wanted to do our part to help qualified candidates in need of financial assistance for education. So, we established the Angela Loving Scholarship for the communications schools at Virginia Wesleyan and nearby Regent University. It has been very rewarding to meet with the young scholarship recipients and see them graduate.

Just as business success often begets more success, volunteering and donating to great causes has a way of snowballing as well. Such was the case with the Neptune Festival of Virginia Beach. It started forty years ago to extend the season in Virginia Beach and also encourage the locals to come to the Oceanfront in September. After closing several blocks of Atlantic Avenue during the first few years to allow street art and food vendors to participate, the organizers realized that the Neptune Festival had real potential to make a much more profound contribution to the city. Nancy Creech was appointed fulltime CEO of the festival, and a local volunteer board started to move the annual event into a great party spread over many days and events. It has also become a major opportunity to raise money, especially for the smaller charities. Our radio stations always sponsored various aspects of the Neptune Festival.

Each year, a selection committee names a Festival king. It's an honor typically bestowed on someone who spends several years devoting time to the Festival, often first serving as a "triton." While my business participated in the organization in several ways, I was little more than a spectator and certainly never among its inner circle. One day a group of people arrived at my office unannounced, came in and closed the door, saying they were the King Neptune nominating committee and that I had been selected to be the next year's King. I was stunned. I knew that being King was more than a one-weekend job: it required a yearlong commitment to attend events, make speeches, interact with community organizations and help plan future festivals. I discussed the commitment with Angie who gave the green light. This was too big an honor to decline. Only one other individual, Tom Barton of Beach Ford, had been selected as a King Neptune without having been previously part of the festival at some level.

It was a wonderful experience, and educational because I learned about things going on in the community that I never knew much about, and it exposed me to scores of people who do good around town, discreetly, without receiving much recognition. I made it a point to thank as many of these great folks as I could. I've handed out trophies at Special Olympics events, visited several of our region's military bases, ridden in local parades, and hosted a senior citizens' ball. I can't thank enough those who give so much to the Neptune Festival every year, and the committee that anointed me King Neptune XXXI. I'm still wearing the ceremonial ring I was given.

Mayor Oberndorf congratulates just-crowned King Neptune XXXI and "Queen Angie."

Neptune King officiating at one of the many events staged throughout the year, here greeting citizens at a Senior's F

"King Gene" with longtime Neptune Festival Executive Director Nancy Creech, affectionately titled by all past Kings as "Queen Nancy."

"Queen Angie" and "King Gene" enjoying another meal, one of their many "duties" during Neptune Week at the Oceanfront.

• • •

In 1989, Don Clark, one of the principals at the law firm of Clark and Stant, invited me to become a trustee and board member of Tidewater Health Care, which among other things owned and operated Virginia Beach General Hospital. I had a special interest in health-related issues, having spent so much time in hospitals after our daughter developed cancer, and due to my experience with Operation Smile. Over the next few years, I ended up on the Beach Hospital Executive Committee, and eventually was named board chairman. During my tenure, Don Clark served as chairman of the hospital's parent organization, Tidewater Health Care. Don had started negotiating a possible merger with Sentara Healthcare, a nonprofit company that owns several of the region's hospitals.

As chairman of Beach General's board, I attended most of the meetings with Sentara. The merger made sense. Stand-alone hospitals like Beach General have a very difficult time financially under the changing insurance rules of Medicare and Medicaid which makes up so much of the patient population. After the merger I was invited to be one of five Beach people to join the Sentara board, where I remained until 2012. I had a chance to learn a great deal about important issues that impact everyone.

I already knew that the cost of health insurance for our employees at MAX Media was the biggest single expense, after the payroll itself. I learned how insurance companies price their product, and why rates are going up. Along the way, I met a lot of interesting people from all over Virginia. Most impressive were David Bernd and his wife, Helen. David was CEO of Sentara for the entire time I was on the board, and he recently retired after thirty years leading that company. We remain friends, exchanging visits between our place in Fort Lauderdale and their vacation home in Duck, North Carolina.

Throughout all of my years of volunteering, I never forgot about my professional roots. I was a member of the board of the Virginia Association of Broadcasters (VAB), holding various positions including president. I was named the CT Lucy Award winner, the VAB's highest honor. My former college, renamed Virginia Commonwealth University, also inducted me into its Virginia Communications Hall of Fame. And Virginia Wesleyan created an honorary doctorate degree program, bestowing the degree on me and three other local leaders . I was especially gratified to receive my degree along with the late Frank Batten, who was the founder of Landmark Communications, best known for creating The Weather Channel. The Batten family has been a major benefactor of Virginia Wesleyan and many other public institutions. Another surprise was winning the Silver Medal of our Tidewater Ad Club, where I attended meetings but never formally joined. The Ad Club flew my longtime friend John Wilson in from Tampa to make the presentation.

Advertising Club of Tidewater

Third District, American Advertising Federation

P.O. Box 282 Norfolk, Virginia 23501

Gene Loving 1979 Silver Medal Winner

Deeply involved in area radio, TV and concert promotion, Gene Loving is at the forefront of the Tidewater entertainment scene

Many local residents who grew up in Hampton Roads during the '60s vividly recall a tall, thin, blond-haired disc jockey known as "Lean Gene." Whether he was emceeing concerts, starring in Disc-O-Ten (WAVY-TV's local version of American Bandstand), or spinning the latest records on his afternoon show for WGH-AM, Gene Loving was always at the forefront of every major happening on the local pop music scene.

Today, at the age of 37, although he has virtually disappeared from the local airways, Loving remains firmly entrenched in the broadcasting and entertainment business. As president of Bay Cities Communications, Inc., the parent company of radio stations WQRK-FM and WTJZ-AM, he is the operating partner of one of Southeastern Virginia's leading broadcasting operations. His partnership of many years with Dick Lamb and several local businessmen in AGL Productions still brings many of the world's leading concert attractions to town. And as a stockholder and driving force behind the establishment of WTVZ (Channel 33), Loving is on the ground floor of one of local television's most innovative operations.

That Gene Loving has grown into one of this area's true media powerhouses comes as no surprise to people familiar with his dedication to the entertainment and broadcasting businesses. Referred to by one associate as the "grandfather of the local concert promotion business," Loving combines many years of experience with instinctive promotional talents and an aggressive style of doing business. Loving's fascination with broadcasting and the entertainment business began very early in his teens when his parents gave him a tape recorder. Loving and a neighborhood friend began to experiment, and recorded their version of a pop-

ular Richmond radio program called the Harvey Hudson Show. Their tape was eventually played by Hudson on his program, an event which marked the beginning of Loving's career.

From that moment, according to Loving, he was hooked on broadcasting. An illegal neighborhood radio station, set up

in his Richmond home, quickly drew the attention of the FCC, and the Richmond newspapers and resulted in publicity that helped Loving land his first actual job in radio—working as a "gofer" for a new Richmond radio station, WLLY. During his high school years he held various con't next page

This was one of the Advertising Club's first awards to an individual not in advertising as a career focus.

'Gene Loving' continued

(from front page)

other radio-related jobs; at station WEZL (weasel radio) Loving hosted a daily program from 3 to 7 a.m., and took care of the station's mascot, a pet weasel. Following graduation from high school, he took several broadcasting and diction courses at Richmond Professional Institute and worked for the Richmond Top 40 giant, WLEE.

Concurrent with the development of his broadcasting career, Loving began to develop a strong interest in the concert promotion field. Through an association with Ned Grossberg, who owned a chain of bowling alleys, he began promoting regular concerts at Richmond's Mosque. With Grossberg's financial backing, Loving was able to attract the top stars of the late '50s and gain some valuable concert promotion experience while still in his teens.

It was Loving's association with Grossberg that eventually led him to temporarily give up his broadcasting career in order to move to Tidewater to become the advertising manager for Grossberg's Tidewater bowling operations. Through a series of bowling promotions on WGH, whose management staff then included several former WLLY executives, Loving once again found himself back in broadcasting. What was to be a one-night, last-minute substitution for Bob Calvert (who had suddenly left WCH for WNOR), ended up lasting eight years.

Loving's career blossomed during the WGH years. An alliance with fellow WGH disc jockey Dick Lamb led to the formation of AGL Productions and their association also brought them to Tidewater television as hosts of the fondly remembered Doc-O Tm program. These years marked the era of Loving's highest public visibility. Not only was he tremendously popular locally, but through his connections in the concert promotion field he was able to achieve international attention with exclusive interviews about the Beatles.

Loving proudly recalls his association with the Beatles. After being denied an opportunity to promote a Beatles concert in this area, he was invited by their booking agent to witness the group's first U.S. appearance in Washington. During his trip, Loving met the group, as well as Beatle George Harrison's sister, Louise Caldwell, who lived in the United States. Loving's friendship with Caldwell provided him with a unique source of information on the group. He began regular, on-the-air phone calls to Caldwell to talk about Harrison and the rest of the group. Eventually, Caldwell invited Loving to travel to England and spend some time with the group while they were filming A Hard Day's Night. This provided him with access to the group that virtually no other air personality could obtain. The interviews that he gathered on that trip and a subsequent trip to the Bahamas (where Help was filmed) were soon syndicated throughout the United States and several foreign countries.

By 1970 Loving realized that the kind of music he was playing on WGH was now being played by some FM stations. Because of the superior sound quality of FM radio, Loving felt it was just a matter of time before listeners were attracted there. So when the job of general manager of WNOR-FM was offered to him, Loving could not turn it down. He recalls feeling, "If I was going to have a real future in radio, I had to go where the listeners were." While Loving's departure from WGH stunned many local listeners, it demonstrated his keen business sense and knowledge of the industry.

The five years that Loving spent at WNOR were marked by a dramatic increase in FM listenership and innovative programming. He takes special pride in the station's late-night progressive music programming, which became the key to the ratings success of WNOR-FM. This marked the beginning of progressive music programming in Tidewater and verified what Loving was witnessing at concerts: "Progressive music was the future of the business."

Loving's years of experience and dedication culminated in 1973 with the formation of Bay Cities Communications, Inc. and the acquisition of WQRK and WTIZ (then WTID). With co-stockholder Martha Davis, Loving was able to achieve what he calls the goal of every disc jockey, owning his own station. Almost immediately after getting his radio stations off the ground, Loving began working on opening an independent UHF television station. A chance meeting with Joel Cooper revealed that Cooper was also working on establishing a UHF station. Loving and Cooper decided to join forces, marking the beginning of an association that ultimately resulted in WTVZ signing on the air in 1979.

Loving sees the 1980s as an exciting time for radio and television. He forecasts a resurgence of AM radio, directly related to the imminent development of AM stereo. He also foresees the continued development of video discs, home video tape units, pay television and cable television as a growing challenge to those involved in the commercial television business. But whatever trends do develop in radio and television it is certain Gene Loving will be there to meet the challenge and continue as the youthful "grandfather" of the local entertainment scene.

Reprinted with permission from the publisher of METRO MAGAZINE, Norfolk, Virginia.

Gene in heyday with fans, Fabian, Ringo and Lamb

John Wilson (left) Harvey Hudson (center) at my Silver Medal event. All three of us worked together at WLEE in 1960, when Harvey, one of our mentors, was the king of Richmond radio, taking a chance on two kids who wanted to be in broadcasting.

I mention this list of awards and recognition because I am obviously proud of these accomplishments and feel very fortunate to have been singled out for the honors. And there are so many other deserving individuals. By serving on the boards of these various organizations, I got an opportunity to get to see firsthand the great work of others and to give something back to the place that has been so generous to me. I never plunged into these philanthropic endeavors to gain kudos. At the point in my life where I was asked to serve, I didn't need recognition or to make contacts. I did these things for my soul—not my wallet. My service was a way to say "thank you," not to be thanked. The act of giving and helping is in and of itself rewarding. I have grown spiritually from working with others to improve our community and its worthy causes. Helping people is deeply rooted in my faith and the teachings that continue to guide me. My hope is, if you have hesitated to become active in some community organization that interests you,—Jump in.

EPILOGUE

When the big financial meltdown started in 2008, advertising was one of the first expenses many businesses cut. Revenues at MAX Media and at most radio and TV stations across America declined by a third or more within twenty-four months. Compounding the bad news for us was the collapse of the real estate market, coupled with the turmoil in the auto industry. Both sectors are huge advertisers on radio and TV. Banks withdrew from car financing and, without it, new-car sales almost stopped, especially those gas-guzzlers, as prices at the pump spiked. When jet fuel hit $5 a gallon, we sold the company airplane.

Several of the biggest industry players in broadcast suffered; some newspapers had even steeper financial declines. Some were forced to liquidate holdings or merge. Clear Channel, which is now iHeartRadio, Sirius and XM, and the Tribune Co., are examples. For satellite radio to survive, Sirius and XM merged.

The post-Great Recession years have been very difficult for many in the media business. We were lucky that all of our senior debt had been refinanced by private investment firms, which included some of the best in the world: Guggenheim, Goldman Sachs, and MSD Capital, which is Michael and Susan Dell. We were able to negotiate loan extensions in exchange for giving our lenders an equity position in the company. Others in the media business with large commercial bank loans were not so fortunate, and their lenders took over.

We actually benefited from a couple of those misfortunes. A lender asked us to take over two FMs in Denver, giving us 51 percent controlling interest; the original investors lost more than $25 million. Another bank asked us to take four FMs on the Outer Banks of North Carolina.

As I write this in 2016, MAX Media is still viable. To pay down debt, we have been able to slowly sell off some of our stations over the past three years as the economy mends. And we expect to continue in radio for the foreseeable future in Norfolk, and in Missouri, Illinois, North Carolina and Colorado. Our only remaining TV holdings are in Bowling Green, where we have CBS and NBC, and the independent TV stations in Puerto Rico.

It strikes me as ironic that, after all these years, I am still mostly a radio man.

• • •

The successes I have experienced far outweigh those that were less than fruitful. My partners and I made money on this journey, more than I ever imagined. My crystal ball helped me to see the potential in FM radio back in the late '60s. We got in early on UHF television and quickly built a portfolio of independent stations. We signed on with the upstart FOX network and then found big investment firms hungry to finance media acquisitions. Each step we took was a foundation for the next.

Along the way we met many of the biggest names in music and entertainment, of whom Jack Benny is still my favorite entertainer. And those early days with the Beatles seem almost surreal now.

Of all the people I have met, I have the most admiration for Pat Robertson and Bill Hybels because each has contributed so much towards improving the lives of others. Pat, especially because he started both Operation Blessing and Regent University from nothing. Bill Hybels for founding Willow Creek Church in a suburb of Chicago. Willow Creek has thirteen thousand member churches in forty-five countries. Bill also established an annual speaking forum featuring the biggest names in business and politics who focus on how to make a positive impact on the lives of others.

Angie remains dedicated to her volunteer work with CHKD (Children's Hospital of The King's Daughters) and with Women Helping Others (WHO).

• • •

The political system in the US is dependent on our participation. All politics is local. Even our US senators and congressmen have local offices. The broadcast business is regulated by the federal government via the Federal Communications Commission. From time to time you have to call on your congressman or senator regarding the agency (FCC) that has authority over what you do for a living. We have gotten involved over the years at the city, state, and federal level. Several pages of this book could be filled with pictures taken with presidents, federal legislators, governors, and dozens in state and city government. Several more pages could feature paragraphs about each of those we have gotten to know who impact the laws that govern all of us. Many of the events and fund raisers feature speakers who are not running for office but also participate in their own way to contribute to the public dialogue.

• • •

I can't help but wonder sometimes how all of this good fortune fell into the lap of a tall skinny kid from Richmond who liked spinning records and the sound of his own voice on the radio. *Why me?* It's an imprecise, cliché question with a fuzzy answer. I attribute much of my success to the people around me.

For whatever reasons, I have had mentors who took an interest in my career, and in me personally, and then took a chance on me financially. I am not exactly sure what my early mentors saw in me, but I can say this much—I was determined and I was persistent.

I thank—and blame—my workaholic tendency for many of the opportunities that crossed my path. Fifteen-hour workdays were my routine, and I was never afraid to try something new. When I was young, some people saw the potential in me. As I got older, I saw the potential in others. I also learned early that it is easier to win as a team than as an individual. There is an old African saying that goes something like this: If you want to go fast, travel alone. If you want to go far, travel with others.

When I was young I was too naïve to fail or be scared off. As I got older, doing deals and taking risks became a compulsion. It was exhilarating—both the money and relationships forged. I tried to get along with others and never intentionally screwed anyone, although I know those who were fired may not see it that way.

When I won, I brought others along; when they won, they brought me. I learned very early that business is symbiotic, and when it's built on relationships and trust there can be lots of winners. People partner with you, or entrust you with their money, because they believe you're fair and will make them a profit. When you do that, you develop a track record upon which to build even grander dreams.

I'm often asked, "What was the best experience, or thing, that happened during your career?" I can answer that now, looking back, understanding what is really important.

I was able to lead others to build brand new broadcast stations, which led to the most important thing someone in business can do—create jobs. A job means so much to an individual, a family, the economy and the community. Altogether there were several hundred new jobs which still exist today. Additionally, it was also bringing new free entertainment to markets where many people do not have the resources to pay for restaurants or a movie, or a sporting event. Today, millions can watch or listen at home after a tough day on the job, or raising a family. If alone, they have the company of TV or radio.

Having lived many of my dreams, I'm still looking to the future as we evolve with the changing media digital revolution. How many more years will "communications" be part of my life? Dick Lamb and I have been to the funerals of the DJs we worked with in the 1960s, and only the two of us remain alive out of the Swingin' Six at WGH who worked together the longest. We have a bet on which of us will go first.

I'm worried about how I'm going to collect my winnings.

I had an opportunity to spend time with Mayor Rudy Giuliani on two occasions talking at length about non-political topics, like his favorite restaurant in New York City and his son's golf ambitions.

I accepted the opportunity to meet Donald Trump when he came to Regent University just before the 2016 election. No matter your political views, meeting a future president is always a special occasion.

Angie and me with then President George W. Bush, following an interesting conversation about his Scottish terrier, Barney.

I enjoyed meeting two of my favorite national columnists and TV commentators, Laura Ingram and Charles Krauthammer. They were in town for a political debate.

CPSIA information can be obtained
at www.ICGtesting.com
Printed in the USA
BVHW02s1937181018
530631BV00016B/87/P